Brothers and Sisters of Retarded Children

Special Education and Rehabilitation Monograph Series, 9

Brothers and Sisters of Retarded Children
An Exploratory Study

FRANCES KAPLAN GROSSMAN

18064

 1972

SYRACUSE UNIVERSITY PRESS

ISBN 0-8156-2154-X

Library of Congress Catalog Card Number: 73-170664

Library of Congress Cataloging in Publication Data

Grossman, Frances Kaplan, 1939–
    Brothers and sisters of retarded children.
    (Special education and rehabilitation monograph
series, 9)
    Bibliography: p.
    1. Mentally handicapped. 2. Brothers and sisters.
3. Family. I. Title. II. Series.
RC570.G76   155.9′2′4   73-170664
ISBN 0-8156-2154-X

Manufactured in the United States of America

Editor's Foreword

THIS BOOK presents a refreshing departure from the type of research which has characterized the study of mental retardation for many years. Heretofore, the focus of research has been on the retarded individual—the way he learns, behaves, and adjusts in a so-called normal world. Some research has been undertaken wherein the predominant focus has been on the parents of the retarded, but, with the exception of the work of Louis Fliegler and Jean Hebeler, this work has been relatively superficial. What has been done has been concerned primarily with changes in parental attitudes or performance as the result of some intervention activity.

Dr. Grossman's study is focused not on the retardate *per se* but on the impact of retardation on the developing attitudes of brothers and sisters who perforce share the same parents, home, and social environment. She has modestly subtitled her book "an exploratory study." While this may be true, it is an exploration in depth which employs numerous techniques appropriate to the topic in order to shed light on this complex psycho-social problem.

It is important in assessing this book to observe that the normal brothers and sisters represented in the study were sufficiently advanced in chronological age to be able to enter fully into the interviews, but at the same time were chronologically close enough to the experiences of childhood and youth to be able to attempt accurate assessment of their own reactions, feelings, and understandings.

The current emphasis toward community placement of retarded children for purposes of education and training means that families in increasingly large numbers will retain mentally retarded children of all ages in the home. Under these circumstances, the mental health of siblings of the retarded individual in the home, and the problem of social interaction and family sociometry will become crucial issues for study in the field of mental retardation. This volume is an important contribution to meager literature on these subjects and, although research-oriented, will be useful to parents as well as to professional personnel. For educators, psychologists, and physicians who advise parents and normal children, there is a wealth of important information in this book. Some mature young people who themselves have retarded brothers or sisters will find material in several chapters which could be helpful to them in their adjustment to a sibling's retardation.

Most important, however, is the fact that Dr. Grossman has brought to the study of mental retardation a lucid and important document with a focus on a dimension of human social interactions which has been largely ignored. Although the author points out the limitations, the book is certain to take a place in the list of important literature on mental retardation.

The University of Michigan   WILLIAM M. CRUICKSHANK
September 21, 1971   *Series Editor*

Foreword

SINCE THE TURN OF THE CENTURY there has been sporadic realization that an individual is inextricably embedded in a network of relationships. Because of the complexities of these relationships, some authorities maintain that the usual conception of cause and effect—while perhaps making life simpler for psychological theoreticians—is theoretically unjustified. It would perhaps be more accurate to say that any theory of human behavior must be a social psychological one. It is the realm of practice—the area of human service—that has been most resistant to the implications of the social psychological aspects of the theories on which practice has been based. But even here we can see signs of change, primarily in the work of those who work with families (and even neighbors) instead of the single individual. The emerging fields of community psychology and social psychiatry reflect the increasing recognition that a narrow view in treating the individual is not justifiable either on theoretical or on social grounds.

Nowhere more than in services for the mentally retarded has there been such a concentrated focus of diagnosis and treatment on the individual. How and with what to diagnose the retarded child, the types of treatments that might be appropriate, issues of school and institutional placement, etiology and differential diagnosis—these were the questions which almost exclusively occupied the minds of those concerned with clinical service. Of course the retarded child had parents, grandparents, and siblings. Naturally, these people were affected by the retarded child (what a simplified conception of cause and effect!), and they could try the patience of most sensitive clinicians and aggravate the adjustment problems of the child. These facts were always known, but they were regarded not as part and parcel of the problem but as obstacles to helping the retarded child. The situation was not unlike

that in psychological research where for years it was assumed that
the characteristics of the experimenter (age, status, color, personality, etc.) were not involved in the behavior of his subjects,
and vice versa. Although we know better today, the practice of
research as reflected in the journal literature only minimally reflects such knowledge.

Dr. Grossman's book is a refreshing departure from the traditional literature in mental retardation precisely because she has
taken the social psychological approach seriously. More important, she has formulated and applied it in ways which open up
new avenues of research and practice. The value of the content
of this book—and Dr. Grossman deserves no little credit for pre-
serving for us the inherent fascination of the case material—
resides not only in what we learn about normal siblings of retarded individuals but in the intellectual voyage so well described
here. Dr. Grossman begins with her psychotherapeutic efforts
with a highly complicated young girl with a retarded and institutionalized older brother. It says much about Dr. Grossman's
acuteness, both as clinician and theoretician, that she became
interested in the interaction between the two siblings and particularly the impact of the retardation on the "normal" sister.
Then, for heuristic as well as clinical purposes, Dr. Grossman
organized and worked with a group of normal siblings of retarded
children and as these siblings communicated their thoughts and
feelings by word and deed, it became clear to her that the problem had to be pursued in systematic fashion. It was one of those
instances where one did not have to read significance into the
case material, and where future directions of research were quite
clear. Then began the task of formulating a program of research
which would not only meet the standards of objectivity and
replicability but—and here was the trick—produce data which
would be clearly relevant to hypotheses obtained in the clinical
situation. What frequently happens (because it really is so difficult) is that when clinically derived hypotheses are tested in
formal research the data seem a long way removed from the
original hypotheses. Dr. Grossman has met this test in admirable
style.

I do not consider this to be a book relevant only to the field of mental retardation. This is a book of great import for anyone interested in how family dynamics, organization, and stability are influenced by *any* catastrophe. Dr. Grossman's data on, and discussion of, the social class variable will tell the discerning reader much about our society. And finally, anyone interested in the prevention of human misery will be provided with a solid base for action.

New Haven, Connecticut
May, 1971

SEYMOUR B. SARASON
Professor of Psychology
Yale University

Preface

MY FIRST CONTACT with a sibling of a retarded child was with Cindy, the little girl whose treatment is described in Chapter 2. I was then a junior faculty member at Yale and a staff member at the Yale Psycho-Educational Clinic. At the Clinic, we sometimes worked with individual children in the context of consultation with community agencies. Cindy's family had requested help from the New Haven Regional Center, an organization with which we had many ties. (The Clinic's style of functioning, as well as a description of the New Haven Regional Center for the Mentally Retarded, is described in detail in Sarason, Levine, Goldenberg, Cherlin, and Bennett [1966].)

Cindy's plight stimulated my curiosity about other brothers and sisters, so with Dr. Elizabeth Fox, I established a discussion group of young adolescent siblings of retarded children, also at the New Haven Regional Center and with the support and cooperation of the Center's staff. This project is discussed in Chapter 3. (Chapters 2 and 3 taken together were adapted from an article previously published in *Psychological Problems in Mental Deficiency* [Sarason and Doris, 1969] and in *The Psycho-Educational Clinic: Papers and Research Studies* [Kaplan and Sarason, 1970].) Although these experiences were fascinating in their own right, I had little awareness of the potential significance of a study of brothers and sisters. However, with the encouragement of Dr. Seymour Sarason, then director of the Clinic, I launched into the study of college students with retarded siblings that makes up the major part of this book.

The formal research took approximately five years. During most of that time, financial support for the project came from the Psycho-Educational Clinic. During the last year, I received a National Institute of Mental Health Grant (#MH 18365–01) which enabled me to finish the data analyses and complete the manuscript of this book. Computer facilities were made available by Boston University.

It was only gradually during the time I was working on the college-student project that I began to see more clearly the intellectual and historical context and relevance of the problem. The orientation of the Clinic, under Dr. Sarason's direction, emphasized a psycho-social view of mental retardation, as indeed of other mental health problems as well (*e.g.*, Sarason *et al.*, 1966; Kaplan and Sarason, 1970). It was not until I had acquired considerable experience in settings away from the Clinic that I began to see the prevalence of the view of retardation that we have termed the "change-the-child" approach, that focuses nearly exclusively on the defects in the child and on efforts to influence that child. It was not until then that I had sufficient perspective to begin to see how a study of brothers and sisters of retarded children could only arise out of a psycho-social approach to retardation, and also could contribute to the elaboration of such a point of view. A simpler way of describing my own conceptual development is to say that I could only write Chapter 1, which describes this psycho-social perspective, after I had written the rest of the book.

In recent years a number of other researchers and writers in the area of retardation assume this stance in addition to Sarason (in Sarason and Gladwin, 1959; Sarason and Doris, 1969). Farber's book, *Mental Retardation: Its Social Context and Social Consequences* (1968), and the latest book by the Drs. Braginsky—*Hansels and Gretels: A Study of Children Who Live in Institutions for the Mentally Retarded* (1971)—further develop the psycho-social perspective and have greatly contributed to my own understanding of the issues.

From what I have said so far, it should be clear that the encouragement, support, and stimulation provided by Dr. Sarason, both as a mentor and as a friend, were essential to the evolution and completion of the project. I am greatly indebted to him.

I also want to thank the many siblings of retarded children and their families who shared their experiences with us. (All the names and identifying circumstances have been changed to protect their anonymity.) Over the years of the college-study project, a number of individuals provided valuable help, and several played central roles in the development of many of the ideas, as well as in carrying out the mechanics of the research. Foremost among this group was Patricia Louis, whose efficient organization of a constantly shifting and very busy panorama of research assistants and student-subjects allowed me to keep my sanity while learning about siblings. Her help is gratefully and affectionately acknowledged. Lydia Holquist, Rhona Weinstein, Coree Wade, Robert Sokolov, and Sandy Hershman all played important roles in the collection of the data, its analysis, and in the production of the final product. Drs. Cynthia Wild, Linda Shapiro, Seymour Sarason, and Enid Friedman, were kind enough to read over a draft of the manuscript and provide helpful comments, which substantially contributed to the readability of the final product. Finally, much appreciation is due to the patience and support of my husband, who lent his enthusiasm for my undertaking, as well as his editorial skills, to the completion of the book.

Newton, Massachusetts   FRANCES KAPLAN GROSSMAN
April, 1971

Contents

Brothers and Sisters of Retarded Children

CHAPTER 1

A Different View of Mental Retardation

MENTAL RETARDATION has been defined as a major social problem for our country, and has cost untold amounts in terms of money, human resources, and personal sorrow and pain. The report from the President's Panel on Mental Retardation (1962) gives some sense of the magnitude of the problem: 10 times more individuals are mentally retarded than have diabetes, 25 times more than have muscular dystrophy. Only 4 major diseases—mental illness, cardiac disease, arthritis, and cancer—affect a greater number of individuals. In 1962, over 5 million Americans were retarded. "More than 250 million dollars was spent in support of special educational programs conducted by the public schools. In 1963, the national government spent . . . in excess of 128 million dollars in its program to combat mental retardation." (Stevens, 1964.) The degree of personal gain and tragedy cannot be described through numbers, but is overwhelmingly apparent to all who have worked in the field of retardation.

No single perspective toward retardation is sufficient to meet the potential and actual problems involved. However, one of the underlying themes of this book is that we, in this country and culture, tend to view mental retardation in a particular way that oversimplifies the situation and, more seriously, limits us in the kinds of questions we think to ask and solutions we can imagine. This work, and the research and clinical experiences on which it is based, demonstrates what can happen when we think about the problem in a different way and consequently focus on aspects not usually emphasized. Hopefully, the book also illustrates the value of the particular approach taken in leading to relevant and useful knowledge.

1

In our culture, mental retardation and other serious handicaps often are viewed and treated as if they were primarily—or only—problems residing in the affected individual, or at most in the family. (We are considering here only that proportion of retarded people with demonstrable, or assumed, organic damage—approximately 20 percent of the total population of people diagnosed as "retarded." As Braginsky and Braginsky so well illustrate [1971], the myths and misconceptions concerning the other 80 percent—those who are from the lower socioeconomic class and who have no demonstrable central nervous system pathology—are even more prevalent and destructive.) According to this view, if a child has Down's Syndrome (Mongolism), or is brain-damaged, or crippled, something has to be done for him and his handicap. For example, we provide him with medical care and physical therapy, with day care and residential treatment, with psychotherapy, occupational therapy, and speech therapy—all to help him grow, develop, and, above all, to change. In other words, we act as though the child and his slow development—his retardation—are the whole of the problem, and if we can only help him to be different than he is, we will have solved the problem. As a further illustration of our nearly exclusive emphasis on the afflicted individual, a highly regarded review of research in mental retardation does not have a single chapter on the family or the community; the focus is on the handicapped child and the possibility of achieving personal improvement in that child through changes in care or treatment (Stevens and Heber, 1964).

All of these forms of education and therapy are indeed helpful to many individuals, families, and communities. Unfortunately, a major side effect of this "change-the-child" approach is that it leads families to see the retardation of a child as necessarily tragic, devastating, and traumatic for all concerned. And not only the families of the retarded are infected by this view. All of us, even professionals in the field of mental retardation, have been led to regard the mourning reactions of the family and community toward a retarded child as inevitable, as if these reactions were intrinsic to the handicap and are the only possible way to respond to such an occurrence.

What this perspective ignores is that even an organic handicap in a child is also, and at times primarily, a social-psychological event for the affected family and community as well as for the child. The direct consequences of the disability on the family may be objectively negligible, either because the child's handicap is slight, or because the family's financial resources are such that the disability is not a physical or economic burden. Yet, the total impact of the handicap on the family may be powerful and destructive because of the interpretations and reactions of the individuals and groups involved. For example, a mildly retarded child may be quite capable of functioning as a member of a family, to which he contributes as much as the other children. A moderately retarded person might well play a useful role in keeping his elderly and isolated parent company and giving him or her some purpose in life. However, if the first-mentioned child is viewed as a blemish on the family's reputation; if the moderately retarded person is seen primarily as a deviant—or as divine punishment inflicted on the parents for their "sins"—then these views, fully as much as the actual abilities and handicaps of the retarded person, determine the total impact of the child's defect on the family. Similarly, but more positively, the effect on the family of a seriously handicapped child who is viewed by that family as providing a special opportunity for them to learn and grow together is greatly influenced by that view, at least as much as by the child's actual inabilities.

Sarason and Gladwin (1959) were probably the first to formally state this position in their farsighted monograph, *Psychological and Cultural Problems in Mental Subnormality: a Review of Research*. They illustrate the importance of the cultural response to retardation in determining its impact with Eaton and Weil's description of the Hutterites (a strict communal Christian group with several colonies in South Dakota). They point out:

> The standards of adequacy set by the culture appear to be wide enough to embrace most people who function at anything but a pathologically deficient level. . . . Finally, the Hutterite society is so organized that it can take care of *all* persons, whatever their level of functioning, within itself without resort to special institutions or other devices. (p. 531)

Mentally defective people are generally accepted among the Hutterites, and there is little social stigma attached to the condition. Consequently, retardation tends not to be the major catastrophe for a Hutterite family that it often is for a family in our culture.

Our cultural view of mental retardation as almost inevitably traumatic for all involved is not an intrinsic part of the handicap itself, but stems from our culture and the values that go with it. (Farber, 1968, has elucidated some of the reasons for the point of view taken by our culture, as well as how our institutions maintain it.)

This emphasis on the importance of social and psychological factors in determining the effect of a handicap on an individual and his social world is not unique to retardation. Wright (1960) takes a similar position in discussing the impact of physical handicap on the individual. She points out that the presence of a physical handicap in an individual is an ecological, and not a psychological, event. The reactions of the individual and of the social setting he inhabits determine what the psychological consequences will be, both for the individual and the people around him. (Also Ausubel, 1952; Hanks and Hanks, 1948; Macgregor, Abel, Bryt, Louer, and Weissmann, 1953; Meyerson, 1948.)

In introducing this chapter, the point is made that the way we view retardation influences (and in some ways limits) the kinds of questions we think to ask and the possible solutions we consider concerning actual and potential problems. As an example, if we see a particular reaction of families and communities as an inevitable and intrinsic aspect of the retardation itself, then it does not occur to us to raise questions about why the culture stigmatizes and isolates handicapped individuals or about possible ways of changing that societal response. Or again, this perspective does not lead us to ask why families feel as they do about it, or why some families feel and behave in one way with respect to a retarded child and some in quite another.

Because, in fact, and despite this cultural framework, enormous differences exist from family to family in how members react to, and cope with, the presence of a handicapped child. Many variations seem to involve social-class differences in values and perspectives (*e.g.*, Felzen, 1970). However, dealing with children with similar handicaps within any given social class makes it obvious that families vary tremendously, both in the way they cope and in their effectiveness in dealing with issues raised by the handicap.

In addition to supporting our own[1] view that a family's response is not intrinsic to the handicap itself and therefore inevitable, this variation suggests the possibility of learning much more about how and why some families are able to cope in ways that provide valuable growth experiences for all members of the family, while others are damaged or limited by the experience. (In fact, increasing numbers of professionals in the field of mental retardation are focusing on the families and are attempting to help them cope more effectively with a handicapped child, *e.g.*, Farber, 1968.)

In our search for knowledge about how families might cope successfully with retardation, our interest was drawn to a less studied component of the social system affected by, and itself influencing, the retardation of a child. We began to wonder about the effects on the normal brothers and sisters in these families. For example, we wondered if, for some normal children, the experience of growing up with a retarded sibling might be a positive experience, and felt that if we could find such children, we might be able to learn from them how to be more helpful to other children with a handicapped brother or sister. More generally, we were curious about some specific effects of growing up with a retarded sibling, such as how this influenced the normal boy's or girl's curiosity or self-concept or feelings toward his or her parents.

We also felt that a family's response to the presence of a handicapped child must have similarities to the family's reactions to any other unexpected event, or to a serious disappointment. That is, the problems associated with mental retardation seemed to us to be related to a host of more general social and psycho-

1. The "our" and "we" are sometimes editorial, referring only to the author. More often, "they" refers to the author in collaboration with one or more of the many individuals who at one time or another have participated in, and contributed to, the research and its formulation.

logical problems. Consequently, study of the former issues promised to shed some light on these broader questions.

By the time we began writing this book, we had had a variety of experiences with brothers and sisters of organically retarded children. We had come to know literally hundreds of people—young children, teenagers, college students, adults—with one or several retarded siblings. By then it was clear that, over-all, the great majority of these people were quite "normal," *i.e.*, they had no more, nor fewer, problems than the rest of us. Most shared a belief in the importance to their lives of having a retarded brother or sister. A large number bore the imprint of the experience in a variety of subtle ways—in the direction of their interests; in the fantasies, wishes, and hopes they brought with them into adulthood; in their fears and anxieties. A few were seriously troubled by their experiences and had not yet successfully come to terms with the impact of their brother's or sister's handicap on their family life and on themselves.

That this is a significant experience, regardless of the shape and value of its ultimate impact, is illustrated by the excerpts from interviews quoted in later chapters.

Thoughts, fears, and fantasies are experienced by countless brothers and sisters of retarded children. For most they form a backdrop to normal, well-functioning lives. But for some few they come to dominate and overwhelm, an inextricable element of serious mental disturbance. Such a little girl was Cindy, whose psychotherapeutic treatment is described in the next chapter. The outcome of Cindy's treatment was disappointing. However, her attempts to come to understand her older brother's retardation and the thoughts and fantasies she had about it are not unique to this one disturbed child, and can be seen with unusual clarity, both because of her disturbance, and because of the extended treatment relationship.

CHAPTER 2

Fears and Fantasies of a Younger Sister: A Case Study

ALTHOUGH CINDY HERSELF was a seriously disturbed girl, her story is told here primarily for the light it sheds on the concerns of normal brothers and sisters of retarded children. Cindy's conviction that she was "sick" like her retarded brother, her belief that her curiosity about his handicap was evil and dangerous, her assumption that Marvin was retarded because someone had intentionally damaged him, all represent rather common fantasies of well-functioning brothers and sisters. One of the few differences between them and Cindy, albeit an important one, is that they are able to keep their fantasies and fears from dominating their lives. Because Cindy was in therapy for a long time—some 18 months—it was possible to learn about these very private thoughts and worries that children are ordinarily reluctant to share, even with people close to them.

Cindy's story is also the story of her parents. And here again, although her parents were in a great deal of psychological difficulty, their reactions to their son's retardation and, subsequently, to Cindy's birth differ more in degree than in kind from the reactions of parents who are better able to cope. Consequently, they too can teach us about the stresses and strains on parents of retarded children, and how these pressures can complicate their dealings with other children in the family.

Finally, the description of this one family's experience suggests some ways of thinking about how professionals and others might help normal children deal more comfortably and adequately with a retarded brother or sister.

7

THE BACKGROUND

Several years ago I began a psychotherapeutic relationship with an 11-year-old girl, little suspecting that the questions raised by this experience would be the impetus for a full-scale research project on siblings of retarded children. Because many of the issues that emerged in the course of the treatment remained central to the research, my experience with Cindy is described in some detail as the proper introduction to it.[1]

The experience of treating this child is worthy of description in its own right, as well as in the context of siblings, as her case clearly illustrates the way that our prior conceptions of a child and of a category of dysfunction or "disease" so often enormously influence how we behave toward that child and ultimately become self-fulfilling prophecies as the child in turn responds in accordance with our expectations. Although at the time this was written Cindy's future was at best uncertain, her response to psychotherapy and to me suggests what might have been had parents, teachers, and other people in her life treated her differently, or had any of these people seen her problems as potentially remediable and, consequently, brought her for treatment earlier. In this era of reawakened concern for all handicapped and troubled children, Cindy's story underlines the need for early intervention and for preventive approaches to mental health problems. This "might have been," tragic as it may be in this particular case, can still be possible for other similar children.

Finally, this case illustrates once again what we are slowly coming to realize: the "case" is never just the disturbed child, the retarded infant, the delinquent adolescent. The "case" is the entire social system, influencing and being influenced by the identified child's problem. It always includes the family and often the neighborhood, the schools, and the community (e.g., Farber and Ryckman, 1965; Sarason, Levine, Goldenberg, Cherlin, and Bennett, 1966). Cindy's pathology consisted not only of the difficulties in thinking and feeling which she experienced; it was also part of an entire network of family interaction and patterns, which had in

1. Originally published in Sarason and Doris (1969).

turn been deeply affected by Cindy's older brother, a severely retarded boy.

THE INITIAL CONTACTS

Cindy's parents, Mr. and Mrs. B, first came to an agency that services retarded children because they were puzzled by what they described as her strangeness and were troubled by her increasingly inappropriate behavior in school. They decided to approach an agency for the mentally retarded because they considered Cindy retarded, as did the school, which had placed her in a class for such children. They expressed an interest in recreational activities for Cindy—with other retarded children—but did not seem to consider the possibility that whatever difficulty was causing her "retardation" and bizarreness might be, in part at least, remediable.

The social worker who visited the home reported that the mother suspected Cindy's difficulties to be due to an allergy to milk, since an older brother had such an allergic reaction. However, the social worker also expressed some puzzlement about his impressions of Cindy: she did not talk the way a retardate usually does. She had insisted on being present while he spoke with her parents, and she repeated such phrases as, "My life is over—I'm going to end it all. I'm very frustrated." He responded to her implicit pleas for help by referring her to me for a psychological and intellectual evaluation and possible treatment. Before I met with the B's, previous test material, doctors' reports, etc., were collected. They all gave a picture of a retarded, strangely behaving, brain-damaged child, and in fact she was diagnosed by several in just that way. The reports implied or stated that the neurological, organic defect was the basis for her retardation and strangeness. On the other hand, it was not clear to me how the diagnoses of brain damage "explained" this child's behavior. For example, the reports rated her reading as being at a high level, although she was given an IQ test score in the 60s. Why this discrepancy existed was not explainable in terms of an organic deficit. Consequently, it was with some feeling of puzzlement that I came to the first meeting with the B's.

The B's were a middle-class Jewish family who showed signs of the strain they had been under. Mrs. B, a heavy, well-dressed woman, was quite overwhelming in her aggressive manner of talking, her demandingness, and her real sorrow. Mr. B seemed to be a somewhat subdued man who let his wife do most of the talking.

Cindy herself appeared noticeably small for her age. At that time she was prepubescent, and looked nearer 8 or 9 than her actual age of 11. She had a somewhat strange appearance, probably due to the disarray in which she kept her clothes and hair. Nonetheless, she had a decided charm about her when she talked. In this first meeting, I was torn between an impression that she was an extremely "out of it," disorganized, and/or retarded child, and the occasional sharp realization from her comments of her acute and sophisticated awareness of what was going on.

Mrs. B actually provided the first major clue to Cindy's difficulties with her very first sentence to the therapist. Pointing to the one-way mirror in the treatment room, she said, "Oh, I know about those mirrors. They showed us how they work when we took Marvin to the institution." Thus, the identification in Mrs. B's mind between Cindy and her severely retarded, institutionalized brother was made clear from the beginning.

Although this tie between Cindy and Marvin was relatively clear at the outset, many other aspects of that first interview with Mr. and Mrs. B and Cindy became comprehensible only over a period of 18 months and over 100 hours of treatment. Several aspects of this family's way of relating to each other were obvious even at first. Mrs. B did most of the talking, describing their recent difficulties with Cindy with considerable affect and involvement, becoming tearful at points when she told of their fears that Cindy would become like her older brother. Cindy managed to look "crazy" and "stupid" during this discussion; she rolled her head around, played with her saliva, and maintained a silly grin. However, when her mother began likening Cindy to Marvin, she burst out, "You don't love me! You want to send me to an institution!" indicating she was more in touch with the conversation than she looked or acted. However, she also "undid" this angry comment shortly afterward by going up to her mother and nuzzling her as a small baby might—touching her face, leaning against her, etc. Mrs. B responded to this by touching Cindy, stroking her and telling her she loved her. Thus, any real anger Cindy might have felt and expressed was withdrawn, as it were, and their "loving unity" reestablished.[2] Even then, the B's fear and conviction that Cindy, like her brother, was "incurable" and would end up in an institution was obvious.

Mr. B was generally quiet and let his wife do the talking, saying only that it bothered him when Cindy did all these strange things because he knew it was not normal. He added that he knew she could not help it. I spent a brief time with Cindy alone at the end of this interview. Despite her peculiar, seemingly unrelated, and "unintelligent" behavior, when I suggested she might come back and talk with me, she said, "Yes, we should set up a schedule!" Thus, she indicated from the beginning a strong desire to be helped and to establish a relationship.

The history of the difficulties—some of which the parents gave during this hour, some of which emerged over the year and a half of contact—began at least as far back as the birth of their second son. Their firstborn, Richard, was a healthy boy, and two years later they had another son, Marvin. It shortly became evident that Marvin was retarded, and they began the troubled journey taken by so many parents of retarded children—from doctor to doctor looking for advice and assistance. Much is unclear about this period of time, except that they kept Marvin at home for approximately 10 years, and that during this time Mrs. B became very closely attached to and involved with this younger son. She maintained him as a complete infant, assuming he was totally unable to help himself and treating him accordingly. The decision to institutionalize him was extremely difficult for the B's to make and to carry out.

2. One of the clearest characteristics of this mother-child relationship was its "double-bind" nature, i.e., the mother's behavior communicated two contradictory "messages" which can have the effect of keeping the child in a state of anxiety and uncertainty. This characteristic has been noted in the relationship between schizophrenic individuals and at least one of their parents, usually the mother. (Bateson, Jackson, Haley, and Weakland, 1956)

By their account, after Marvin was institutionalized, they took their first vacation since his birth and on that trip accidentally conceived Cindy. (At another time, they reported she was born before their decision to institutionalize Marvin.) In either case, the intimate connection in their mind between the loss of Marvin and Cindy's birth was apparent.

From the time of Cindy's conception, they desperately feared she would be defective. Mrs. B was convinced she could not bear a healthy child. When Cindy was born, although no defects were apparent, they began taking her from one pediatrician to another, unable to believe she was not defective despite the physician's reassurances. By the time she was three, their prediction began to come true; she was beginning to seem somewhat slow in development. She was sufficiently "immature" at age five to be held back a year before starting kindergarten, then was kept in a combined first and second grade for three years, also because of "immaturity." Interestingly enough, Cindy did rather well those years. She had a sympathetic teacher who liked her, and she was able to learn some academic material despite some strange mannerisms, a reported short attention span, poor coordination, and other indications of difficulty.

When she finally left this class to begin third grade, with a different teacher and more emphasis in the curriculum on academic performance, she began to deteriorate. She cried, screamed, needed constant reassurance from the teacher, and could no longer maintain her previous level of academic work. At the social worker's recommendation, she was transferred to a special class for educable retarded children, where, however, she continued to deteriorate. She frequently hit herself in the head saying, "I'm stupid, my brain doesn't work." She was frightened of being touched and screamed when another child accidentally brushed against her. She stopped doing any academic work. It was at this point that her parents appealed to the Center for Retardation for assistance.

I began to meet with Cindy twice weekly, while a social worker met regularly with Mrs. B and occasionally with Mr. B. In addition to the treatment sessions themselves, I immediately established contact with the school Cindy attended to find out what was happening and later to attempt to influence their handling of her.

FIRST THREE MONTHS OF TREATMENT

Cindy quickly established a relationship with me.[3] She made it clear she liked to come, and although she was silent much of the time, she was clearly involved in the process and thinking about it, in and out of sessions. The earliest focus of my comments, once she was comfortable with me, was the contrast between her rather sophisticated style of speech and high-level ability to understand and her seeming inability to learn at school. After being confronted with this a number of times, she began to reply with such comments as, "I can't do things any more, I think my mind is broken."

This theme of her inability to learn being associated with her own view of her "head being broken," of something being "wrong with my brain," ran through the first year of treatment, and she objected with increasing vehemence when this position was challenged. (At no time did she voluntarily mention her brother Marvin, who did indeed have "something wrong with his head.")

Seemingly related to Cindy's learning difficulty was her curiosity, which was obviously both strong and inhibited. She began acting out sexual questions using dolls—such as having them hug and kiss and then asking me what they were doing. When I offered to answer any questions she had about anything to the best of my ability, she became—for her—unusually direct and active in asking what people do when they are married, how babies are born, etc. Since she was prepubescent at the time, I also discussed menstruation with her in some detail. She was fascinated by these discussions and remembered in detail essentially all the facts we discussed, giving further evidence of her ability to learn under certain conditions. However, when I commented on her intense curiosity she told me, "That's my sickness."

3. Since the focus of this account is Cindy as a sibling of a retarded child, no attempt was made to describe the psychotherapy in detail. Only those aspects relevant to the general issue are described here.

It never became entirely clear why curiosity was so dangerous in the B's family. (Difficulty with curiosity has turned up in a large number of "normal" siblings of retarded children. This is discussed in detail below.)

The other major theme, which was already present in rudimentary form from the beginning, was her inability to express her enormous fury at her mother. A major concern of Cindy's was that if she showed her hatred, she would be sent away. In fantasy, she imagined it would cause her total destruction. At this early point in treatment, I was aware that Cindy did not express an "expectable" amount of anger at her mother or at me, and talked with her about it. I was not aware for many months of the intensity of rage that would be released when it began to emerge.

THE NEXT NINE MONTHS

Cindy was extremely upset when I left for a month's vacation, and became increasingly symptomatic. By the time I returned, she looked pitiful and bizarre, and I found it hard to be with her without feeling guilty and somewhat helpless. One symptom consisted of holding her breath and then tightening her entire body in a spasmodic manner; at its height, she repeated this many times a minute. She also began "wiping faces," rubbing her hand down over her nose and gesturing as if she was wiping an invisible substance off her face and discarding it. At times she hit herself in the nose with her hand, occasionally hard enough to give herself a nosebleed.

The treatment of a child with a learning disorder can most effectively be carried out in close cooperation with the relevant persons in the school setting (Sarason *et al.*, 1966). Although Cindy's special-class teacher wanted to help Cindy, her own point of view, as well as the orientation of the entire school system, resulted in treating children in special classes like "retarded children." That is, it was assumed that they could not understand things and that they would not be able to do very much work, academic or otherwise. In addition, Cindy's symptoms frightened the school personnel, causing them to treat her as if she were extremely fragile as well as retarded. Given this attitude and the series of expectations it set up, Cindy could only continue to behave as she had been doing and so confirm her own and others' views of her as incapable of learning or of behaving more normally.

After a relatively short attempt to influence the school and teacher, the need for a different setting became apparent. Several months after school began in the fall, Cindy was transferred to a private school that specializes in work with children who have learning difficulties. I talked frequently with the principal and each teacher, emphasizing her ability to learn and to function normally.

Partly as a result of these efforts, partly by virtue of their own orientation and skills, they responded to Cindy as if she were a normal child. They behaved as if they expected her to act normally and to learn, thus making it possible for her to attempt to behave in these ways. This was undoubtedly the first time in her life outside of therapy that anyone ever acted toward Cindy as if she could be normal and intelligent. After an initial period of adjustment, when she first began to perceive this attitude, she became shocked and expressed violent disagreement with this view. We spent many hours talking about her alleged stupidity and I reiterated what I deeply believed, that nothing about the way she was born made it impossible for her to learn. Since she did not mention Marvin, I asked her about him. She did not want to talk about him at first, and, when I asked, she said she did not know what was wrong with him. Since she had been taken along once or twice a month for many years whenever the family visited him in the institution, it seemed highly unlikely that she did not know and I commented on this to her. Finally, she suggested: "Someone hit him on the head—I don't know who." This fantasy that he had been willfully damaged (by her mother?) must have greatly aggravated her fears of displeasing her parents.

Once Marvin came up for discussion, the fight over whether she was defective began in earnest. She insisted that she was, demonstrated it repeatedly by acting totally stupid (*e.g.*, not being able to find a paint brush when it was lying in front of her on the table), said repeatedly she was just like Marvin and that she was born with something wrong with her brain. Finally, in utter desperation at her inability to convince me of her point of view, she said: "I'm sick like my brother. I don't have any originality, and my coordination isn't very good!" I told her I was aware that she thought that, and furthermore that her parents thought that as well. I discussed with her my idea that her parents had been so frightened that something might be wrong with her that they had come to believe there was. However, I pointed out numerous instances where she had been able to learn and again restated my disagreement with the family point of view about her.

After several months in the new school with the treatment focused on learning, she began one day in therapy to write a list of spelling words on the board, something she had never done before. Then she wrote a list of all her courses and a time schedule and a list of her teachers' names. I was delighted but afraid to talk directly to her about it for fear this new development would prove to be a mirage! However, my next visit to the school found the teachers jubilant. Cindy had started to learn. She seemed to have given up her previous view of herself as a nonlearner, which finally opened to her the possibility of learning. The spurt in academic work was impressive. In some fields, such as social studies, she rapidly began to catch up to the grade level of children her own age, though arithmetic remained difficult and tedious. But for the remaining time in treatment, even when her emotional life was utterly chaotic, she continued to progress in school, proving rather convincingly that her previous "retardation" was not a necessary result of neurological deficit, but also a response to her parents' and teachers' negative expectations— that she could not learn.

Other events and issues were taking place concomitantly. Only a few major themes will be mentioned here. Her curiosity about sexual matters progressed to a more specific concern with what her parents were doing in bed together, what her newly married eldest brother did with his wife, and the forlorn question to me: "What's an 11-year-old girl to do?" Hints of some primitive sexual fantasies came up in her play, but at this time she did not share these thoughts.

Despite progress in several areas, however, I began to experience the hours as difficult, frustrating, and unproductive. Cindy was frequently silent the entire period, and often her behavior was stereotyped and rigid. Her behavior at home was more focused, having lost its previous diffuse and irrelevant quality, but she began having more temper tantrums. In particular, Mrs. B and Cindy had a major battle each morning before school. Although at this time I had no conscious awareness of the problem obstructing treatment, the information was available in the details of the morning battle had I but realized what I knew.

Cindy did not get up in the morning, despite her mother's scolding and finally screaming that she should. Then Mrs. B would come in and undress, wash, and dress Cindy in bed like an infant (or like a profoundly retarded child). Finally, Cindy would get up and go to the bathroom on her own. When the school bus arrived, Cindy would scream and cry, "Don't send me, don't make me go!" and Mrs. B would feel she was killing her if she did insist. Sometimes she was able to get her on the bus; at other times she would give in. She described herself as being as upset as Cindy at forcing her to leave but also hating Cindy for putting her through such a difficult scene daily. When Cindy got to school, her behavior usually changed dramatically; she became pleasant and cheerful, with no signs of the early trauma.

The incredible infantilization and associated symbiotic intimacy, the rage and death wishes associated with separation, and the intimate relationship between Cindy's pathology and her interaction with her mother, were all present in these incidents. (Staver, 1953, has described a similar family pattern in a group of children with severe learning difficulties.) However, I did not yet see the problem clearly, but only knew I was getting increasingly discouraged about the treatment. Further, Mrs. B began cornering me in the hallway and talking in a very depressed and demanding way about the need to institutionalize Cindy. Cindy was getting more and more difficult, according to Mrs. B, and in particular she could not tolerate more of these morning scenes. Mrs. B implied she herself was approaching a "nervous breakdown."

Since the social worker was leaving at this time, I decided to take over the contact with the parents, but in a different form. I continued to see Cindy twice a week individually, but met with Cindy and her parents together weekly for family treatment.

Two Months of Family Meetings

Within an extremely short time, the central issue in the family pathology was unmistakable. These parents, and particularly the mother, were totally unable to accept *any* anger from Cindy. The family solution to this, with which they all conformed, was that she disguise her fury as "craziness" and that they view her expressions of anger as unmotivated, uncontrollable pathology. In the second family meeting, Cindy said to her parents with feeling: "I hate you!" They immediately responded by saying, "You don't really hate us, do you? You can't really feel that way!" When I commented on their discomfort with Cindy's attack, they both said, "She doesn't really mean it." Cindy then ceased any direct expressions of anger, reverting instead to more "crazy" behavior, which involved running through a variety of symptomatic behaviors—all of which made her appear bizarre and also greatly irritated her parents.

In the next several meetings, Cindy expressed her rage and fury more and more openly. In one dramatic meeting, when they had been reminiscing about what a beautiful baby she had been, she stood up and yelled at them: "I hate you, it's your fault, you didn't take care of me!" and then covered her face and, for the first time in my presence, cried. Mrs. B also cried, and then both became increasingly guilty and depressed. Mr. and Mrs. B again began talking about the possibilities of institutionalization.

In individual sessions Cindy was openly angry and at the same time less symptomatic and indirect than she had ever been. She also began using individual sessions to share her fantasies and private thoughts. One fantasy that preoccupied her for many months was that she would stop up the toilet, then defecate in it; the toilet would run over, and her feces would entirely cover the house and her parents. Although the primitiveness of some of these fantasies was at times startling, I felt it represented significant therapeutic progress for her to be able to share and discuss her private world.

Although she was moving rapidly in treatment, the problem that eventually led to the destruction of the therapy had already begun to cause trouble. Cindy was unable to maintain the distinction between talking about her fury and acting out many of these fantasies and thoughts. She became increasingly destructive at home, tearing some curtains, breaking a window, and writing on the wall. She stopped up a toilet and did defecate in it, which was more openly expressed aggression and pathology than her parents were able to tolerate. The situation was rapidly reaching a boiling point.

The Last Two Months

At this point in time, several events unfortunately coincided. I left for a month's summer vacation and during this time Cindy's maternal grandmother, who had been very close with both Cindy and Mrs. B, died while vacationing with the B's. Aside from the real deprivation and the fantasy concerns this caused Cindy, the major disruption was the loss to Mrs. B, who had received considerable support from her mother. She felt herself to be even more deprived and resented Cindy's needfulness. Simultaneously, she tried to turn more to Cindy for support. Cindy's expressed anger was, of course, increasing the distance between them rather than allowing them even their previous closeness and any support Mrs. B had derived from that.

Within a month of my return from vacation, it was apparent that Cindy could go no further while living in the home, since her parents could not tolerate her aggression. She had to begin to deal with her hatred before any further progress was possible. Further, she herself was at times overwhelmed by the intensity of anger released and the anxiety it aroused, and at least once became acutely disorganized in school at which time she uncontrollably screamed and ran up and down the halls. Mrs. B called me to say she could no longer tolerate Cindy at home, since she herself was on the verge of collapse. Her depression was sufficiently severe for me to have some real concern about her. Finally, but only in the last several weeks of this chaos, Cindy's behavior made it impossible to maintain her at school, even with medication and with considerable flexibility in the programming at the school.

It is a gross understatement to say that the period just before Cindy's hospitalization on an acute psychiatric ward was trying. Mrs. B dramatically stated the conflict in a family meeting by saying she could not stand to have Cindy at home any more, she was driving her crazy, but she also could not and would not tolerate any separation from her! I finally insisted on the separation, saying I could not in good conscience continue working either with Cindy or them unless they accepted this recommendation. We met daily for several days, during which time Mrs. B's stability was seriously in question. It became apparent that one factor making a breakdown seem attractive was the fantasy that if she could not be with Cindy at home, she could be her roommate in the hospital. I told her firmly that if she needed hospital support for a time, she would go to a different hospital. With this, the crisis subsided, and Cindy was hospitalized.

The end of the story is a sad one. Cindy profited greatly from two months of separation from her parents, but then needed a long-term residential setting to provide the necessary structure and treatment. Obtaining a place in a good residential facility for a disturbed child who performs within the retarded range on intelligence tests and whose parents cannot afford to spend many thousands of dollars a year for the placement is virtually impossible, and despite repeated attempts I was unsuccessful. After a brief period at home, Cindy was placed in a nearby private residence for retarded children. That need not have been antitherapeutic had the personnel been able to enforce some separation between Cindy and her parents. They were not able to do this, and at last report Cindy seemed to be functioning as a mildly retarded institutionalized child.

But the important issue is not whether Cindy would have made her way to health at this point, but rather that if we could have gotten to her when she was younger, this child could have functioned far more adequately. If we had gotten to her parents to help them cope more effectively at the time when their son's retardation became apparent, or when they had to institutionalize him, or later when they began to express fears about the new baby, or even when Cindy was held back in the first grade, Cindy might then have had a chance.

Let me be explicit on one point. I do not mean to imply that Cindy was not brain-damaged or not functionally retarded. She appeared to be a child who came into the world less equipped to deal with it than some children (she did show a number of signs of "minimal brain damage"). Similarly, her parents undoubtedly were not the most psychologically fit people before they had a retarded child, but they were then required to handle a situation difficult for the healthiest of parents. If professionals in the field of retardation and mental health could have provided some assistance at any one of a number of points when the difficulties were first beginning, Cindy's story would be very different from what it is today.

SOME FURTHER IMPLICATIONS

Cindy's story has broader implications for our understanding of normal brothers and sisters of retarded children. Her parents' fear and expectation that she would be retarded like her older brother is not unusual; only in intensity and degree of conviction does this distinguish them from other families with a retarded child. Cindy's resulting view of herself as retarded, expressed most amusingly as well as most poignantly in her comment: "I'm sick like my brother, I don't have any originality, and my coordination isn't very good!" is also not atypical. In its more general form of at least partial identification with the handicapped sibling, it can be seen again in the discussions of the young adolescent siblings described in the next chapter.

Cindy believed that Marvin had been "hit on the head by someone" and so damaged. Normal siblings, particularly young ones, often attribute their brother's or sister's defect to such an attack and consequently fear bringing that same attack down on themselves, for some transgression they cannot imagine.

Finally, Cindy believed her curiosity was bad and dangerous. She feared to ask or to know about sex and also about Marvin's retardation, yet her lack of information about these most important topics led her into further difficulties: in particular, unrealistic fantasies and fears.

In addition to shedding light on the thoughts, fears, and fantasies of brothers and sisters of retarded children, Cindy's story illustrates well the limitations of what we have termed the "change-the-child" approach to mental retardation. Treating Cindy, and before her Marvin, as if the children and their intellectual limitations constituted the whole problem was to ignore the major psycho-social dimensions of the situation. Cindy's handicap alone would have caused minimal disruption in her ability to grow and develop in a supportive family situation. It was not her actual limitations but the meaning these perceived defects had for her parents and for the community in which they lived that led them to respond in such a disastrous and tragic manner.

CHAPTER 3

Young Adolescents Talk

THE CASE HISTORY OF CINDY was presented because it highlights some of the fears and fantasies found in brothers and sisters of retarded children. This chapter describes some clinical contacts with two groups of siblings of retarded children, young siblings and teenagers who participated in a discussion group. In addition to adding to an understanding of how young people come to understand and deal with retardation in the family, the material provides much support for our view that Cindy's concerns were not unique to her or only to other disturbed children. These normal teenagers expressed many of the same anxieties.

For example, Cindy felt she must be retarded since her older brother was. The group members struggled with a similar question: if I have a handicapped brother or sister, does that mean something must be wrong with me, too? Cindy felt her curiosity about her retarded brother was her "sickness"; the adolescents graphically described and illustrated how difficult it was for them and their parents openly to discuss their siblings' handicaps.

Finally, this chapter may serve as a rough guide for those interested in working with teenage siblings in a group setting.

Several years ago, in our cinical contacts at a regional center for retarded children, the weight of evidence began to accumulate to suggest that siblings of retarded children are often adversely affected.[1] Parents frequently voiced concern to us about their normal children and the effect the retarded child had on their lives. Because of the emphasis of the staff of this facility on serving the entire family in its natural setting—the home—the clinical staff was brought into increasing contact with the siblings. One

1. This chapter was coauthored by Elizabeth Fox, and previously published (Kaplan and Fox, 1968).

staff member described a normal sibling who had unconsciously begun to imitate the petit mal attacks suffered by her older sister. There were no grounds for suspecting actual neurological pathology in this "normal" girl. Rather, all the available evidence suggested she was acting out her identification with her sister. This 10-year-old became quite depressed when her sister came into residence at the retardation facility. When I talked with her, she denied having any troubling thoughts or feelings—with one exception. When she went to bed (her sister previously shared the room with her) she would suddenly become afraid the "boogey man will come and take me away," and then she was unable to stay alone in the room. Although she rationally knew why her sister was institutionalized, and that it would not happen to her, her fantasies reflected the underlying fears common to many siblings that perhaps it could happen to her. Another fantasy was the idea that she might in some unknown way be defective herself. All of these experiences underlined the need for further study of the problem. A search of the literature revealed little work on siblings, although the need for professional aid has been noted from time to time (e.g., Carver, 1956; Caldwell and Guze, 1960; Graliker, Fishler, and Koch, 1962; Farber, 1963; Farber and Jenné, 1963). Farber and Ryckman (1965) reviewed the literature on family interactions when a retarded child is present and concluded that the family relations of normal siblings are seriously affected. Our first article (Kaplan and Colombatto, 1966) described a project with younger siblings of retarded children in a Head Start program. Schreiber and Feeley (1965) described the only service program reported in the literature. They met with a selected group of 10 adolescents who had indicated an interest in participating in a meeting in which they could discuss the questions and problems they had in dealing with their retarded brothers or sisters. The project with young adolescent siblings described below, and the one described by Schreiber and Feeley, arose independently to fill a need experienced by staff members working with families having a retarded child.

GROUP DISCUSSION FOR ADOLESCENT SIBLINGS

To pursue the questions about the sibling population, a project was undertaken to learn about young adolescent siblings of retarded children. Our interests were both to learn about siblings and also to learn when and in what ways preventive intervention might be effective. We had a chance to learn in at least two ways. First, we could find out if the kind of group we were establishing could alleviate and help resolve existing problems which, although not currently being treated, could lead to more serious disturbances in the future. Second, we could begin to explore, through retrospective analysis, what difficulties the siblings encountered when they first became aware of their brothers' or sisters' retardation, and how they might have been helped at that time. Unlike many functional disturbances, the problem of mental retardation as a family concern can often be traced to a particular point in time when the retardate was identified. Since a professional person is usually involved at that point, again unlike the situation in the development of most psychological disturbances, the chances for preventive work with other members of the family are maximized. Hence, if we could learn from these adolescents what pressing questions and fears they possessed related to having a retarded sibling, the opportunity to use such information for a preventive program would be great.

A third issue of major relevance which could be explored in a sibling program would be the extent to which such a program could have therapeutic effects on the retardate. We felt that any effective program for the "patient"—in this case the retarded child —must involve family members. Participation in this group was seen as one method of helping the normal child modify his behavior toward his defective sibling. In this way, the group could help not only the siblings involved but could also help effect change within the network of family members' relationships and attitudes toward the retarded child.

With these interests in mind, we initiated a pilot project with siblings of retardates at the regional center. The specific aims of this project were to understand more clearly the special problems of siblings of retarded children and to explore ways of meeting their needs.

This pilot project lasted approximately four months. At that point the program was reviewed, and on the basis of this evaluation a second sibling program was established. Before describing the second group in more detail, we will briefly discuss some of the many problems which arose in establishing the pilot project.

The co-leaders originally tried to organize the group through the staff members at the regional center. The idea of such a group had been raised at a number of staff meetings, and the leaders felt the staff had some basic understanding of the group's goals and possible therapeutic effects. The staff was asked to refer any siblings between the ages of 12 and 16 who they felt would benefit from the group, and to contact their families to see if they would be interested in having these children come. Some contacts were made in this fashion, and most of the families expressed an interest in the group. However, when a date for the first meeting was made, very few adolescents planned to come, and the inadequacy of this approach became apparent. Largely because of our own lack of clarity about how the group would function, the staff had little understanding of how the group was going to work and what it was going to accomplish. As a result, they could not easily feel that helping to organize the group was worth a substantial effort on their part. And due to the deep concern parents had about their children participating in such a meeting, it required a determined effort to maintain the parents' commitment to the program. This parental resistance represented a major obstacle, since the children were completely dependent upon their parents for transportation.

The project could have been abandoned when this lack of motivation became apparent. However, we were convinced that one cannot always wait for clients to come on their own to professionals—sometimes mental health workers must actively seek out those who may need help. In fact, our experiences in community mental health work suggests that it is those who do not come easily and willingly who most need the time and attention of professionals in the field (see Sarason *et al.*, 1966). This group seemed to us to be important enough to these youngsters to warrant an intensive recruiting effort on the leaders' part.

We called all of the adolescents recommended, including

those who had already been approached by other staff members. In most instances, the call was followed by a home visit, designed to explain the group further to the sibling and to deal with the many questions and concerns of the parents. The parents seemed primarily apprehensive that their children would reveal things about the family and the retardate which they wished to keep secret. One father, after talking with a co-leader about the group and its purpose of providing a place for these young people to talk about their problems, agreed to his son's participation, then turned to the boy and said, "O.K., start talking. I'd like to hear what you have to say." Although he had agreed to having his son in the group, he was still worried about what the boy might say.

We subsequently discovered that retardation was not discussed openly in many of these families and that many parents were afraid of having their children even consider the subject. They seemed worried about the kinds of questions the siblings would ask, what they might say about how the parents treated the retarded child, and what the siblings' attitudes toward the retarded child might reveal. These home visits, and the opportunity they provided for talking with the parents, seemed to be sufficient to deal with their concerns. We felt fairly confident that they would prove reliable in providing transportation.

The adolescents contacted varied widely on a number of dimensions. In particular, no attempt was made to equate degree or type of retardation among their siblings, so their brothers or sisters ranged from a moderately retarded child with Down's Syndrome and a severely physically involved cerebral-palsied girl to several mildly retarded children in educable classes in the public schools. Of that group, four were in residence in the regional center and several others attended the day program. In addition, no attempt was made to screen the adolescents themselves, so their own intellectual level, degree of psychological health, and even social class varied fairly widely.

THE PILOT GROUP

The meetings of the pilot group were conducted by the author and a then third-year psychological intern. The group met one evening a week for an hour and a quarter and refreshments were served. With the consent of the members, all meetings were tape-recorded.

The leaders opened the first meeting by defining two major goals of the group. One was to help the psychologists learn what it was like to be a brother or sister of a retarded child, how it affected the normal siblings' lives, what difficulties it caused them, if any, and what implications their experience had for people working in the field of retardation. The second was to provide the siblings with an opportunity to share their own thoughts and feelings with others in a similar situation in the hope that this sharing might be both interesting and helpful to them. The leaders provided no specific format for the meetings, but told the members that it was up to them to decide how they wanted to run the meetings and what they wanted to discuss. In general, the co-leaders sought to encourage open discussion and expression of ideas and fantasies by the group members, and to avoid being perceived as experts who had the answers to all questions.

Although these ground rules may have been appropriate in the long run, they seemed to lead to tension and discomfort during the early meetings. These adolescents were not used to talking openly about retardation and their retarded siblings, especially with strangers. They had great difficulty in finding a level of discourse which was neither banal nor anxiety-provoking. For the most part, they preferred to keep the conversation at a relatively superficial level and depended on the leaders to suggest topics and keep the conversation going. The co-leaders also had difficulty in deciding when and how to intervene in the discussions because of our inexperience with "normal" siblings and our uncertainty about what a group of "normal" adolescent siblings would be able to discuss. Occasionally, a member would bring up extremely anxiety-provoking ideas which aroused great discomfort and seemed to confirm their feelings about retardation. At the second meeting, for example, the conversation was dominated by the concerns and fantasies of a boy whose comments seemed quite disturbed and disorganized. He began by talking about seizures and said that his sister looked dead when she was having one. He later went on to say, when the discussion turned to the causes of retardation, that his sister's slowness was caused by a lump on the back of her head which secreted poison. He felt that she would be all right if doctors could remove the lump. Both of these topics fascinated every member of the group. However, raised in this way, and at this stage of group development, these subjects tended more to frighten group members and to discourage participation than to involve them in meaningful discussion. (In the second group, when the siblings had come to establish strong ties to each other and to the group leaders, many of them were able to discuss these same topics with relative ease.) The siblings' anxiety interacting with the difficulties of the co-leaders led to long, painful silences which only the most courageous could break. At least 3 of the 14 members stopped coming, and all the others felt continued uneasiness.

Another factor contributing to difficulties in discussion was the constantly changing membership of the meetings. Contrary to our initial hopes, parents were not wholly reliable in providing transportation, so that even if the siblings wanted to come to the meetings some of them were unable to do so. The uneven and disturbing quality of the meetings contributed to erratic attendance, for some group members would stay away a week or two after a particularly upsetting meeting. As a result of all these problems, attendance varied from a low of 5 to a high of 14 people, and each meeting had a slightly different membership from the one preceding or following it.

Despite these numerous difficulties, the co-leaders felt that the group was fulfilling some of its aims. A number of fruitful and intriguing discussions had taken place. Siblings who attended fairly regularly began to show strong loyalty to the group and indicated its importance to them in many ways. For example, they were hurt and angry when, after several months, the leaders proposed adding new members to the group. One member who had never missed a meeting expressed his resentment by boycotting the meeting following this discussion; *i.e.,* they felt they were "advanced" members who had learned a good deal and did not want to start back at the beginning with anyone new. In various ways, then, the leaders were encouraged to continue with the group if some of its major shortcomings could be overcome.

Issues Considered in Forming a Second Group

Issues such as transportation and parents' resistance could be approached more effectively than had been done in the pilot project. However, the co-leaders felt that some additional change was probably necessary to help adolescents verbalize their feelings in the group situation. One possibility was to limit group membership to highly motivated, relatively stable, and verbal siblings, as Schreiber and Feeley (1965) had done. In addition, we could have given the discussions an educational orientation and restricted the discussion to a relatively factual level. However, these possibilities seemed contrary to the original purpose. If the unmotivated, disturbed, or nonverbal youngsters were eliminated, the group would not be reaching those adolescents who most needed it. It was not consonant with our philosophy to restrict the group to those who came without urging and who could participate freely and appropriately. Similarly, limiting the discussions to an educational focus did not seem to be the solution. Only a relatively unstructured situation would permit and encourage the expression by the members of their underlying fantasies about their retarded brothers and sisters and about themselves, and we felt this to be essential to our understanding of the problems facing them, as well as to their own growth.

An alternative to placing limitations on group membership and discussion was suggested by a staff member of the Regional Center. He proposed that the group spend part of its time doing volunteer work with some of the residents at the Regional Center. Group members had asked, from time to time, if they could do volunteer work at the Regional Center, and the idea of combining volunteer activity with the discussion group intrigued the leaders. This activity might allow the siblings to express themselves about retarded children without having to talk explicitly about their own brothers or sisters. Further, their contact with other retardates would help broaden their perspective on retardation and help them to think through their relationships with their own siblings. In addition, this experience could provide a common basis for communication and help stimulate group discussion. When this combined activity-discussion group was proposed to the siblings, they responded with enthusiasm.

Various changes were incorporated into the establishment and functioning of the second group. The meetings, held only every other week, lasted for 2 hours, the first 45 minutes being spent with some of the retarded children in residence, the rest of the time devoted to a group discussion about what the siblings had done, what children they had watched or played with, and what ideas and questions they had as a result of these contacts. We were able to offer transportation to about half the members of the group.

Experience with the pilot group had underlined the importance of enlisting the parents' support and of allaying their anxieties as much as possible. To this end, after letters were sent out announcing the changes in the group and inviting several siblings who had not been members of the first group, we telephoned each family to give further information and encouragement. Both the parents and siblings were invited to the initial meeting, the parents meeting separately with one leader while the siblings held their meeting with the other.

A majority of the siblings had at least one parent present at this meeting, and these parents shared a number of feelings about having their normal children involved in such a program. Their attitude was highly favorable, but they also expressed some concern that their children might betray family secrets; they all indicated tremendous curiosity about what their children were saying. Their concerns and fears were clarified and discussed with them. Somewhat surprisingly to the leaders, the parents indicated rather strongly their wish for a similar group of their own, led by a co-leader of the sibling group. Finally, they arranged to meet occasionally with one of the co-leaders to discuss how things were going.

THE SECOND GROUP: PHASES OF DEVELOPMENT

The new teenage group started with 14 members, several of whom had participated in the original group. The development of the new group seemed to fall into several phases. During the first several meetings the members were excited and fascinated by the experience of meeting the retarded children and of becoming acquainted with the Regional Center. They also seemed to be buoyed up by the feeling that this group was going to "work," and that, frightening as the prospect might be, they were going to have a genuine opportunity to discuss their retarded brothers and sisters.

In contrast to the meetings of the pilot group, these first few meetings were characterized by active participation, with people frequently interrupting each other. During the time spent with the retardates, the co-leaders worked actively to help the siblings interact with them. At this stage, the siblings wanted to do things for the retardates: organize activities, lead games, etc. As the novelty of the contacts wore off, the siblings realized that it was not easy to keep a game going with a retardate, and that it was often difficult just to remain with one for any period of time.

This realization led into what seemed to be the second phase of the meetings. Although the prolonged and painful silences which typified the pilot meetings did not recur, the siblings began to turn away from the problem of retardation and their difficulties with their brothers and sisters toward thinking of the group as a club for organizing social activities for the children at the Regional Center. For example, they wanted to pay dues which they could then use for parties for the retarded children. What little they said about their experiences with the children indicated that the siblings were having trouble thinking of activities for them and that they felt frustrated and helpless in trying to interact with them. In a group of nonsiblings, this frustration might have been expressed and dealt with in an open way, but with these siblings it seemed to reactivate their feelings of helplessness toward their own retarded sibs, which was a difficult subject to discuss.

The group indicated by some of their comments their own awareness that they were avoiding important issues. The co-leaders again raised the question of the purpose of the meetings. At the meeting where they had agreed to collect dues we asked them if that was really what the meetings were for, and whether they wanted the meetings to turn into an organization to plan organized social events for the retarded children or whether they wanted to talk about their own siblings and the problem of retardation. The siblings replied that they really did want to talk about their brothers and sisters. That was why they met, wasn't it? Several of them were able to influence the group to give up the idea of collecting dues, and members began in greater earnest to approach problems concerning the Regional Center children and their own siblings.

From that point, members of the group were able to keep more of the conversation directed toward topics related to their siblings or toward different problems associated with retardation. Before discussing these topics in detail, the interaction between the siblings and the children at the Regional Center and the effect of this contact on the meetings will be described to provide the context for later discussions.

Relationships with the Retarded Children

Just as the tenor of the meetings changed, so did the relationships between the members of the group and the children at the Regional Center. The retardate group consisted of 30 high-functioning retarded children who often spend their evenings in a large living room in their residential unit containing couches and chairs, a TV, and various games and books.

Originally, the siblings felt that they were there to think up things to do and games to play with a fairly unresponsive and possibly recalcitrant group. They expected to put effort into the interaction, but did not really feel that any would be expended by the retardates in return. This seemed to be the case for the first several weeks. However, as soon as the retarded children realized that the group would visit regularly, and as soon as they began to know some of the siblings, they started making definite demands on them. The siblings no longer had to seek out the retarded children—they sought out the siblings instead. It was no longer necessary to think up activities, since they emerged quite naturally within the matrix of friendship. Although this change did not occur with all the siblings, it occurred frequently enough to be considered a stable phenomenon.

In reviewing the ability of this group to deal with issues of retardation and their relationships to their siblings, it would appear that meeting with children at the Regional Center facilitated their discussions in several respects. Perhaps its most important function was to serve as a "half-way house" in their approach to an anxiety-arousing topic. Having this common experience with retarded children other than their own siblings allowed them to share thoughts and feelings which did not necessarily implicate themselves and their own siblings. *Their experiences with the children at the Regional Center provided a safe context within which to discuss the problems.* And the problems they had with these children mirrored those they encountered with their own siblings.

These meetings also seemed to provide the siblings with some perspective about the nature of retardation. For many, retardation had in the past been defined for them solely by their brother or sister. The contact with the Regional Center children broadened their perspective and gave them a somewhat more objective view of their siblings.

Issues Raised in the Discussions

Given this framework of discussion, in which the group members could approach their problems either in terms of their experience with the Regional Center children or directly in terms of their own brothers or sisters, these adolescents were able to discuss a number of central concerns. For example, the issue of being similar to or different from the retarded sibling permeated many of the meetings and seemed to be a source of enormous concern for all of the group members. In fact, the experience with this group suggests that the main task of siblings of defective children is to avoid identifying with them. At times, group members frantically attempted to maximize the differences between themselves and their siblings. At one meeting, a boy described two normal siblings he knew from school. One was very fat and the other excessively thin. They all were impressed that two children so unlike could be from the same family. Implicit in their discussion was the question: if a very fat and a very thin child can come from the same family, can a very slow (retarded) and a bright child also come from the same family? In other words, is it possible for us to be normal, even though we have a retarded sibling?

A second issue that bothered members of this group was how their brothers and sisters understood their affliction, and, more generally, how the retarded children understood the world and what feelings they had about it. Group members agreed that retarded children have feelings, just like everyone else, but they were not sure how much their siblings could understand. This issue is complicated by the fact that the brothers and sisters of the group members represented a wide range of difficulties and levels of functioning, so that, for example, several of the adolescents with severely handicapped siblings seemed to feel that these siblings had little appreciation of their differentness from the normal population, and that it would mean nothing to explain this to them. Others saw this as a real problem. For example, one girl had a sister who was in an educable special class and who probably entertained expectations of getting married and pursuing goals similar to those of her normal sibling. As the normal sister put it: "What do you do, just sit her down and say 'Guess what, Susie. You're retarded!'?" Another problem in understanding was whether the retarded children could tell right from wrong, and whether their destructive behavior was intentional.

This last question is integrally connected with another common problem: how do you control and discipline your brother or sister? Most of these siblings had younger retarded brothers and sisters, and often acted as parent-substitutes in caring for their siblings. Do you hit your brother or sister when he or she does something bad, or do you just ignore it? Most of the group members seemed to agree that normal tactics do not suffice—their retarded siblings seem to persevere much more than normal children. Some felt that perhaps their retarded siblings do not understand enough to be punished, but others felt that their brothers and sisters know when they are doing something wrong, and should be dealt with accordingly. All seemed to agree that their parents were the final authorities and that they had little say (and did not want to have more to say) as to how their brothers and sisters were handled. They were able to admit that they hit their brothers and sisters from time to time, and received group acceptance of this behavior.

A problem about which all group members felt strongly was how they and their families related to the community. They described, with mixed feelings of contempt and injury, the reactions of neighbors to the retarded sibling. Many had been harassed and had watched the sibling insulted and stared at by others. They did not know whether to defend the sibling or just to withdraw him from the situation. The question of what to tell their friends was also raised. Some had been teased at school; others seemed to have escaped this, but most felt that they could tell only their good friends, and then only if their friends would have to come into contact with the retarded child. They described varying degrees of involvement with their siblings outside the house. Some felt comfortable in taking their siblings on special trips, or having the sibling come along when they went shopping or to a movie. Others seemed to have as little to do with the sibling as possible. The sensitivity of these adolescents to the reactions of others was seen in miniature in the living unit at the Regional Center, since three members of the group had siblings in residence there. They had been remarkably reluctant to share this information with the group and the group equally adverse to perceiving it. One member's irregular attendance was probably due to his concern about being identified with his sibling. This issue is, of course, another part of their concern about being the same or different from their retarded siblings.

Another core topic which was approached less directly by the group, and which continued to evoke a great deal of anxiety, was how discussions about retardation were handled in the family. We had explicit statements from both siblings and their parents that talking about retardation was like talking about sex. One mother expressed this opinion in a parents' meeting, going on to say that she and her husband always answered any questions the children asked. Clearly, many questions never get asked. Some questions that were left unanswered, or at least not answered to the siblings' satisfaction included: What are seizures all about? Why should (or shouldn't) retarded siblings marry, and how is it that sometimes retarded people have children? What effects will having a retarded sibling have on their ability to have children that are normal?

It was apparent that the normal adolescents in this group developed a real capacity to express their thoughts and feelings about their retarded siblings. Parallel to this was the development of a strong attachment to the group and to individual members of it. Many of the young people seemed to have benefited from the experience. Several of their parents told us how much more comfortable the adolescent seemed with his or her own sibling. Some of the young people told us themselves how much they had enjoyed the group. Many would have liked the group to continue, and others who had not participated asked if they might join.

From our perspective as co-leaders, we felt it had been a strenuous experience: we had worked very hard to get the young people to come regularly and to help stimulate active and useful discussions. We also felt it had been worthwhile from two perspectives. We did feel it benefited many of them. And we learned from the group, as well as from the individual clinical contacts described at the beginning of the chapter, a great deal more about the problems and potentials of young brothers and sisters of retarded children.

Whether such group discussions are the best way to help young adolescents remains unclear. Although, as we have said, many members of the group liked this approach, the effort required by us to maintain the group was prohibitive; we could not sustain it for an extended period of time. Possibly, either a slightly younger group—all late latency-age children—or a slightly older group—all middle to late teenagers—would accomplish as much as we were able to do, with less resistance.

CHAPTER 4

College Students: Who Talked With Us

So FAR, we have described a series of clinical observations of normal siblings of retarded children. The clinical impressions and hypotheses they generated led us to embark on a more formal and full-scale study of the issues.

Because the research was a direct outgrowth of our view of the problem, a brief restatement of that view might clarify why we chose the approach we did. As stated in Chapter 1, we were convinced that retardation is not simply a defect that occurs to, or resides in, an individual. Rather it appeared to us to be an event that involves and includes the total family unit and often parts of the larger community as well. This is most strikingly illustrated in those cases where the functional retardation itself is a result of family dynamics (*e.g.*, Staver, 1953); it is perhaps less obvious but equally true when the original retardation has an organic basis which then comes to have a variety of meanings for the family. These meanings and the methods family members use to deal with their significance affect how the retarded child and all other members of the family are encouraged and allowed to develop. Too often the eventual adjustment of the family limits and distorts one or more possibilities for growth. That some families seem to thrive despite or because of the retarded child suggests that there are potentially adaptive ways of coping with retardation. An awareness of this fact opens the possibility of providing guidance to assist families in finding an adaptive and productive adjustment.

By this time, too, we were committed to the view that preventive interventions can no longer be limited to developing ways of decreasing the incidence of defective children, although obviously this is vitally important. Prevention must also include helping families who already have a retarded child to cope in a way that enhances, or at least does not hinder, the family members' opportunities for growth and development. The precursors of our sibling research suggested the importance of several factors: the way the family talks about retardation and the problems of the retarded child; how parents deal with their own aggression toward the retarded child; how they teach the normal children to do this; how they handle community relationships with the retarded child; and how they assist their normal children in understanding and explaining the issues involved. Relatively little effort is required by professionals to talk with families about these issues at the time the retardation is first discovered, when families are so needful of support and information. In contrast, trying to undo damage accumulated over many years is often impossible and at best an inefficient use of community resources.

Even more broadly, we were coming to see the problem of a family dealing with a retarded child—and all this means to them— as one instance of a universal experience: how a family copes with unexpected disappointment and trauma. Few families can avoid such experiences, whether it be in the form of a retarded child, a chronically ill member, a serious accident, or some other extended stressful event. Despite the many specific differences in these experiences, the core issue seemed to us to be how a family responds to severe and continued stress, which often occurs without warning. One could argue that it is only when professionals and others can begin to see that retardation does not represent a unique set of problems unrelated to all other mental health situations will the artificial separation between these areas disappear and fruitful interchange occur.

The formal research was developed and executed over a 5-year period and focused on 83 college siblings of retarded children. In this chapter, the college students who talked with us, as well as our method of recruiting them, are described.

WHO PARTICIPATED

Although we learned a great deal from the group described in Chapter 3, talking only with young adolescents who are often uncomfortable when discussing personal issues with a strange adult was not entirely satisfactory as a means of obtaining information about siblings of retarded children. For that and other reasons, we chose to study college students. Our experience and that of our colleagues had suggested that they tend to talk freely and openly about themselves in an experimental situation. Many are bright and verbal. While memories of their earlier relationships to siblings are undoubtedly distorted to some degree, we believed that their relative independence from the family group would make it easier for them to discuss the situation without the need for massive defensive maneuvers. Finally, their attendance at a college implies a degree of adjustment beyond that found in an unselected group of college-age young people. This degree of adjustment undoubtedly facilitates their ability to talk comfortably about their experiences with a retarded sibling.

Our initial sample consisted of men undergraduates at an Ivy League college. (These men are described in detail below.) After collecting and analyzing this data, we were impressed by the further need to learn about women siblings and about young men and women from more varied social-class backgrounds. We were able to get permission to carry out the research at a competitive, small, private women's college, and at two noncompetitive community colleges (hereafter referred to as Community U or, when differentiation between the two schools is required, as Community U1 and U2). Our method of recruiting subjects and our research procedures were virtually identical for all students. The names of students were obtained from the dean's office or school directory, and personally addressed letters were sent out to all members of several classes at each school. The letter described our interest in college students with a retarded brother or sister and requested their participation. A brief form and a return envelope were enclosed with each letter. The letter requested that each student return the enclosed form after indicating on it the age and sex of any siblings, and if any was mentally retarded.

They were asked to sign the form if they were interested in participating as a brother or sister of a normal or handicapped child. We offered $1.50 per hour for their participation. Arrangements were made for the forms to be deposited in a box centrally located on each campus.

The response rates varied from 36-percent returns at the private women's school and the Ivy League school, to 7 percent at Community U1. In all, 37 brothers of retarded children volunteered from the Ivy League college, 25 sisters from the women's private college, and 29 men and women siblings from Community U. A small additional group of siblings of retarded children (SibHs) was obtained by writing to all college-age siblings of children at the community Regional Center for the Mentally Retarded.[1] These last were included with the SibHs from the two Community U's, since their backgrounds and educational experiences were comparable to those of the students in these groups. (Table 1 shows the number of letters delivered to students at each school, the number and percentage of responses, how many of these volunteered to participate, and the proportion of SibHs and siblings of only normal children [SibNs] responding in each group.) All SibHs who volunteered were contacted by postcard and/or telephone and an appointment time arranged. Several from each sample were eliminated from the final analyses on the basis that their sibling's handicap was totally unrelated to mental retardation or clear organic damage affecting psychological functioning. All of the students who volunteered and whom we considered appropriate for the study remained in the research. Our persistent and enthusiastic pursuit of potential "no-show" subjects made it virtually impossible for a subject to drop out once he had given his initial consent. (Our "pursuit" included making innumerable phone calls, once interviewing a girl in her dormitory room, etc.)

The last section of Table 2 shows the final four groups of students—one each from the Ivy League school, the women's private school, and men and women from Community U, as well as the religious affiliation of their family, the number of children

1. In response to 86 letters sent out, 13 replied that they were in college and would participate.

in the family, and the sex of the handicapped child. All were college students ranging in age from 18 to 25. All but one were white, and we did not know that one was black until he volunteered the information. The majority were from Protestant families; Catholics comprised the next largest religious group.

A comparison among the four groups of SibHs on such demographic variables as social-class background and the number of children in the family showed that the most striking differences were in social class. (The actual scoring for these and all other items is described in Table 10. The details of the statistical analysis of these demographic variables are in Table 3. Table 4 shows the interrelations among these demographic variables and the scores reflecting the severity of H's handicap within each sample.) While students from the private women's and Ivy League colleges came primarily from middle- and upper middle-class families, Community U students came from upper lower and from lower middle-class families. (Because this social-class difference plays such a large role in the interpretation of the results of the study, a breakdown of the four samples by class is shown in Table 5.)

CHARACTERISTICS OF THE HANDICAPPED CHILDREN

The handicapped brothers and sisters (Hs) of these college students varied enormously on all important dimensions, such as severity of mental or physical handicap and their age relationship to the age of SibH.[2] Although several suffered brain injury following an illness in childhood, most were retarded from birth or shortly thereafter. (Their specific diagnoses are listed in Table 2.)

No significant differences existed among the four samples in severity of mental or physical handicap (Table 6). (In the popu-

2. The "diagnosis" used in the research was arrived at by first asking the SibH how H was diagnosed (and occasionally having SibH write the parents for information if he or she did not know). We used this information in conjunction with detailed information about exactly what the handicapped child could do, e.g., what self-care skills he or she had, if the child talked, etc. Although some H's undoubtedly were misdiagnosed at least partially, either in terms of label or intellectual level, in general we feel the ratings sufficiently accurate to be relied upon for the purposes of this research.

lation at large, severely retarded children are evenly distributed across socioeconomic class groups [Kushlick, 1960].) As Table 7 shows, 17 percent of the retarded children fell into the severely or profoundly retarded category (IQ less than 25), 35 percent into the moderately retarded category (IQ between 25 and 50), and the largest proportion, 48 percent, into the mildly retarded category (IQ above 50). (This last group also included a few H's who were cerebral-palsied but not mentally defective.) The distribution was approximately the same for the degree of physical handicap or stigmata, but with the largest group being moderately physically handicapped or marked.[3] Over-all, 25 percent of the sample was diagnosed as having Down's Syndrome (Mongolism).[4]

Retarded male children outnumbered females in each sample. In all, twice as many male Hs were represented by their siblings as female Hs. (In the population at large, more boys are retarded than girls, but only by a few percentage points.)

Finally, there were significant differences in the age at which the retarded child was institutionalized and the total amount of time he or she spent in residential facilities between the retarded siblings of students from the private women's and Ivy League colleges, on the one hand, and Community U on the other (Table 6). The handicapped children represented by the former group were institutionalized earlier and for longer periods of time than the children represented by the Community U students. (These data, and their importance, are considered in detail in Chapter 12.)

THE CONTROL GROUP

Of the siblings of normal children (SibNs) who volunteered, 66 were selected on the basis that they, as a group, were similar to

3. Although in the total population a high proportion of retarded people fall into the mildly retarded category, the classification includes cultural-familiar retardation, which is concentrated in the lower classes (*e.g.*, Kessler, 1966). Our sample is comprised primarily of children with retardation due to organic causes, who tend to be lower in IQ.

4. In the population of organically impaired retarded children, Down's Syndrome constitutes the largest single diagnostic entity (Wunsch, 1957).

the SibH group in academic-year level, number of children in the family, sibling position by order and sex, and the religious affiliation of the family. Because our primary focus was on the SibHs, and because of the time and expense involved in seeing each student and processing the data, a much smaller number of SibNs were used as a control group. In the final sample of SibNs, there were no significant differences between the SibHs and SibNs within each of the four samples on the dimensions of social class, religious orientation of the family, the number of children in the family, the sibling position of Sib, or the intactness of the Sib's parents' marriage. Table 8 shows the distribution of men and women subjects in the SibN and SibH groups in each of the four samples.

Is the Sample Representative?

Of vital importance to the research is the question of the representative quality of our volunteer SibHs. That is, did we get nearly all of the brothers and sisters of handicapped children in these college populations, and if not, can we say anything about the characteristics that distinguished those siblings who volunteered to talk with us about their experiences from those who did not respond to the letter? As a beginning attempt to answer this question, we decided to obtain a 100-percent survey of some small but representative group of students from one or more of these college populations. This was possible for both the private women's school and the Ivy League school, but not for Community U1 or U2. In each of the former two schools, we selected a living unit that was representative of the college population and approached each student in that unit personally—not on the telephone. Each student was asked the same questions we had indicated on the form: if he had any siblings and how many there were, if any were handicapped, what the nature of the handicap was, and the family's religious orientation. Although it is possible for a reticent sibling to lie to the interviewer, we doubt that this occurred with enough frequency to influence the results; this approach seemed to give an accurate picture of the population.

In the Ivy League school, 312 students were surveyed. (Only 2 from that dormitory unit could not be reached.) Of these, 7 had handicapped siblings; 3 were already in the research, 3 others were not in classes that had received the letter. In the women's private school, 133 women were queried and of these, 7 had handicapped siblings. Five had volunteered originally, the other 2 had not.

The proportion of siblings of handicapped children was higher in both surveys than in the returns from the research letter. In the Ivy League school, 2.2 percent of the students in the 100-percent survey indicated they had one or more retarded siblings, while in response to our letter, 1.2 percent acknowledged having a handicapped brother or sister. As we noted, in our 100-percent survey data, 3 of the possible 4 SibHs who had received the letter had volunteered. The data from the private women's school were similar. Of those who returned the forms, 2.1 percent said they had a retarded sibling, while the percentage found in the 100-percent survey was 5.3 percent. Five of the 7 potential SibHs who had received the letter had volunteered.

These data raise an important question: why was the proportion of siblings of handicapped children higher in the 100-percent survey than in the response to the research letter? It is undoubtedly true that, with such small samples, random variation in proportion is great. Further, the discrepancy between volunteer and nonvolunteer siblings of a retarded child was small among the survey sample: of 11 potential SibHs who received the letter, 8 volunteered. However, the fact that in both cases more siblings of retarded children appeared in the 100-percent survey, and that not all we found in that survey had volunteered, suggests that some number of potential SibHs did not respond to the letter. To the extent that these nonresponders varied in some systematic way from the SibHs who did volunteer, the bias has to be considered in any interpretation of the research findings.

Several possible factors could have deterred some potential SibHs from volunteering. Some people characteristically tend to volunteer to participate in research more than others (e.g., Rosenthal and Rosnow, 1969). Further, in most psychological research, some proportion of those who volunteer never come to their appointments. Rosenthal and Rosnow suggest that these "no-shows" are psychologically similar to nonvolunteers. As was mentioned, we were able to keep all potential no-shows in the study, and consequently do have data on individuals similar to nonvolunteers. Their potential "no-showing" is reflected in our "lateness" score, which rates the degree of difficulty the Sibs had keeping their research appointments. [Table 10, V (6).] Since few significant differences on our psychological measures appeared among students varying on this lateness dimension, we have reason to believe this quality is not related to the dimensions of interest to us and consequently could not introduce any significant bias.

The more important factors deterring some siblings of retarded children from volunteering for this study probably relate more specifically to retardation and the difficulty people have in discussing it. Some inferences regarding the probable nature of this bias can be drawn from a comparison of two family characteristics of the SibHs and the over-all college population, represented by the survey data, from the two colleges for which these survey data are available (Table 9). In both samples, the SibHs, in contrast to the general college population, tended to come from larger families. In particular, a much smaller proportion of our SibHs came from two-children families than did students in general at both the private women's and Ivy League schools. In the former, significantly fewer SibHs were Jewish than in that college population.

(The siblings of normal brothers and sisters who volunteered to participate did not differ in any systematic way from the survey population. This suggests that the selective factor in responding was not simply due to the way the letter was phrased or some other research artifact unrelated to having a handicapped sibling.)

Some types of retardation, such as Down's Syndrome, are associated with the age of the mother, and hence occur more frequently in larger families when the mother is still having children at an older age (Jervis, 1959), and one quarter of the siblings in this sample carried this diagnosis. To some extent, this could account for the discrepancy in family size between our sample and the total population. However, it seems unlikely that this was the only factor, particularly since there is no evidence available that fewer retarded children of organic etiology (as are most of these Hs) are born to Jewish families, or, with the exception of Down's Syndrome, in smaller families. Further, again excluding Down's Syndrome, mental retardation does not occur with any greater frequency at any place in the birth order (Benda, 1960).

Another interpretation of these data is that students from families most traumatized by the handicap did not identify themselves as SibHs and did not volunteer to participate in the research. The impact of retardation seems to be much greater in smaller families than in larger, where other children can help to meet the needs and expectations of the parents for their offspring. Several researchers (e.g., Stubblefield, 1965; Zuk, Miller, Bartrum, and Kling, 1961) have found that Jewish families have more difficulty coping with a retarded child than do Protestant or Catholic families. Thus, siblings from smaller families and from Jewish families (which also are often smaller) may be sufficiently troubled by the issue to want to avoid discussing it.

Rosenthal and Rosnow (1969), in their summary of articles discussing the effects of anxiety level and psychopathology on volunteering, report that nonvolunteers, particularly for interview studies that might be anxiety-arousing, tend to be less well adjusted and more anxious. Westley and Epstein (1969) found that a far greater proportion of parents of college children rated as disturbed by the researchers refused to participate in their research, compared with parents of students rated as healthy.

These findings support our inference that those students who did volunteer were probably better adjusted and came from families less traumatized by the retardation than the nonvolunteers. To the extent that this is the case, any negative psychological effects of having a retarded sibling that we found in our data would probably be greater with a more complete sample. In other words, at least for the students from the private women's and Ivy League schools, our subjects were probably the ones who were less negatively affected by the experience. In addition, for the results that focus on the relationships within the SibH population and their families, the sample bias would tend to reduce the variation along a number of dimensions. This degree of homogeneity reduced the probability of obtaining statistical significance of predicted relationships. Although a more complete sample would be preferable, the impact of the likely sample bias on these data was to strengthen our confidence in significant results that did appear.

Another question raised by the data on the proportion of students responding to the questionnaire involves the comparability of the samples from the women's private and Ivy League schools, on the one hand, and Community U1 and U2 on the other. The fact that the proportions responding to the letter from the former two schools were both similar, and relatively high, as well as the apparently similar biases in the selection of who replied, suggest some comparability of samples. That is, these data permit one to assume that in general terms the meaning of the letter, of the research, and of the students' responses to it, were approximately comparable among the groups from the Ivy League school and the private women's school. Consequently, and for purposes of clarity, these schools are referred to as "Private U" hereafter.

There is no reason to believe that the research had the same comparable meaning to the students in the two other colleges (as it did to students of Private U), or among the individual Community U students. Not only is the proportion of respondents very much smaller, but the entire process of recruitment was different in these two settings. (The lower rate of return of this upper lower and lower middle-class sample is consistent with results of many other studies [Rosenthal and Rosnow, 1969].) In Private U, lists of students and their places of residence were available, as well as a systematic method of contacting them by letter established by the schools themselves. In neither Community U1 nor U2 was it easy to get such a list, nor was there any systematic and reliable means of distributing letters to students. On the college campus of Private U, the authorities could point out a centrally located spot for a box for returns. On neither Community U1 nor U2 campus did such an obviously central location exist. Certainly the fact that one of the two latter schools was not primarily residential—and in fact had many students attending nights, part time, etc.—changed the character of the college considerably. All of these factors undoubtedly influenced both the way the research letter was viewed by the students, and the factors involved in their decisions to participate or not.

Our research contacts with these students supported the assumption that they were quite different as a group from the students at Private U. Students attending both Private U schools are extremely homogeneous as a group, relative to the students in Community U1 and U2. Although there is some variation in social-class background among these men and women from Private U, all come from families where education is highly valued. Most come from upper middle-class backgrounds, and the students themselves all had to be bright enough and motivated enough to meet the very selective admission requirements. They tend to be proud of their schools and of their participation in them, and, by and large, view social science research as a meaningful aspect of their total college experience. Further, because we obtained a higher percentage return from these groups, we are confident that our data do represent the population, with the biases as we have described.

The student populations at Community U1 and U2 are extremely varied. Both schools have noncompetitive entrance requirements and are inexpensive to attend. Neither stresses academic excellence. Students attend these two schools for a variety of reasons. Some, for example, have little interest in, or knowledge about, higher education and it did not occur to them to try to go to a better school. At the other extreme are students whose families have so little money that although the student is bright and motivated he cannot afford to go elsewhere. Some students attend these colleges because they are also holding jobs in the community, because their spouse works in the community, or because the student is too psychologically disturbed to manage a more competitive situation despite high ability. In other words, the motivations, family backgrounds, ability levels, etc., are extremely varied.

Given this variation, in the context of a low rate of return to the initial letter and the absence of a survey in either Community U1 or U2, we have less confidence in our ability to generalize to the total population of SibHs in this population. However, the interrelationships that existed among these data did raise important hypotheses about the similarities and differences between this population of SibHs and those from Private U.

CHAPTER 5

College Students:
What We Asked Them

OUR PRIMARY METHOD OF LEARNING about these young men and women was by talking with them: asking questions and listening to all aspects of their answers. We introduced the interview by describing how we had become interested in the topic. We told all of them that there were no secrets involved in the research and that they could ask any questions they wanted to about the interview or any other aspect of the research. Some did ask questions, which we answered to the best of our ability. (Interviews were conducted by the author and several highly trained research assistants.) The interview was semistructured; interviewers followed a set order of items that they could alter readily if the student showed a strong inclination to follow up a thought of his own or develop a different idea. We asked detailed questions about the handicapped sibling, other members of the family, and how the normal sibling felt he or she was doing in college. (The total interview schedule is in Appendix C.) The interview took approximately an hour and a half to complete and was tape-recorded.

After the interview we gave several tests. One consisted of four subtests of the Wechsler Adult Intelligence Scale (WAIS): Information, Vocabulary, Block Design, and Similarities. These were administered following the standard instructions (Wechsler, 1955). Then all subjects were given several self-administered paper-and-pencil tests to complete before they left.[1] An Information Test to measure the subjects' factual knowledge about mental retardation was constructed for the research. This contains 15

1. Actually, several other tests were given as well. They have not been included in the discussion and consequently need not be described here.

items, each worth 2 points, and takes approximately 20 minutes to complete (Appendix D). Finally, the subjects took the Test Anxiety Questionnaire (Sarason and Mandler, 1952), which is a 39-item test asking them whether they experience a variety of anxiety symptoms in school test situations. (The rationale for using a test-anxiety scale rather than a general anxiety test is that this specific test has proved to be a more powerful predictor of a variety of other measures [see Kaplan, 1966].)

The interview and tests often took at least two meetings to complete. At the end of this procedure we again offered each student the opportunity to ask questions about the research, and also to talk with the author (if another interviewer were seeing him) if he or she had further questions or concerns. (Many took advantage of the offer to discuss the research with us.)

SCORING

Each interview was given a code number and transcribed. Only the number remained on the protocol for purposes of identification. When all protocols were typed, the scoring procedure was as follows: each interview was scored according to a rating scheme devised for this research (Table 10). Because these items are so important to understanding the results of the research, they are discussed in some detail here. Brothers and sisters of retarded children were scored on all items; siblings of only normal children were scored on all items not directly involving a retarded sibling.

Each part of every interview was marked as belonging to one of seven broad areas of content, such as "characteristics of the handicapped child" or "curiosity." Initially, two markers determined in which category any part of the interview fitted. However, since agreement was nearly 100 percent, only one rater was required for subsequent interviews. Occasionally, when the material overlapped, two categories were indicated for part of the interview.

After the marking was completed, scorers were assigned.

However, each scorer was assigned only one item within a category to be scored at any given time. Thus, for example, if a scorer was assigned to score the amount of open discussion and curiosity SibH felt about H, he or she would score all protocols on that item, reading only that portion of the interview marked as dealing with open discussion and curiosity. That same scorer would not score the other items within the open discussion–curiosity category.

This method provided several safeguards against scorer bias. By reading only that aspect of the typescript relevant to a particular item, the scorers did not read other information about the subject (or about H, in the case of SibHs) that might bias their judgment either in support of the hypotheses of the study or in any other systematic way. Second, by having different scorers score items in any given area, we eliminated a generalization of scoring response to all the items in the area. This made it more likely, for example, that a family where parents really were inconsistent in their handling of curiosity would receive different scores for the items under curiosity rather than receiving a consistent score produced by the scorer's implicit expectation of consistency.

Four trained scorers, two of them unfamiliar with the hypotheses, did all the scoring. During the training process, all of the scorers rated every item they would ultimately score on five interviews. The scoring was then compared and discussed. Difficult items were scored on an additional five interviews that were again compared and discussed. For the final scoring, all items were rescored, *i.e.*, the practice scores were not used. Following the training, the scorers did not discuss the scoring with each other until it was entirely completed. Nearly all of the final scores were averages of the scores of two scorers. When possible, the scoring on each item was done by one unfamiliar with the hypotheses and one sophisticated scorer.

The scoring of the WAIS subtests and the Test Anxiety Questionnaire was conducted according to the systems described in the relevant literature. The Information Test items were scored by a procedure developed by the author.

INTERVIEWER AND INTERSCORER RELIABILITIES

We wondered if our own personal characteristics, interests, etc., influenced the way we conducted the interviews with the students, and, if so, if this might have affected what they told us about their experiences. An analysis of variance was carried out to compare subjects' responses to various questions when asked by different interviewers. Because one interviewer did more than half of all the interviews, scores of her subjects on potentially influenceable items were compared with scores of all other subjects. Only on two items—wonder about the family [Table 10, IV (3)] and curiosity about sex [Table 10, IV (2a, b)]—were there any significant differences. However, since this interviewer talked with roughly an equal number of SibHs from each sample, we were not concerned about this having any significant impact on the final results.

Interscorer reliabilities were computed on all items used in the final analyses. The range from the high 70s to the high 90s was considered satisfactory.

STATISTICAL ANALYSES

Two types of statistical analyses were used to evaluate the results. Analysis of variance was carried out to compare the scores of the SibNs and SibHs, as well as to compare the four samples of SibHs with each other.

The primary analytic process was the partial correlation. Ideally, in research of this nature, major independent variables would be controlled by sampling procedures. For example, to look at the effects of the severity of mental handicap on other variables, samples of siblings of mildly, moderately, and severely retarded children would be selected, with all other important factors such as social class, age relationship between H and SibH, etc., held constant by the sampling. However, such a procedure was not feasible in this study. Given an extremely small population of college brothers and sisters of retarded children, and given the great difficulty of locating and recruiting them, it was necessary to fully utilize all available SibHs.

Major differences among the family situations of siblings within any one group needed to be dealt with by some procedure other than sampling. To accomplish this we employed partial correlation coefficients. This method allowed us to examine the relationship between two variables while statistically eliminating the influence on that relationship of other potentially influential factors.

Two principles guided us in deciding which variables to partial out of which relationships. First, the severity of H's handicap—including both the degree of mental retardation [Table 10, I (1)] and of physical handicap or stigmata [Table 10, I (2)]—was statistically controlled in virtually all analyses (unless otherwise noted) because of its apparent centrality to the data. Second, in any instance where a major demographic variable (number of children in the family, religion of the family, etc.) correlated significantly with either of the two variables under consideration, that demographic factor was statistically controlled in the analyses. This is a slightly conservative approach; some statisticians recommend partialing a variable out of a correlation only when it correlates significantly with both of the variables of interest (e.g., Blalock, 1961). It was dictated by our concern with being able to see the underlying meaning of any statistically significant relationship.

(The effect of the academic-year level on the Sib's responses was statistically considered and found to be inconsequential. In all subsequent analyses, academic class was disregarded.)

POSSIBLE SOURCES OF BIAS

Relying heavily on interview data, as this research does, leaves open the question: what evidence is there that the students were not telling us what they thought we did (or did not) want to hear? How do we know that the data have any validity?

With regard to these points, several potential sources of bias exist. The most obvious is conscious distortion if the subjects did not take the research seriously or if they had an interest in undermining it. Unconscious distortions of memory and reporting for a variety of reasons are also possible. The subjects may have responded primarily to the social desirability of their answers. Finally, they may have responded to the experimenter's subtle communications of his expectations as to how they should respond (Orne, 1969; Rosenthal, 1968).

As to the first issue, the SibHs indicated in a variety of explicit and implicit ways that they took the research seriously, thought it important, and considered it a way in which they could make a contribution that might help other families with retarded children. Several refused to take money for their participation, and nearly all obviously were trying to be as open and honest with us as they could be.

A second line of evidence concerns the relationship of the relatively factual information obtained from the students about their siblings and family groups and what their parents said in answer to the same questions. In the pilot projects with the first 10 college students, we requested permission from the subjects to write their parents and to include a questionnaire for the parents to fill out. Many items, such as the request for a description of the handicapped child, or an estimate of the importance of religion to the family as a whole, were the same as the questions we asked each SibH. Of the 7 families who completed and returned the forms, with no important exceptions, the data from the parents and from the SibH from that family were identical. This gave us confidence in the relatively factual information we obtained from SibH.

The more complicated issue involves those questions which concern attitudes and feelings, and particularly those involving retrospective reports of what SibH thought or felt. Obviously, such data cannot be considered as an accurate factual description of what went on in the past. However, if it can be demonstrated that it was not simply a response to the social desirability of the answer or to the demand-characteristics of the research, then it can be considered meaningful data in its own right. That is, it is interesting in itself to know how young adults describe their earlier experiences with a retarded brother or sister and how they have come to understand and evaluate this experience, even if what they tell us is not precisely what they thought and felt as young children in that situation.

Two sources of data provide partial answers to this problem. Some questions asked in the interview involved answers easily evaluated on a social-desirability continuum. For example, the questions: "Were you in general curious about H's handicap when you were young?" and "How do you feel toward H?" each have responses that college students feel somewhat pressured to give. ("Yes, I was curious," and "I like H.") If we found most students giving these responses, we would have some reason to doubt the validity of the data. In fact, the responses did not follow this pattern. For example, of our first sample of 28 men students, 7—in describing their own curiosity about H's handicap—said or implied they had little or no curiosity about H; 8 said they had been extremely curious; and the remainder distributed themselves in between. In describing how they felt toward H, again the distribution of scores is approximately normal, with 5 of the 28 subjects saying or implying that they disliked H very much, 8 expressing strong positive feelings, and the rest at points in between. (The data are comparable in the other samples.)

Second, a number of responses to interview items showed interrelationships with each other that seemed to demonstrate a meaningful internal consistency to the data. For example, SibHs in one sample who said they spent much time with H also consistently reported liking H more than other SibHs and thinking more about H's future. If the answers were primarily in terms of the social desirability or the social pressures in the interview situation to give a particular answer of the responses, those items having obvious social desirability "pull" would not necessarily correlate with other items for which this dimension is irrelevant.

The third type of evidence involves the relationship between responses on interview items and other kinds of data less subject to situational factors of the research. For example, the Information Test would be particularly difficult to influence. In two samples, SibHs who reported their parents as being more willing to discuss H's handicap and themselves as more curious about it also demonstrated that they know more about mental retardation, suggesting that their report of what used to occur has some validity.

To summarize, while incidental features of the research design, such as the fact that all the interviewers were female, undoubtedly influenced the data, we are not aware of any systematic distorting biases. In particular, there is evidence that neither social desirability nor conscious distortions played a significant role. We therefore feel some confidence in the value of what these college students told us.

CHAPTER 6

Private U Family Styles

AFTER WE HAD SCORED all of our interview and test material and carried out a variety of statistical analyses, we struggled to integrate what seemed to us to be a vast amount of often confusing results. The findings were too complex to lend themselves to any easy interpretations or summaries. After living with these data and puzzling over them for some months, a broader formulation of the different life situations and experiences of the students in the four groups of brothers and sisters of retarded children began to emerge. That formulation, which is presented in this chapter and the next, aided greatly in our understanding of the specific results and is presented first in order to give the reader a framework within which to consider the specific findings.

The picture that began to emerge was of markedly different life situations of students from Community U and Private U, as well as of men and women students. These differences seemed to have major consequences for the lives of the students, and particularly for the way they experienced relationships with a retarded brother or sister.

A critical dimension that affected the experience and that differentiated Private U students from those at Community U is what we term the "sociocultural status" of the family. Numerous researchers, particularly those focusing on the development of various psychological characteristics of children and their families, have noted the overriding importance of socioeconomic class (*e.g.,* Farber and Jenné, 1963; McCandless, 1970). However, for the groups of students participating in this study, socioeconomic status alone did not reflect all, or even the most important, aspects of differences between the family styles. "Sociocultural status" (SCS) includes the criteria used to establish the more conventional status ranking: father's education level and current occupation. However, it also reflects something about the families' interests in education for the children, as well as related cultural and social expectations.

In our research population, the families of Private U students whom we call "upper socioculutral status" had, in addition to the high educational and occupational status of the parents, one or more children attending an expensive and highly competitive college. We contrast them in this study with Community U families who were primarily of lower middle-socioeconomic status but who did have one or more children attending college (*i.e.*, who had children who are upwardly mobile, obtaining more education than their parents). Further, and in contrast to the Private U students, the colleges these students were attending were inexpensive and noncompetitive local schools.

In this chapter, composite or prototypical pictures of men and women students and their families from the Private U groups are presented, with excerpts from interviews used to illustrate and amplify our impressions. Community U students and their families are described in Chapter 7. The specific research findings and clinical data that led to our general formulations are presented in Chapters 8 through 12.

PRIVATE U STUDENTS

The population of families represented by these Private U students is unique in some respects. College students attending an expensive and highly competitive university are, with their families, a highly favored group. Most of these families have the advantages of money and education, and have been sufficiently effective in their use of these resources to enable a child to attend a highly selective school. (The fact that the colleges here referred to as "Private U" had an increasingly high percentage of scholarship students does not substantially alter the picture presented. Less well-to-do families whose children can get into such universities share many of the characteristics typical of Private U families.)

In addition, many of these family units are psychologically close. Involvements among family members create an intense atmosphere in which family relationships take on a high degree of importance. (Stuckert, 1962–63, notes that among upper and upper middle-class families, compared with lower middle-class families, a much higher proportion have what he calls a "nuclear family orientation" in contrast to a "non-family orientation." Similarly, Green, 1946, talks of the "personality absorption" of the child that often occurs in middle-class homes, where all of the child's interests and energies are absorbed by the family, and he remains intensely involved with it.) The fact that many of the fathers in these Private U families are away at work for long periods of the day does not seem to lessen the intensity of ties, although in some instances it does remove the father from the center to the periphery of this closely knit group.

The intensity of parent-child relationships is heightened by one of the major shared goals of these families, which is the maximum possible psychological, social, and academic development of their children.

These and related characteristics enormously influence the impact of a retarded child on a family. In this sample of families represented by the Private U students, no family was limited financially from obtaining the services it needed or wanted for the handicapped child. Families who had decided to institutionalize their child were able to pay for private care, and in no instance was a family unable to get residential care within a relatively short time of that decision. Similarly, these families were able to afford medical care for H. Although we did not ask whether they had domestic help, and only a few students volunteered that information, nearly all of the families could have afforded help if they needed it to share the burden of caring for the child. None of the Private U siblings made important sacrifices of material possessions, and few were unable to take advantage of opportunities such as private schooling because of the retarded child. In many of the families, the parents seemed to make a specific—and often successful—effort to protect the normal children from all inconveniences and deprivations that might be caused by the presence of the retarded child. (Westley and Epstein, 1960, noted that more integrated families tend to shield their children from financial difficulties.)

The availability of financial resources minimized the practical hardships and inconveniences experienced by these families. The consequences resulting from the presence of a retarded child in such a setting are primarily psychological. As Farber (1964) has described it, the retarded child affects such upper middle-class parents primarily through his or her frustration of their aims and goals, both in terms of what they want from their children and their image of a "happy family life." (This is in strong contrast to the situation in lower socioeconomic-class families, who experience what Farber calls the "role crisis," precipitated by the reorganization of roles that occurs as the family attempts to cope with the actual requirements for care of the child.) The heavy emphasis placed on the growth and development of the children inevitably heightens the psychological impact on the well-to-do family of a child with limited ability to develop.

Most importantly for the normal siblings, the intensity of interpersonal ties within the family magnifies the importance of relatively subtle feelings and reactions toward H, which come to have a major impact on the family. Thus, in the data from this sample, it was such psychological variables as the normal sibling's perception of his mother's and father's reactions to H that were of central importance in the student's experience of H, rather than such factors as the extent or type of H's handicap.

Private U Men

The young men from these Private U families were in a different situation from Private U women. The role-expectations for a son are quite different from those for a daughter in such a family (e.g., Aberle and Naegle, 1952; Farber and Jenné, 1963). Few of these men were expected by their families to play a major role in the direct care of their siblings, and, generally, the more handicapped the retarded child and the more direct physical care he or she required, the more the son was exempt from providing this care. This factor sheltered these SibHs from the intensity of sustained nonvoluntary experience with H, in contrast to the Private U women as well as in contrast to SibHs from Community U families, and further minimized the direct impact of H's handicap on the normal male child.

The following quotations and comments from a Private U man illustrate the intense psychological involvement in the family and the emphasis placed on protecting the growth of all of the normal children, as well as the lack of financial or other real hardship caused by the retarded son. More subtly, the interview excerpts highlight the relative lack of awareness and involvement of this SibH in the day-to-day care problems of H, despite his intense interest in his handicapped brother. There were four children in this Private U Jewish family. H (Sam) was the youngest, a four-year-old with Down's Syndrome. SibH was the oldest. He first talked about the intense interest and concern of the entire family when Sam was born, how preoccupied they were with his development, etc.

"I don't know—I always felt as if I were very much a part of Sam.[1] It is almost as if he has five parents, because all of us are so much older and when—it takes a good deal of attention on my mother's part. You know, having to stay up at all hours of the night, and he never did sleep very well at night until about two years ago. And, as a matter of fact, I wasn't even aware for a long time that she was up so much. Later it came out, and I was somewhat shocked because I should have realized."

He talked then about his mother's great involvement with mental retardation in parents' groups, day programs, etc., then described his younger brother's research on chemical causes of genetic abnormalities in rats. He then talked about his father.

"My father is—I mean—I've said before this year that I felt my relationship with my parents was more of a friendship more than it was a father-son, mother-son relationship. I don't think that's quite accurate, but we used to have long discussions about all kinds of things that would last until all hours of the night."

1. Dashes are used to indicate pauses.

In describing his father, he talked of his father's temper, then continued:

"My parents only had one fight in my entire life that I can remember—that is, a big one. I mean where they—that was in '61, so that was before Sam—. My father is very concerned, I think, with being a parent. He tries to respond in a way that's proper. And I think as a result of this, he expects my mother to have the same kind of attitude. When Mother would get too involved with medical auxiliary and a couple of other things during the week, he would try to make very sure that she was not neglecting Sam, that she wasn't throwing some kind of burden on us."

More briefly, this comment by another Private U man, one of four children, also with a younger brother with Down's Syndrome, emphasized the degree to which this normal son was protected from being in any way imposed upon or limited by H.

"I get a kick out of him, I really do. He's a lot of fun. I don't know—maybe it's because I have all of the privileges of him without the real responsibility. I remember one vacation, I had bunk beds in my bedroom so he slept with me. And one night he got sick or something during the night, and Mom came. And I ended up in her bedroom, and she cleaned it up. This was the type of thing. Mom always took care of him, so that I just got to see the really good side of him. He's sharp; he was a funny little guy."

PRIVATE U WOMEN

These women, because of their sex, were in somewhat different positions from their male counterparts at Private U. As daughters in the families, they were expected to be involved with and participate in child-rearing activities with younger siblings and with H, at least to some extent. Possibly because of this, these women seemed to reflect a somewhat different perspective in viewing their families. Our impression is that they were closer than were Private U men to sharing, or at least perceiving and understanding, the perspective of their mothers in responding to the question about the effects of a handicapped child in the family.

The following excerpts are from the interview with a Private U woman, Mary, oldest of four children. The youngest child, Diane, a severely retarded 14-year-old, was institutionalized several years preceding the interview. As our student-subject described her, Diane was (at the time of the interview) strange-appearing, nonambulatory, and did not recognize most people. The excerpts illustrate the intensity of family relationships and the real difficulty SibH had in expressing unhappiness or anger about Diane and the burden she created. Incidentally, the progression of this young woman's increasing expression of her anger at her mother, as she recalled her mother's inability to cope with H and the effects of that inability on herself, is fascinating to observe.

"How do you think Diane feels toward you?"

"All of us were very close when she was little, when she was living at home, because we had to help Mother with babysitting and so forth, take care of her and change diapers, carry her around when Mother—you know—couldn't manage her. But since she's been at Southbury, Diane doesn't remember any of us now, especially me because I was the first to leave—."

"How do you feel toward her?"

"The problem is, I still recognize her as a 3-year-old, possibly 4-year-old child, except she's much larger than that. And I think it's getting harder for all of us kids—my parents are really used to it—it's getting harder for us to accept the fact that she will never develop, you know, the same way we do. And especially now when she's becoming—beginning to look more and more retarded, it's harder for all of us. We all love her very much but I tend to put things in the way of getting over to see her—. It's really a horrible experience to walk in there and see a 40- or 50-year-old woman [living in the same cottage] grab a hold of you and start shrieking at the top of her voice—. She—when she's home it's just right. It's kind of hard on Mom, because Diane's already heavy and hard to carry; she weighs more than I do. But when she's at home it's more of a normal atmosphere than it is there. She hasn't been home since Easter. We wouldn't have her this summer because Mom was kind of contemplating going to a sanitarium—."

She talked of how much time her mother spent with Diane, teaching her to walk, etc.

"How much time did the other children spend with her?"

"Well, I was the oldest, I always took more. But I don't know, my brother really didn't want to do much with Diane, or change her pants or anything like that. So we usually stuck him with emptying the garbage or something like that. [She laughed.] But Glen and I did more of it."

"How do you think Diane's handicap has affected you?"

She described her interest in mental retardation, and the volunteer work she's done. She continued:

"It's just—it's sad. Several times my mother has commented—you know—it might have been better if she had died, especially when she was so sick. I don't think so. It's just something—we all got through it together; it's just wonderful what you can do."

"When you were little, how much time would you spend with Diane?"

"She had to have attention the whole time. She'd yell unless you did, and you couldn't hit her or tell her 'no'—she didn't understand that too well. So we all had to play with her. Mostly Mother would put her on her stomach on the floor so that she could use her back muscles to sit up. I remember sitting by the hour. Coming home from school, and having work to do or wanting to go out and play, and Diane sitting on the floor yelling for one of us [laugh]. And one of the three of us would sit there and color with her or play dolls with her—. One Christmas my sister and I made her about 40 outfits of doll clothes, we were so tired of making them during the year! We all took a pretty good amount of time, but like I said, she was eight when she went away."

"What do you think has been the effect on your father?"

"Uh, Dad isn't one to show affection. I've never seen him cry or anything else. But Mother told me that when he found out, he sat down and cried. But he's always been able to face problems, just straightforward, and to do with them what he could. And he's done that with Diane, and I think that in the beginning it hurt him a lot. But it becomes fairly commonplace. Not commonplace, but you get used to the idea after a while, and it becomes a regular part of your life—. It may be that's why he has the possibility of an ulcer—part of the reason or something—but I don't think it's affected him adversely."

"What do you think has been the effect on your mother?"

"Well, she's the one now they're working with in ———. They're trying a new drug; she's been in the sanitarium about once a year—. It started right about when Diane was born, and they have repeatedly said that it's not because of my sister. Whether that is to make our family feel better, I don't know. But let's see—after Diane was born, mother was in the sanitarium, and this was before she knew that—well, she knew that something was wrong, that Diane wasn't responding right. But they didn't know what, and ever since then she's been in the 'san' off and on. Maybe Diane has had more influence on Mother than we know. This could be part of the reason she gets sick, but she's never said anything about Diane. It's always been something else she says is driving her crazy. She—when she gets mad, she gets mad at the little things, she doesn't get mad at the big things. And then all of a sudden, she needs to go to the sanitarium—."

"Would you describe your parents?"

After briefly describing both parents and her relationships with them, she went on to say she is particularly close with her father:

"We're both very stubborn and when we get into a fight, there's never been a worse fight. I think he enjoys it though! [Laughs.] We're both very close, I think maybe because I've always understood Mother. My brother has always been the one to say, 'Mother's not sick! Mother's O.K.! Don't talk that way about her.' Daddy would talk to me about something Mother had said. Or once in a while he used to have me around more or less as a spy to make sure Mother wouldn't do anything crazy. But, uh, I sort of begrudge them the responsibility that was thrown on me since I was little. And I can never respect Mom for always being in the hospital at the wrong times. And it's very hard even now for me to love her. You know, it's kind of hard when she tells—she announced to my brother that she no longer loved him one night. How the hell can you possibly respect a person who would say that to her child!"

A Brief Recapitulation

The availability of extensive economic and social resources allowed these Private U families to face a minimum of reality hardships related to the retarded child. This freedom from major deprivation and disruption, in the context of intense family ties, enabled more subtle aspects of the family members' reactions to the retarded child and his or her handicap to assume greater importance. The college students from these families tended to be acutely aware of, and affected by, their parents' feelings toward H. On the other hand, issues such as how retarded or physically impaired the retarded child is seemed to have relatively little impact on the adaptation of the normal children in the family. (One could argue that in the case of Mary, presented above, it was the severity of Diane's retardation that made Mary's life so difficult. However, one could equally well suggest that the major complicating factor was not the severity of Diane's handicap but rather the mother's inability to cope with her normal children or the retarded child.)

The young men we spoke with, by virtue of their sex role in their families, had less direct contact with H than did the women and thus were shielded from feeling much of the impact of the handicap *per se*. They, and the women to a lesser degree, also were shielded deliberately by their parents, whose creed involved giving these normal children the maximum opportunity for self-development and achievement.

CHAPTER 7

Community U Family Styles

THE PRIVATE U FAMILIES described in Chapter 6 were educated and affluent, and the life styles of the family members were greatly influenced by those facts. In marked contrast were the families of the Community U students. By and large, they had few resources available to them. Lack of money was often a serious limitation to how much they could do for themselves, as well as for the retarded child. The parents had little education, and many seemed relatively inept at coping with their lives and the problems they encountered. In this context, the primary focus of at least a sizable majority of the families represented by the Community U students was to survive, financially and interpersonally. These families did not have the luxury of emphasizing the growth and development of each child to his or her maximum potential, although many hoped the children would advance themselves through schooling. Rather, as the children became old enough to help out, either by contributing to the family's financial resources or by helping with other tasks, they were expected to share the burdens of coping with the exigencies of family life.

The energy consumed by this effort left little available for intense interpersonal involvement among family members, and generally these families appeared loosely knit and relatively uninvolved with one another (Green, 1946, McCandless, 1970, and Stuckert, 1962–63, have all commented on this characteristic of lower middle- and upper lower-class families.) These Community U students—at least by the time they reached college age—appeared to be relatively free to disregard their parents' views, partly because of the students' own upward mobility which rendered their parents less useful to them as models (e.g., Green, 1946; Stuckert, 1962–63).

The primary impact of a retarded child on such a family situation comes from the real hardships created by that child. Both the financial drain on the family resources, as well as the major investment of time and effort required by a handicapped and dependent child, produce what has been described as the "role crisis" (Farber, 1964) or the "reality crisis" (Menolascino, 1968) which is greatly influenced by such real issues as the severity of H's mental and physical retardation.

Community U Women

Both because of the over-all family needs and expectations, and because of the specific role-demands placed on girls in a family, the women SibHs from Community U had a great amount of direct contact with H, usually in a position of responsibility for him or her. The consequences for them of growing up with a retarded sibling had far more to do with the nature and degree of this contact, and how it was affected by such factors as the severity of H's handicap, than by the psychological reactions of family members to that handicap. (Farber and Jenné, 1963, also concluded that one very important influence of a retarded child on a normal sibling is the increased responsibility often given to that sibling.)

Further, many of these young women felt they knew more than their parents about caring for a retarded child—and in fact many did, by virtue of their training in special education, their volunteer work with retarded children in community facilities, etc.—which further reduced the impact of subtleties of family feelings toward H on these SibHs.

The following long excerpt from the interview with a Community U woman captures many aspects of these families. In particular, it highlights the enormous responsibility given to SibH, partly because of the inability of her mother to cope. It also reflects SibH's relative distance from her parents, reflected, for example, in the casualness and uninvolvement with which she described them. This is in sharp contrast to the intense involvement with parents seen in the interviews with Private U students. Also in striking contrast to the stance taken by the Private U students is this young woman's comfort with describing her earlier resentment toward H, and the matter-of-fact manner in which she discussed H. She was the oldest of three children, with the youngest, Mary, a mildly retarded girl.

"How do you think Mary sees herself?"

"She sees herself like she sees me; this is the way she's always been. I don't know what it is, but she has always been with me. Because Susan, my other sister, is a very independent person. And she's the type that's not sympathetic towards sick people or anything, and she never had patience. And so I sorta like cared. Someone had to stay with Mary, and I always have done it. So she always likes to dress like me; when I decided to let my hair grow, she let her hair grow."

"How do you feel toward her?"

"I love her just like my other sister and sometimes it's a lot easier to love her. But there have been times when I resented having the responsibility for her—. I remember when we were little kids. Like my girlfriend and I always had Mary with us and we used to complain—."

"What do you think the effects have been on you?"

SibH described how her sister was not doing her work at school, and when the school started sending notes home with Mary to that effect, Mary was not delivering the notes and would forge answers.

"Finally, Father caught on. My father took the working of homework and everything away from my mother. He said, 'You're too emotionally involved.' So I took over then, and I went to see the teacher, and found out what Mary had to do and everything. And I started working with the teacher in his class—. I don't regret anything other than the fact that I did lose quite a bit of my privacy, because she just attached herself right to me."

We asked her how much time she spent with Mary in a position of responsibility. She said she spent a lot of time.

"Yeah, my parents are both what you call organization people. They're both members of their union—in fact, officers in their union, and in the American Legion. And my father is in the fire department. So they were involved in lots of things, and someone had to stay home with Mary. And Mary is very attached to my mother and myself, so as long as one of us is around, she's not bad. But she can be very upset when neither of us is around."

"What do you think the effect has been on the family?"

She said essentially that they have grown closer.

"But once in a while my parents disagree. My father tends to be more of a disciplinarian when it comes to Mary. My mother becomes very lenient where Mary is concerned. Once in a while there is some dissent, but generally we're a very tight family."

"What do you think the effect of Mary's handicap has been on your father?"

"Well, where Mary's concerned he sort of walks on thin ice. Twice he really got mad at her, and she deserved it, and he has given her the spankings she deserves. But he has always been shaken afterwards. 'Cause Mary—sometimes she's like a puppy, and whenever you spank a puppy, he goes to a corner and if you come near again, he shies away from you. And that's the way Mary is with my father, especially if she has done something wrong. She's just like another kid to him, although he doesn't talk to her the way he talks to me, I have to admit. I am his pet, and I always have been 'cause I've always done things with him—. When Mary's concerned, he has not had as much to do with her as my mother does. Lately he has taken a big interest in her."

"What has been the effect on your mother?"

"Well, where Mary's concerned, my mother has always been on the defensive. It wasn't easy for her of all people, and she's just not used to it. Like Mary can be treated like a normal person now, and from everybody's point of view it is best for her if everyone insists that she produce what she can do, the best she can. 'Cause people aren't going to be making exceptions, and sooner or later Mary has got to be on her own. But my mother can't—isn't going to face that completely. And she's gotten 100 percent better than when Mary was younger, but she's got a long way to go yet."

Later, we asked her to describe her parents. She told of being close to her father, then said of her mother:

"She's a highly nervous person and she's in some areas very bigoted, but this I think is part of her upbringing. She comes from a marriage—a very strict Catholic family. And you'd think she'd be more lenient, but she got very upset to think that my sister was to marry a non-Catholic boy. She's become better at it now, but there are certain things like mixed racial marriages she is bitterly set against."

A much shorter excerpt, also from an interview with a Community U woman, underlines the relative casualness with which feelings toward other family members, including the retarded child, were treated, and the psychological distance SibH had from them. This woman had a retarded brother, seven years younger than she.

"How do you feel toward Chris?"

"Well, um, I love him very much, and I don't resent him anymore, but when I was younger, I think I did."

"Have you spent much time taking care of him?"

"Well, I've babysat for him, from nine to five during the summer."

"What about during the school year?"

"I've always been responsible until five o'clock."

"Did you ever wish Chris wasn't around when your friends were there?"

"Oh, definitely. I remember—this is really strange—one time when I was about 12 we were in the pool, and I tried to drown him! It was really horrible—my mother almost flipped! Oh, I don't know, I guess it was a horrible thing to do, but I didn't know I was doing it. I didn't understand he was retarded or anything. I just knew, I guess, that I had to babysit for him all the time, and he was just a bother to me!"

"What do you think has been the effect on your father of Chris's handicap?"

"My father is very low intelligence. I think he kind of resents my brother in a way, because my mother gives him all the attention. And my mother, you know, it takes up all her time. She was completely nervous. When she found out that he was retarded, I think she sort of had a breakdown, and now she won't admit that he is retarded. She keeps trying to find help for him instead of just stopping and getting him trained in what he can do."

"What kind of person is your father?"

"Just the average, I guess. Laborer type, because that's what he is. He doesn't do anything. He likes to gamble but he doesn't do it very much because we don't have any money."

COMMUNITY U MEN

These men were not as psychologically involved with their families, and particularly with their parents, as the college men or women from Private U. Many held regular full- or part-time jobs and consequently had achieved financial independence from their parents. Nor were they expected to participate heavily in child-care activities with H, as were their female counterparts from Community U. Superficially, at least, they seemed to be the least involved with the experience, which may be one of the reasons they were the hardest to recruit to participate in the research. Alternatively, other factors than disinterest may have kept them from participating and affected those who did come. These young men, as a group, tend not to verbalize their feelings, especially about a topic as threatening as the physical or mental handicap of a close relative. This factor may have led many to avoid participating in the research and influenced those who came to appear relatively noncommittal.

This first excerpt is from an interview with a Community U man who was oldest of three, with a 10-year-old, mildly retarded brother, Carl. This young man was somewhat atypical in his degree of interest in his retarded brother. The relative casualness about it, as well as his marked independence from his parents, however, is representative for this group.

"How do you feel toward Carl?"

He talked of being close with Carl, enjoying him.

"I miss him a lot, a lot of times—like they went to Florida in February. And while he was gone, I missed him. I don't know, he's just a lot of fun."

"Are there any ways you and Carl are alike?"

"Yes, he enjoys the outdoors—he'd much rather be outside than any other place—and I guess I sort of do too. And he likes doing the same things I like to do—."

"What do you think the effect of Carl's handicap has been on you?"

He talked of his decision to go into Special Education, that he spent a lot of time babysitting when they were younger, and that the practice had turned out to be useful now that he had a baby of his own.

"What has been the effect on your father?"

"It's given him more to worry about, in a way. He doesn't know exactly what to do with or about Carl; things like that. Both Sandra and I were completely different experiences and he just doesn't know how to treat—it."

"How would you describe the effect on your mother?"

"Well, it's been hard on her—real hard on her. Actually it's given her a lot more responsibility, and she tends to worry about every little thing; she worries about him a lot."

"How do you think she feels about Carl's retardation?"

"Well, she's learned to accept it now. And, she didn't know what to do at first, you know, and she tries to help him, and she doesn't know how far to go. 'Cause she didn't know whether it's going to confuse his school work if she helps him or not."

"How do you feel toward your parents?"

"Well, sometimes I feel they're wrong [laughs] but don't we all! Not so much any more. They don't have much of an education. My mother went through three years of high school. And my father went through junior high and that's all. And they don't know much about it, and they don't know that much about teaching him things. And in that way I feel they were wrong about some things. But they've tried their best about it—."

The last excerpt from a Community U man, oldest of three boys, with Doug (the youngest) mildly retarded, is almost a caricature of uninvolvement. Initially, he responded to our question of how severe Doug's retardation was, by saying:

"Well, I think he's educable but I don't know, 'cause they never really talked to me much about it."

"Do you think you could find out the specific diagnosis and let us know?"

"Well, I don't know if they would tell me or not. I suppose I could ask. I don't know if they would be uncomfortable."

"How do you think Doug sees himself?"

"I don't know. I haven't given it much thought lately—. I don't know—I'm sure he knows it."

"How do you feel toward Doug?"

"Well, I like him, of course. He's my brother. I feel very sorry for him because I'm sure he'll never be able to do anything, or to fit into society, I guess. I don't really know what he's going to do. I don't know—that's how I feel towards him."

"How do you think Doug's handicap has affected you?"

"Well, I don't know. I've been thinking about that since I got your letter. I really don't know how it affected me. My parents act very strange about this thing. They never really—really talk to me about it. I always felt they should talk to me about it because I was part of the family, but I guess they never really talked to me about it. So I don't really know how it affected me. When I was younger it used to be very frustrating 'cause sometimes he would be—he would seem very normal and other times he would have a tantrum or something—."

"Do you think it's made a difference in your life?"

"I don't know. I really don't think so. It's been—I suppose my relationship with my whole family would have been a lot closer if he were normal. I realize it's a great strain on my parents and that might have affected my relationship with them."

"Did you spend much time with Doug when you were younger?"

"I used to try and play ball with him, or something. I guess I used to try to do the things I would do if he were regular."

"Did you spend a lot of time with him?"

"I guess not. I babysat occasionally."

He went on to talk about the general tension in his family, the fact that his parents did not get along too well. He said his father tried to act as if Doug is normal, so they made no attempt to teach him anything.

"I really don't know how they feel about it. I can't understand why they don't discuss it. I know I wouldn't be able to say exactly how they felt about it because they never told me. It would just be from observing."

"How do you feel toward your parents?"

"Well, I don't know, I guess—I certainly love my parents; sometimes I get very upset with them. I don't feel they understand me at all; I guess I don't understand them at all either. I guess I have the same feelings that everybody has. They certainly have always been very good to me. They've always taken care of me if I was in any trouble. Now I have a wife that can understand me. It's not so bad any more, but I used to have a really difficult time. I had nobody to talk to about personal things."

These Community U students talked very differently about the experiences they had growing up with a retarded brother or sister than did the Private U students. Many described major disruption and hardships falling on the family because of H's handicap and the care H required. As a consequence of this, as well as of their relative detachment from their parents, they assumed a different position *vis-à-vis* H. The women, by virtue of their role as daughters in the family context, took on a great deal of the responsibility of caring for H and consequently were most affected by such factors as the degree and kind of H's physical and mental handicap. The young men, while also more independent of their parents than the Private U students, had less to do with H and seemed less involved than any in the four groups with their retarded brother or sister.

Finally, these young people from Community U seemed generally more mature than did the Private U students, although all were roughly the same age. Some of the Community U students were married and had begun families of their own, while major ties of the Private U students were still to their own parents. This factor also influenced the way these young people thought about and described their handicapped siblings and the effect on themselves.

CHAPTER 8

Coping With Retardation: Statistical Results

IN CHAPTERS 6 AND 7 we sketched a broad framework within which to understand the life experiences of the young men and women in our four different groups and discussed how these different styles of life influenced the way they viewed and experienced a retarded brother or sister. Starting in this chapter, some specific findings are presented concerning one very important question: whether the over-all psychological health and adaptation of these college students were influenced by having grown up with a retarded brother or sister. We also asked: if they were affected, what factors contributed to this result?

This is essentially a statistical chapter; it describes the variables used to measure adaptation and presents the statistical results. A more general discussion of these results and of their import appears in Chapter 9. (Readers who prefer to skip the statistical details may move on to the next chapter and still maintain the continuity of thought and discussion. For the reader's convenience, in subsequent chapters statistical material is presented in separate sections.)

MEASURES OF ADAPTATION

A major problem in attempting to measure mental health or psychological adaptation is deciding what aspects of functioning to consider. For example, do academic grades, or frequency of dating, or quality of friendships reflect the mental health or pathology of a college student? Or is the way a person thinks and feels about himself a better indication of his mental health?

Westley and Epstein (1969), who were confronted with the same difficulty while designing a way to evaluate the mental health of 30 college students, ended up using three major criteria of health. The presence or absence of psychiatric symptoms was one dimension. The quality of the student's social and occupational adaptation was assessed by evaluating such factors as interpersonal relationships, his relationship to his work (study) and to his "sociocultural environment." Finally, their third criterion was "psychodynamic integration," which included the functioning of such aspects of personality as cognition, perception, intelligence, affect, sexuality, etc., as well as the researchers' judgments of the extent to which the student appeared to be dealing effectively and without undue anxiety with his stage-appropriate conflicts, *e.g.*, in these college students, with identity formation.

Although measures for the sibling research were developed before we saw Westley and Epstein's formulations, our scoring items are quite consistent with theirs, though more limited in scope. "Coping-effectiveness" is our central measure of the quality of the SibH's psychological adaptation to the experience of growing up with a retarded brother or sister, and reflects our clinical impressions of what is a healthy response and what a troubled one to this situation. (This formulation inevitably is based on a number of assumptions about psychological health and pathology, and about personality. Here, these assumptions are spelled out in some detail to allow others to understand our judgments and so be in a better position to evaluate our results.)

In our view, a college student who has come to terms with the fact and idea of having a retarded brother or sister is comfortable when experiencing and acknowledging negative as well as positive feelings toward H. We assume that all close relationships involve some ambivalence, and the one between siblings—normal or abnormal—involves at least as much as most. Students who feel guilty or uncomfortable about having *any* angry or resentful feelings toward H must actively work to keep those feelings from conscious awareness, and pay the price for repressing or denying any aspect of experience. For example, one sibling who insisted that his feelings toward his retarded sister were entirely friendly and positive tended to be very limited in the range and intensity of feelings he experienced or expressed. It seemed as if the only way he was able to avoid feeling angry at his sister was by avoiding feeling any very strong emotion. On the other hand, students who expressed an unrelenting angry bitterness about H's handicap and its impact on the family members also seemed to us to have coped less well than students who were more accepting of their family situation.

Second, for the college students who were still in contact with H, the flexibility and over-all quality of that relationship—of course within the limits of H's capabilities—tells a great deal about SibH's adaptation. For example, a student who spent some time with H and was neither internally driven to be with H all the time nor to avoid him altogether; who currently had some, but not excessive, interest in H's activities; who was fond of H but did not allow that closeness to keep him from embarking on his own life with people outside the family; had gone a long way in the direction of successfully coping with H's handicap and its meaning to himself.

Finally, a student who has been able to cope well does not define his own self primarily in terms of H. This student neither feels, as did Cindy, that because he has a retarded sibling, he must be handicapped, nor, alternatively, that because he is so much brighter and more capable than H that he must be very exceptional. The student's view of himself is largely independent of his view of H.

The actual scores that reflected these judgments were arrived at by at least two raters making separate judgments of each student's over-all coping-effectiveness. Independent scorers, including several who had not previously been involved in our work with siblings and so did not necessarily share our biases about them, were able to reach a high level of agreement on this score despite its intuitive, inferential quality, supporting our impression of the reliability and validity of the measure.

In addition to "coping," two other scores—"embarrassed" and "talks to friends"—also reflect aspects of SibH's effectiveness in dealing with H's handicap. These two, conceptually related, rate on the one hand the personal comfort or discomfort described by the normal sibling about being seen with H, and, on the other, the extent to which SibH shared information, thoughts, and feelings about his or her retarded sibling with friends.

This emphasis on SibH's comfort or discomfort with H "in public" stemmed partly from our clinical impressions that individuals and families who adapt well to having a retarded child in the family tend to be unashamed of the child, often talk openly about the retardation, and even make a point of educating others about such handicaps. These clinical observations are related to a formulation by Farber (1968), who has emphasized the withdrawal of family members from extrafamily life that often follows the identification of a retarded child in that family. (Also Carver, 1956.) To some extent this withdrawal is a direct result of the amount of time and effort required to care for the child. But, as Farber points out, the norms and values of a community are often contradictory to a family's norms with a retarded child, forcing the family to withdraw if they are to maintain an accepting attitude toward their child. For example, when mothers of school-age children get together, they often talk with pride of their children's achievements in school, pointing out how theirs are doing better than other people's children.

This emphasis on competitive achievement is in opposition to the attitude necessary to a parent who has come to accept a retarded child and has had to learn to value the child for other reasons than his ability to compete successfully. Thus, the withdrawal can be seen as an avoidance of dealing with conflicting norms. However, some well-functioning families we have seen seem to adapt by consciously and explicitly working to educate the public. These families are trying to modify external norms enough to make room in the community for retarded and otherwise handicapped children. The extent to which normal siblings relate the retarded brother or sister to their own outside world by talking about him or her to friends, being seen with the child, etc., not only reflects the way the parents and other normal children come to deal with that issue, but also the SibH's own resolution of that potential conflict.

Summarizing, the three adaptation measures directly related to the retarded sibling are:

1. Coping-effectiveness: a clinical judgment of the extent to

which SibH was positively, neutrally, or negatively affected by the experience of growing up with a retarded sibling. High scores mean high coping-effectiveness.[1] [For details of scoring, see Table 10, V (2).]

2. Embarrassed: a rating of the extent to which SibH described him- or herself as being embarrassed, at the time of the study or in the past, when seen with H by others. High scores mean strong embarrassment [Table 10, V (5)].

3. Talks to friends: a score of the extent to which SibH talked with friends about H, based on a specific count of the number of people SibH remembered telling about H. High scores were given to SibHs who said they talked with many people, low scores to those who talked with few or none [Table 10, V (4)].

Four other scores, unrelated to retardation, reflect the general functioning and adaptation of the college students:

1. Academic functioning: the academic performance of SibH at the college he was attending. A student who received high grades received a high score on this item [Table 10, V (1a)].

2. Over-all functioning at college: a composite of five scores, including academic functioning, and the extent to which SibH had friends, dated, participated in sports, and in school activities. These items were designed to reflect current living styles and adjustments and involved little inference in scoring [Table 10, V (1)].

3. IQ: the prorated score from four subscales of the WAIS was used. (The comparisons among the four samples of SibHs on IQ, as well as between the SibHs and SibNs, are included. However, since IQ did not relate significantly to either the demographic or psychological variables in any of the four samples, in subsequent analyses this score was omitted.)

1. The obvious statistical method for comparing groups, and the one used here, is the analysis of variance. However, results of this method of analysis, here and in all subsequent chapters, should be viewed with caution because of the considerable variation within each sample that is not statistically controlled by this method. For example, the groups of SibHs showed significant differences in the religious orientation of the family and the sibling position of SibH (Table 4). Such factors can greatly influence the experience of having a retarded sibling and consequently might well affect other scores. Yet, they cannot be held constant by the analysis-of-variance technique. Because of this, only main effects from these analyses were considered, and even the interpretations of the main effects were tentative unless supported by other statistical findings.

4. TAQ: a score of anxiety in a test situation (Sarason and Mandler, 1952).

The intercorrelations among these adaptation measures are shown in Table 11.

STATISTICAL FINDINGS: ADAPTATION

We found no important differences between siblings of retarded children and siblings of only normal children on our measures of adaptation (Table 12). (Of course, it was not possible to compare them on coping-effectiveness, our central score, since that relates specifically to a retarded sibling. Also, although the SibHs did receive higher scores on over-all college functioning, that can be explained by the sampling bias that resulted in our getting only the better adjusted brothers and sisters of retarded children [Chapter 4].)

Among the groups of brothers and sisters of retarded children, several statistically significant differences were found on these measures (Table 13). Private U students had higher scores on academic functioning and IQ, as was expected from the sampling procedure. And, over-all, the women students had lower IQ scores than the men, primarily because Private U men had significantly higher scores than the Private U women (one of the few differences between these two college populations). As a group, the women talked more than the men students about H, and Community U students more than those from Private U. The men students all expressed slightly more embarrassment about being seen with H than did the women.

THE SEVERITY OF H'S HANDICAP AND DEMOGRAPHIC FACTORS

We next wondered: what factors in the life situations and experiences of the students related to, and possibly influenced, the adaptation of the SibHs within each sample? We decided to look at variables such as the severity of H's handicap and the number of children in the family, on the one hand, and at psychological variables such as the extent to which the parents were described as having been able to accept H and his or her disability, on the other.

Two scores reflecting the severity of H's handicap (the degree of mental retardation and of physical handicap) and five demographic characteristics were considered important.

1. The degree of mental retardation, (MR): the less the retardation, the higher the score [Table 10, I (1)].

2. The degree of physical handicap or stigmata: the less the handicap or stigmata, the higher the score [Table 10, I (2)].

3. Number of children in the family: the score is simply that number.

4. Social class of the family: the score is based on father's education and occupation. Higher scores reflect higher social class [Table 10, III (7)].

5. The sex of H: although sex is not a continuous variable, a continuous scale was constructed for sex to enable us to control its effect in the partial correlations. For any given sample (which, of course, has SibHs of only one sex), the score reflects that H was either the same or the opposite sex as SibH. In all analyses in which the sex of H in itself was important, sex was considered in (two) discrete categories [Table 10, I (5)].

6. Religious orientation of family: this too is a variable appropriately belonging in discrete categories. However, for statistical purposes, religious orientation also was rated on a continuous scale based on the literature, which suggests that Catholic families have the easiest time with the retarded child, Jewish families the most difficult. High scores went to Catholic families, next to Protestant, lowest to Jewish [Table 10, III (6)].

7. Age relationship between SibH and H: as with sex of H and religious orientation, for all important analyses the age-relationship score was divided into discrete categories—those SibHs older than H and those younger. For purposes of control in the partial correlations, a scale was constructed based on the assumption that the older SibH was than H, and the more siblings between them, the less traumatic the experience for SibH. High scores mean SibH was older than H; low scores, younger [Table 10, I (4)].

STATISTICAL RESULTS:
SEVERITY OF HANDICAP, DEMOGRAPHIC FACTORS

In order to examine the effects of each factor alone, partial correlations were carried out in which the relationship between the two scores reflecting the severity of H's handicap, demographic variables, and the adaptation measures were examined, with the influence of all six other variables statistically controlled (Table 14).[2]

Effect of the Degree of Mental or Physical Handicap

Despite the presumed importance of the degree of H's handicap on a family's functioning, we found surprisingly few statistically significant relationships between the severity of handicap and any of our measures of SibH's adaptation. The greatest number (4 out of a possible 12) were in the sample of Community U women. The greater the mental retardation of their sibling, the *better* their over-all functioning at college, and the greater their assessed anxiety. (For Private U women, as well, in the only significant correlation in that sample, the greater the mental retardation of their brother or sister, the higher their anxiety score.) On the other hand, for these Community U women, the greater the *physical* handicap, the *poorer* their judged coping-effectiveness and the lower their anxiety score.

For Private U men, no such relationships appeared with the degree of retardation, but several did with physical handicap. The greater the physical handicap, the better their judged coping-effectiveness and the more they talked with friends about H.

For the Community U men, the less the mental retardation, the more they talked with friends about H.

2. In this and all subsequent analyses, because of the incomparability of scores among SibHs groups, interrelationships among variables in each group were considered separately.

*Effect of the Number of Children in the Family and
of the Family's Social Class*

These two variables are often related—although not in these samples (Table 4). Here they are considered together. One of the few statistically significant findings was a correlation between the number of children in the family and the coping-effectiveness for the Community U women, such that the greater the number of children, the better SibH's judged adaptation. Also, the more children, the higher the anxiety score. In this sample, the positive correlations between social class and both coping and over-all functioning approached, but did not reach, statistical significance.

The higher the social class of the Private U women, the better their academic functioning. The higher the social class for the Community U men, the less open they were in talking with friends about H.

*Effects of the Sex of H, the Religious Orientation of
the Family, and the Age Relationship Between SibH and H*

Considering the sex of H, the only main effect from analyses of variance comparing scores on measures of adaptation of siblings of boy and girl retarded siblings was found in the extent to which SibH talked about H. As a group, siblings of retarded girls talked less about the handicap than siblings of boys ($F = 2.30, p \leqslant 0.05$). All students described more embarrassment over a same-sex handicapped brother or sister than over one of the opposite sex ($F = 4.78, p \leqslant 0.01$), with the strongest effect occurring among Community U men with boy Hs. An interesting additional fact can be derived from the data classifying SibHs by the sex of H. Of the 83 SibHs, 56—or 67 percent—had a retarded brother, and only 27 a retarded sister. (The proportions of handicapped brothers to sisters was approximately the same for the men and women SibHs.)

No significant main effects by religion appeared in the analysis of variance of the adaptation measures.

Finally, in the only significant main effect from an analysis of variance relating adaptation measures to age relationship, SibHs older than H had significantly higher coping scores than SibHs younger than H ($F = 2.51$, $p \leq 0.05$). This finding held for all colleges and both men and women.

PSYCHOLOGICAL FACTORS

As we have seen, the scores reflecting the severity of H's handicap and the demographic variables had relatively few statistically significant relationships with the measures of adaptation. In other words, and speaking loosely for the moment, these factors did not seem to determine or predict how well the normal brother or sister was able to deal with the retardation of a sibling. What factors, then, did relate to our measures of psychological health?

Several psychological variables emerged from the literature and from our clinical experience, and were refined and elaborated during the early period of the research. In particular, five aspects of family functioning, as perceived and described by SibH, seemed interesting in and of themselves, and also conceivably related to the way SibH came to deal with the fact of having a handicapped brother or sister.[3]

1. Mother's acceptance of H: this variable reflects our judgment of the mother's acceptance of H and of H's handicap, as reflected by SibH's discussion of his mother and her relationship with H. Rather than being a simple numerical reflection of SibH's evaluation of his mother's acceptance of H, the score is a result of our clinical judgment from all of the interview material. High scores were given for greater acceptance [Table 10, III (4)].

2. Father's acceptance of H: same as (1), above, but for father [Table 10, III (3)].

3. Family acceptance of H: although often it seemed difficult, if not impossible, to separate the family's acceptance of H from the mother's and father's, in some families a general attitude toward H existed that did not seem to stem from, or even neces-

3. Two others, "Feels Towards Parents" [Table 10, III (1)] and "Feels Towards Normal Siblings" [Table 10, III (2)] were originally included. However, neither item related in any important way to the issues concerning mental retardation and both were therefore eliminated from consideration.

sarily be consistent with, one or both of the parents' views [Table 10, III (5)].

4. Feelings toward H: this score reflects our clinical judgment of SibH's fondness or dislike for H. High scores were given for greater fondness [Table 10, II (3)].

5. Marital integration: we were uncertain whether to consider this a demographic or a psychological variable. This is a measure of the overt intactness of SibH's parents' marriage ranging from no disruption, which received a high score, through desertion of the family by one parent, which received a low score [Table 10, III (8)].

STATISTICAL RESULTS: PSYCHOLOGICAL FACTORS

In Table 15, which compares the scores of the four samples on these psychological items, several important differences appear. Mothers of men students were rated as more accepting of H than mothers of women students, while both men and women from Private U described more family acceptance of H than did Community U students. (Actually, for all three acceptance scores, looking at the means, Community U women reported the least acceptance, Private U men the most, and Private U women fell in between.) Community U students reported more liking for H than did Private U students.

In striking contrast to the relative lack of relationships between the adaptation measures and the severity of H's handicap and demographic factors, numerous strong relationships existed between these psychological variables and the measures of adaptation, particularly in the Private U samples (Table 16). For these two groups, there were consistently high correlations between mother, father, and family acceptance of H and two of the three adaptation measures closely related to the retarded child; students from families judged as being more accepting were rated by us as having coped more effectively and described themselves as less embarrassed by H. For the Community U students, only one significant relationship between these measures appeared: for

Community U men, coping correlated highly with family acceptance.

For the Private U men, also, father's acceptance and family's acceptance correlated *negatively* with over-all functioning at school.

There were few significant correlations in any of the four samples between adaptation and marital integration of parents. For Private U men, the more marital disruption in their family, the higher their anxiety rating. Community U men reported less open talking with friends about H, the less the marital disruption of the family.

The other psychological variable that did significantly correlate to several measures of adaptation was SibH's feeling for H, particularly for the siblings from Private U. In these two groups, liking for H correlated highly with coping-effectiveness and with a report of not being embarrassed by H. For the women, the more they liked H, the higher their over-all functioning and the lower their anxiety scores.

Fewer relationships appeared between adaptation and feeling toward H in the two other samples, and those that did tended to be weaker than those found among the Private U samples. Community U women who were less embarrassed by H also liked him or her. Community U men who talked to friends more about H liked him or her and got lower anxiety scores.

We wondered if the severity of H's handicap and/or demographic factors influenced or related to SibH's description of the family's acceptance of H. The partial correlations between the acceptance scores and each other variable—again with the other six statistically controlled—showed surprisingly few results (Table 17). For Community U women, but not men, fathers were reported as more accepting of H, the less the mental retardation. For Private U women, father's acceptance correlated negatively with the number of children in the family—the more children, the less they were described as accepting H. For Private U men, mothers were reported as more accepting, the less the mental retardation; but mother, father, and family acceptance were all reported as higher, the greater the physical handicap.

From the analysis of variance by the sex of H, mothers and fathers were described as being more accepting of a female handicapped child than of a male (for mother, $F = 4.78$, $p \leqslant 0.01$; for father, $F = 2.93$, $p \leqslant 0.01$) and for fathers, this result was true for all four samples. Looking at the same means, mothers of Community U men and women were described as tending to accept a female H more, while Private U women described their mothers as more accepting of a male H. There was no difference for mothers of Private U men.

From a comparison of SibHs younger and older than H, as well as comparing men and women and students from the different schools, the only significant main effect was that SibHs older than H reported more family acceptance of H than those younger ($F = 2.88$, $p \leqslant 0.05$). No differences appeared in the analysis of variance by the religion of the family.

In Chapter 9, the specific results are considered in light of the broader formulations presented in Chapters 6 and 7, as well as in light of the relevant literature.

Coping With Retardation: What Makes a Difference

ONE PREMISE underlying this book is that reactions to mental retardation are not inevitably determined by the nature and degree
of the handicap itself, but rather depend upon social-psychological factors such as the cultural and familial definition of the
problem. This suggests that the usually unhappy—often devas-
tated—reaction of families of a retarded child in this culture is not
an inevitable response to the birth of a retarded child. We became
interested in finding individuals—in this case brothers and sisters
—who themselves had not been harmed by the experience of
growing up with a retarded sibling and, in fact, who might have
benefited from it. We felt that finding some such young people
would both demonstrate our point about the wide range of possible reactions to a handicapped child and also teach us something about the particular aspects of a family and its functioning
that encourage such a positive result.

In this chapter, we are ready to consider this question of
"benefit or harm" to the normal siblings through consideration
of the statistical findings presented in Chapter 8 on the over-all
adaptation of the normal siblings. These results are examined in
light of the conceptual framework we constructed in Chapters
6 and 7 for understanding the life experiences of the young men
and women in our four different groups, and also with respect
to related findings in the literature.

One note of caution is needed. As we have pointed out several
times, the brothers and sisters of retarded children who volunteered to talk with us about their experiences probably were better adjusted and more accepting than many of the college siblings
in the schools they represented. Thus, although it is extremely

important from our perspective to know if *any* brothers or sisters can benefit and grow from the experience of growing up with a retarded sibling, the *percentages* of students in our samples whom we judged to have benefited cannot be given great weight. In addition, since these young people had already demonstrated a degree of adjustment by their very presence in college, we suspect that they, as a group, would reflect far more adaptive coping with retardation than an unselected sample of college-age siblings.

OVER-ALL BENEFIT OR HARM?

One of the most impressive general findings is the extent to which we judged some students to have benefited (as reflected by high scores on coping-effectiveness) rather than being harmed by the experience of growing up with a retarded brother or sister.

Considering all 83 of the student-subjects, 37—or 45 percent—were judged by the scorers to have benefited, in contrast to having been harmed or showing no net psychological effect (Figure 1). Thirty-eight—or 45 percent—were judged to have been harmed, and eight were considered neither benefited nor harmed, so that the net result of positive and negative effects canceled each other.[1]

In our clinical judgments, those who had benefited had a greater understanding of people, more tolerance of people in general and handicap in particular, more compassion, more sensitivity to prejudice and its consequences, more appreciation of their own good health and intelligence than many of their peers who had not had this experience, as well as a sense that the ex-

1. As we have said, these percentages of students whom we judge to have gained or been harmed cannot be taken as an accurate description of the total group of college siblings. However, we can make some educated guesses as to the true percentages in the population. From the schools we refer to jointly as "Private U," our 100-percent survey indicated that about one-half of the total college population of siblings of retarded children had volunteered to participate. If one assumes as a most extreme estimate that all of the Private U students with retarded siblings who did not volunteer were harmed, and then recomputes the proportion of those who benefited versus those who were harmed, then at the very most, approximately 73 percent could be considered harmed and 23 percent estimated to have bene-fited. (Our lack of comparable data about the total population at Community U makes it impossible even to estimate the possible percentages there.)

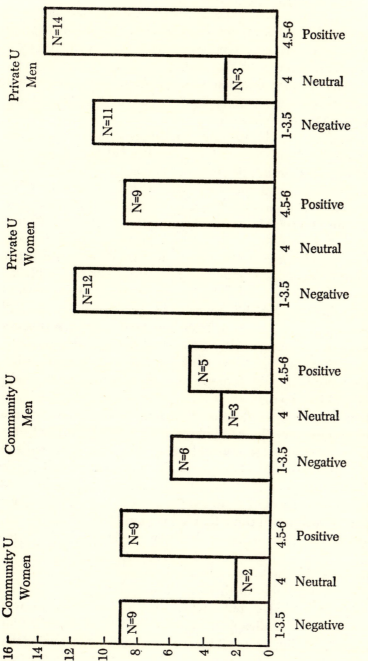

Figure 1. Graphs of number of siblings of retarded children in each sample judged to have positive, neutral, or negative over-all psychological effects: coping-effectiveness.

perience had drawn the family closer together. The following was said by a Private U man who was expressing a point of view similar to that of many of the siblings we judged as effectively coping. (Our scoring decision was not based on this passage alone.) He was talking of the effects on him of having a younger brother with Down's Syndrome:

"It's taught me to be tolerant. I mean, from a very early age I've learned people are different, and you have to make exceptions and you have responsibilities to other people. And you just need love and patience and understanding to get along with other people. And I've always been geared to just being aware. And being aware of prejudice and misconception. James is different but he's not *that* different. That's one thing it's undoubtedly taught me—that there are not only normal people and crazy people but there are shades, and it's just getting used to that fact."

This young man was both highly sophisticated and introspective in his discussion of the impact of his brother on him. Not all brothers and sisters judged to have benefited were as introspective; some were more matter of fact about it. The following excerpt is from the interview with a Community U girl with a mildly retarded, slightly younger brother. When asked how she felt toward him, she replied:

"Well, I'm in Special Education now, so it sort of puts a different outlook on things. I always felt that I could help my brother in some respects. I would spend time with him, and this sort of thing—just the extra special things that he didn't get in school—the individual attention. And, and I guess I love him just as much as, say, I would a normal person. Just the way he shows affection towards me—I think that helps considerably."

Later in the interview, we asked how she felt he had affected her.

"Well, I don't think I ever would have gone into Special Education. I never thought of that as a little girl. I always thought I wanted to be a teacher, but I never thought I would work with people who were handicapped, because I thought I would be just too sympathetic. But having it in your own house and realizing that this is the worst thing that could ever happen for a kid makes you think. I figured I should try Special Ed just to see if I was able to do it. And just trying to help out all those other people—parents, who don't know what to do with their kids—is very satisfying. And I'm sure that I've influenced a lot of my friends. I've convinced a lot of people to try it and see."

A final, quite interesting statement by a subject judged to have coped well is one by a Community U man, second oldest of eight children. Marty, the youngest, a boy with Down's Syndrome, was six at the time of this interview. We asked him how he felt toward Marty.

"I just love him. I prefer him, he is the person in my family I like the most, because he is different but he is—I don't know—we consider him 'heaven sent.' You know. He teaches us so much —he is so innocent all the time. Even though he's six years old now, he is still as innocent as he was. And no matter what company you're in he will always be the same. He'll never change his ways, in front of good company or bad company. He'll always be the same old Marty—whether he wants to be stubborn or cry or be happy, he is always the same person. And I think I like him a lot for one, because he is so lovable and, two, because especially when you are grown up—when you are out of your childhood into your adult years—you tend to become sophisticated and see things from a complicated instead of from a simple point of view. And then when you come to Marty—you see how he does it—it sort of brings you down to where you should be, you know."

Later we asked whether Marty's handicap had made a difference in his life.

"Yes, if I stop and think about it, it makes me appreciative of how much I really have when I see how, at the present, how limited he is. And I never thought of myself as being very smart, but compared to him I realize I have a lot of unused potential, where it seems he is using everything he's got."

These reports by some of the siblings of a sense of having gained from their experiences, as well as the researchers' concurrence in some instances, is consistent with data collected by Kramm (1963), who reports that 76 percent of 50 families he interviewed felt they had benefited from having a child with Down's Syndrome, and described their growth in many of the same ways as did some of our SibHs.

On the other hand, it would be naive to suggest that the presence of a retarded child in the home never has negative consequences for the siblings. As was mentioned above, we judged 45 percent of the SibHs to have been harmed, and in the general population of college siblings, and particularly of college-age young people in general, the percentage is undoubtedly much higher. Some of the psychological costs we noted include shame about the handicapped child, and guilt about the shame; a sense of being somehow tainted or defective; a sense of guilt for being in good health and, more often, for harboring negative feelings about the retarded child; a feeling of having been neglected by their parents, who were preoccupied with the handicapped child; and at times a strong belief that the handicapped child had put considerable stress on the parents' relationship, which in turn negatively affected the rest of the family. The following statement was made by a Private U student who was a younger brother of a severely retarded institutionalized boy. We thought this student had been hurt by the experience. When asked what the effect on him had been, he replied:

"I don't know, probably just thinking about him is slightly depressing and slightly bothering—. I mean, just thinking about him in that state—thinking about him and what kind of life he's leading and how it affects my parents and how it affected their behavior towards their other children."

We asked what he said to friends when he mentioned his brother.

"Well, that he exists, basically. That I do have a brother—mentally retarded—not much that we can carry on conversationally. It makes other people feel uncomfortable, usually, to hear you talk about a family tragedy."

A more articulate and self-aware description of a negative effect was given by a Private U woman. The older of two girls, her sister was mildly retarded. First she described her sister as extremely shy, and as worshipping her. She continued:

"I'm the only normal adolescent that she's known and she idolizes me and she thinks that it's really neat—all the things that I do when I go out. If I take her anywhere, which my mother likes me to do a lot, because she feels that it's good for her to get out of the house because she doesn't do much but sit in front of T.V.—so if I take her shopping with me, she'll follow so closely behind me that if I stop she would step on my heels. And if I bend over to touch a sweater or something like that she'll touch it [on] exactly the same spot at the same time! She just mimics me!"

"How do you feel toward her?"

"I feel terribly guilty—not guilty—just wishing I could do more. Both my father and I have very bad tempers. He has a worse temper for flaring up than I do, but I just don't have much patience. And I wish I could have the patience to—to be unselfish enough to spend a lot of time with her. Because I know she loves it. But I'm home so rarely, and I'm so used to being always on my own—I've been away at camp, to Europe on my own. It's very strange to be thrown in suddenly to this suburban home life with a sister like that, who is not normal, who you can't talk to, and all of a sudden having the responsibility after having only taken care of yourself for so many years. And I realize that it could have just as easily been me, and I just feel terribly sorry for her. But I do usually lose my temper an awful lot; it drives me crazy the way she idolizes me. She drools down my neck and it makes me a complete nervous wreck, and I just have to control myself every minute! It's terribly hard for me!"

Finally, a Community U woman, oldest of three, responded to the question of the effect of her youngest sister's retardation on her own life:

"For me, it made me be dependent [sic]. Before my sister was born, my younger sister did take a lot of attention away from me. And when my little sister (H) was born, seeing she was very ill, my parents even more and more drifted away from me. So I became very dependent, and I was doing mostly everything for myself. And it still is the same way. I don't want any help from my family unless absolutely needed; I'm very dependent."

At this point, the interviewer asked: "Independent?"

"Independent. I don't depend on them for anything at all other than the bare necessities."

The ambivalence reflected in the repeated slip ("dependent" for "independent") as well as the underlying rage at her parents, is striking, and she was judged as having been damaged by the experience.

COMPARISONS AMONG THE FOUR GROUPS

No differences in coping-effectiveness appeared among the four groups of students. Both groups of Private U students did better academically than did Community U students, as was expected. The men received higher IQ scores than the women, primarily because Private U men had significantly higher scores than Private U women, as is consistent with the academic ratings of the two Private U schools.

As a group, all women received higher test-anxiety scores, which is a common finding in the literature, *e.g.*, McCandless (1970), Maccoby (1966). Taken in conjunction with a greater willingness to talk about their retarded brother or sister with friends and a lesser degree of reported embarrassment with H than reported by the men students, the findings suggest an important sex difference in the psychology of young adults that influences their way of coping with a retarded sibling, as well as other aspects of their functioning. (The finding that Community U students reported themselves as talking more openly with friends than did the other two groups is accounted for primarily by the far greater frequency of such discussions reported by Community U women.) In general, these girls seemed less concerned about possible negative consequences of what they expressed, whether it be fear and anxiety or feelings and thoughts about a retarded sibling. Partly, their freedom to be expressive came from the relative de-emphasis on independence and autonomy in our culture's socialization of girls.

Community U women talked much more about H than did the Private U women, largely because of the high proportion of Community U women participating in a Special Education major, where discussions about handicapped children are frequent. As one girl said, when asked if they talked about H with friends:

"Oh yeah, especially at school, because I find that a lot of other kids in Special Ed will have relatives or friends [who are retarded or who have a retarded child]."

WHAT INFLUENCES ADAPTATION: THE SEVERITY OF H's HANDICAP AND DEMOGRAPHIC VARIABLES

Degree of Mental Retardation and Physical Handicap or Stigmata

The general assumption in the literature is that a major factor affecting the normal children in a family is the way their parents come to cope with the presence of a handicapped child. If this is the case, then factors affecting the parents will also have an important influence on the normal children (*e.g.*, Carver, 1956; Graliker, Fischler, and Koch, 1962; Kramm, 1963; Ryckman and Henderson, 1965; Schonell and Watts, 1956). Several writers have stated that one factor affecting parents is the severity of the retardation, with more severe retardation causing more difficulties for the parents (*e.g.*, M. Adams, 1966; Hall, 1961). Kirk and Bateman (1964), in partial confirmation of this, report that a high degree of dependence on the part of the retarded child negatively influences the siblings' over-all adjustment. This finding supports Adams' clinical impression to the extent that the more serious the retardation, the more dependent the child.

Further, Farber's study (1964) suggests that upper socio-economic-class families have more difficulty than lower socio-economic-class families when the child does not require inordinate amounts of care but primarily represents a frustration of aspirations for the family. On the other hand, children requiring a great deal of care would seem to cause more difficulty for lower socio-economic-class families and siblings.

In these data, there were surprisingly few relationships between our measures of adaptation and the severity of H's mental or physical handicap. We have emphasized the importance of factors directly and concretely affecting the relationship between SibH and H for the Community U women. Consistent with this point of view, the largest number of significant relationships between the severity of H's handicap and the normal sibling's adaptation occurred in respect to this group. For these women, the less the physical handicap of H—and presumably the less the physical dependence on the part of H—the better off they were (the higher coping-effectiveness score they received), and, generally, the better their over-all functioning at school. This result, consistent with Kirk and Bateman's finding, supports our assumption that these young women, who spent a great deal of time with H and played a major role in taking care of H, were most affected by factors that directly influenced the nature and quantity of that contact.

On the other hand, the *more* the mental retardation of these Community U women's siblings (with the degree of *physical* handicap controlled), the better their functioning. On the face of it, this result seems surprising. However, a number of women—as well as students from other samples—stated directly that, all other things being equal, mild retardation was more difficult to think about and deal with than more severe retardation.

The following was said by a woman from a two-child family, with a mildly retarded younger sister, Carol. When asked what was wrong with Carol, she replied:

"She's not severely mentally retarded, but in my opinion, it's the worse [*sic*] sort of mental retardation. Because she's severely retarded enough not to be able to cope with things—she can't get along with people her own age."

She went on to describe all the things Carol would never be able to do.

"But it's so bad because she knows she's mentally retarded—she knew there was something wrong with her before, and then my mother did tell her. And naturally she sees normal people and wants to be like them, but they are cruel to her. And she knows that there is something wrong with her and it's very frustrating. And it's much worse than being so severely retarded that you don't know."

One seeming contradiction in the data from the Community U women is the high test-anxiety scores of women who also received high scores on coping and school adjustment. However, this apparent discrepancy may not be as contradictory as it seems.

As has been shown before (e.g., Kaplan, 1966), the test-anxiety score may reflect a style of dealing with potentially disturbing or disruptive affect, as well as the presence of a certain quantity of that affect. Given that acknowledgment of anxiety is socially acceptable for girls, and hence the norm in this culture, girls who experience and acknowledge very little anxiety seem to be relying excessively on such defenses as repression and denial, and appear more pathological than girls who experience and describe moderate amounts of anxiety. And, in fact, although girls in this study who scored low on the anxiety scale received extremely low scores, the "high" scorers in the group were not near the top of the scale but rather received moderate scores on anxiety. This suggests that in this study, as in others, extremely anxious subjects did not volunteer, which left the volunteer "highs" at a moderate, rather than extreme, position. In these data, women who were sufficiently comfortable with their thoughts and feelings to admit to moderate amounts of anxiety appeared more adaptive than those who did not. The anxiety scores had no relationships with measures of adaption for the men in the sample.

For the Private U women, as with the Community U women, the greater H's retardation, the higher SibH's anxiety score. However, for these Private U women, the severity of H's physical or mental handicap had no other relationships with the measures of adaptation. Similarly, no relationships existed between the severity of retardation and adaptation for Private U men. These findings strongly support the view that, for siblings from upper SCS families, it is not these reality issues but more subtle psychological ones that are critical in determining the impact of a potential crisis, such as a retarded child, on the family. As Farber and others have said about upper socioeconomic-status families, the primary reaction to mental retardation lies in feelings about the label and its implications, rather than responses to reality issues such as the degree of retardation and the consequent need for care.

An interesting finding is that for Private U men, the *more serious* the physical handicap or stigmata, the better their coping and the more they talked with friends about H. While the degree of physical handicap seemed to affect the Community U women primarily because of the enormous amount of care they themselves were asked to provide for a physically disabled sibling, the degree of physical evidence of handicap seemed to have psychological implications for the Private U men's families.

One possible explanation is that children with physical handicaps presented their families with a more clear-cut need than did children with no physical evidence of disability, thereby reducing the ambiguity of the family's role with the child. It is obvious that a severely involved cerebral-palsied child must be cared for and protected. It may be less obvious what to do with, or for, a child who has difficulty functioning yet has no obvious physical defect.

Similarly, parents of a child with Down's Syndrome and physical stigmata, or those of a cerebral-palsied child with motor disabilities, realize definitely and usually early in the child's life that something is wrong, and have some means of assessing the future course of the child's development. On the other hand, parents of a possibly mildly retarded or somewhat disturbed child and/or a child with a "learning problem" with no handicaps or stigmata are seldom clearly aware of what is wrong *or* why or how it happened, and they have no way of predicting what the future course of development might be. In our sample, these families seemed to remain uncertain as to whether something was really wrong with the child or whether the child was "lazy" or "faking," and never seemed able to give up what appeared to be unrealistic expectations that if only the child would try harder, or if only they could find the proper treatment, the child would be normal. (Parents of obviously retarded children also frequently hold tenaciously to such fantasies. However, the confusion and ambiguity were much more striking in families with children with no physical stigmata or handicap.)

As the brother of a younger "handicapped" brother with no physical signs said:

"Well, he (H) has a lot of trouble reading in school—it seems to be his main problem. Otherwise he seems to be fairly intelligent. He just—he *won't* read; he just doesn't want to read."

At a later point, he was asked more specifically about the nature of H's handicap.

"That's what's so hard to understand, because he just seems too intelligent, but one of his main troubles then, I think, is that he just won't work."

In summary, the influence of the degree of mental or physical handicap is extremely complex, and depends upon a variety of other factors such as the interpretations made in regard to the handicap, the sex of the normal brother or sister, and the role-demands made on that sibling. As Wright (1960) so cogently states with respect to physical disability, so it is also in retardation: the event itself does not carry either the psychological impact or importance of the event. Those stem from the interpretations given to it, and the context in which it occurs.

Adaptation, the Number of Children and the Social Class of the Family

The clinical literature suggests that retarded children have less of an impact on larger families than on smaller ones. For Community U women, the larger the family, the better their coping and the higher their anxiety score. (As observed earlier, high anxiety scores for these women are consistent with psychological health.) The larger families seem to protect them from excessive involvement in care by providing siblings who share some of the burden.

No other relationships appeared between adaptation and family size, probably because of the relatively small number of two-children families in our samples. As we have suggested previously, we have some evidence to suggest that the SibHs from two-children families are more traumatized by the experience and consequently did not volunteer to participate in this study.

Despite the lack of statistical evidence, the clinical material does tend to support the impression that mentally retarded children are often less disruptive in larger families. One Private U man said of his younger brother, a child with Down's Syndrome in a family of 10 children:

"He hasn't really been that conspicuous because there are so many boys around."

On the other hand, several families in our samples with only two children were markedly disrupted. The following excerpt from an interview with a Private U man from a two-child family illustrates his great sense of pressure to make up to his family for his brother's lack of success:

"I have to achieve because I'm the only one in the family, the only offspring who can achieve. Also, my father is a very prideful man and it's hurt him a great deal that Timmy can't achieve. He wants so much to be proud of his sons. That focuses it all on me."

When asked how he felt toward his parents, he said:

"I really feel sorry for them. Because I know—having a retarded son, especially when you have only two children—it's been a very devastating thing. And in some ways I kinda wish they had had more children."

Another, the younger brother of a mildly retarded boy, when asked how H's handicap affected his parents' goals for him, said:

"It's as though I were the only child but worse. That's, I suppose, why I'm being pushed to be the opposite of what he is. It's also been the cause of my being spoiled. Basically, it caused them to center their hopes on me a bit more than they would if I had a normal brother."

Few relationships appeared between measures of adaptation and ratings of the socioeconomic status of the students within each sample because of the marked homogeneity of social class within each college group. (The more valid index of the impact of social class and what we term "sociocultural status" is in the very different patterns of relationships among the variables in the four samples, as has been mentioned.)

There was a tendency for higher socioeconomic-status girls in the Community U sample to get higher scores on coping and over-all functioning. (This is somewhat in contrast to the findings reported by Westley and Epstein, 1969, that measures of health of boys, but not girls, correlated directly with social class.) Also, the higher the socioeconomic status of Community U men, the less open the student was in talking with friends about H. This finding is consistent with the result already noted, that Community U men were more open as a group in talking about H with friends than Private U men, who were of a higher social stratum. It suggests that for men—in marked contrast to women—the higher the socioeconomic status, the more limitations are placed on their freedom to talk openly about such a potentially difficult topic.

Adaptation and the Sex of H and of SibH

The sex of the child and the parent makes a difference in the impact of the child on the parent. Farber (1964) summarizes this literature and concludes that in all families, at the beginning, mothers are more disturbed by the birth of a retarded girl and fathers by the birth of a retarded boy, underlining the initial effects of identification with the child. This reaction is most marked in mothers in lower- and lower middle-class families, which have the most marked sex differentiation in family roles. As time goes on, while fathers remain more disturbed by a retarded son, mothers also begin to be more troubled by such a son than by a retarded daughter. Presumably, the roles demanded of a boy in a family and society are more dissonant with what a retarded child actually can do than the roles demanded of a girl. These findings are consistent with Farber and Jenné's report (1963) suggesting that the sex of the normal brother or sister has an important effect on the ultimate impact on that sibling.

All students in our samples were more embarrassed by a same-sex handicapped sibling than by one of the opposite sex, possibly because of the greater sense of identification with H and H's handicap. Also in these data, brothers and sisters of retarded girls talked less about H to friends than did siblings of retarded brothers, which might well be related to the greater proportion of siblings of boy Hs willing to come and talk with the researchers. Either a girl H caused more embarrassment to the normal students or, more probably, she was less important or interesting to them.

We searched for some examples from the interviews that might illustrate or clarify some of these effects, but found virtually no direct comments about the impact of H's sex. Apparently, whatever the impact of the retarded child's sex on the sibling, it operates at a less-than-conscious level.

Adaptation and Religion

There is considerable discussion in the literature about the effects of religion on a family's acceptance of a retarded child. Stubblefield (1965) reports that Catholic parents are more accepting of a retarded child than are Protestant or Jewish families. The explanation given for this is that the Catholic religion specifies that parents have no need to feel guilty about bearing such a child, but rather should see themselves as specially chosen to be given the child who requires special treatment (also in Stone, 1967). Zuk, Miller, Bartrum, and Kling (1961) also found Catholic mothers more accepting, and found that those Catholic mothers who were more faithful in church attendance more frequently showed greater acceptance of the child. Similarly, Kirk and Bateman (1964), from their survey of the literature, report that the marital integration of Catholic families is not affected by whether or not the retarded child is institutionalized, while non-Catholic families had lower marital integration scores when a retarded boy was kept at home. However, Ehlers (1966) intensively studied 24 mothers of retarded children and found no relationship between religion and feelings of acceptance, and Stone (1967) found no religious differences in her study of 103 families of young children with Down's Syndrome. (Also Felzen, 1970.) A partial explanation for this discrepancy is suggested by Zuk *et al.* (1961). They point out that different measures of maternal acceptance do not all correlate highly with each other, so the results vary depending on the measures used. (Their explanation for the seeming instability of the variable is that parents inevitably are ambivalent about a handicapped child, although with varying amounts of acceptance. Different measures seem to tap different aspects of the ambivalence.)

F. K. Adams (1966) reports the only study relating religious orientation directly to an adolescent sibling population. He found that while Protestant siblings of retarded children showed a poorer over-all adjustment in their home interpersonal relationships than a matched group of Protestant siblings of a normal child, Catholic siblings of a handicapped brother or sister were *better* adjusted than Catholic siblings of only normal children. The bulk of the data on religion seems to suggest that a strong religious belief that parents are not guilty for having a handicapped child can reduce guilt and increase maternal acceptance. As several authors have noted (Stone, 1967; Zuk *et al.*, 1961), Jewish families seem to have the most difficulty as a group, since their religion does not help directly, and the frequent strong emphasis on education intensifies disappointment with a child who learns very slowly.

Our data yielded no clear and meaningful relationships between adaptation and religion, in part because of the sampling bias that resulted in disproportionately few students from Jewish families. Despite the lack of statistical findings, a number of the comments of the students about the significance of religion in their own and their family's ways of dealing with H were revealing. The following quotes are from brothers and sisters from Catholic families who did rely heavily on their religious beliefs to support them in the crisis.

The first statement is by a Community U male, older brother of a boy, Marty, with Down's Syndrome:

"My father always tells the kids that we should look at Marty almost like an angel. And most likely he won't be with us too long. So be happy, feel privileged to do anything for him because he is like a gift from God, and whatever you do for him is like an act of love towards God."

Later in the interview, we asked about the role of religion in their understanding of Marty's handicap.

"Yes, my father had that saying: 'This child that we have is so innocent that he is not capable of sin, so he must be almost like an angel. And so because he is so holy and so special, and because he probably won't be with us too long, we ought to be glad to do anything for him.' This is exactly what my father used to say: 'Whenever you do something for Marty, you ought to just think it is like putting in a word with God. When he dies and goes to heaven, he will put in a good word for you.' "

In another large Catholic family with a young retarded boy, the normal sibling described his mother taking H to Lourdes, France:

"Where miracles happen. Well, she took him over there to Europe when he was two, or one. He was one, and it's kinda miraculous because we don't know how he would be now if he hadn't gone—if he would have been better or worse. My mother always sort of thinks in the back of her mind that this might have helped. Plus my mother used to get constipated all the time—this is really funny—and when she came back from over there she never needed to take those pills she always had had before. And whether this was psychological—but I don't think it is because, you know, she had the prescription. She thinks going to Lourdes might have had something to do with it."

The third comment is by a man from Community U, with just the one retarded sister. We asked how religion affected his view of H.

"Well, I do know she's retarded. I know there's brain damage. And I feel that God wanted her this way for some reason. So He made her this way for some reason. And you accept her, you do all you can for her. Because He says: 'What you do to the least of my brethren, you do unto me.' And these children can't do for themselves, so someone has to do it."

The use of such explanations seemed to occur much less often in Protestant homes and least in Jewish. The following statement by a Private U woman from a Protestant home is relatively characteristic of their attitude. The family was moderately religious in that they attended church services periodically. SibH was asked if religion had affected her view of her retarded brother:

"No, I don't think so. I remember a relative once saying: 'How could God do this to you?' And my mother said: 'Well, I don't really think that God had that much to do with it. I think it's more, you know, within the power of man.' She never really explained to me why it happened, 'cause I guess she doesn't have any explanations herself. But I think she was very upset that this person should say, 'How could God let this happen to you?' "

In summary, the lack of statistical results relating the normal sibling's adaptation to his family's religion is at least partially explicable in terms of the sampling bias resulting in many fewer Jewish students. Also, the apparently greater comfort felt by siblings from more religious families was not always seen by us as genuine and positive coping, and was not rated as such.

The anecdotal evidence from the interviews does support reports in the literature that Catholic families at least make *more* use of religion in coming to terms with H's handicap than do Protestant or Jewish families.

Adaptation and the Age Relationship Between the Normal Sibling and H

Older brothers and sisters in this study received consistently higher coping scores than did those who were younger than the retarded child. (Over twice as many older siblings volunteered to participate in the research than younger: 56, compared with 27.)

There is little in the literature to help explain this result, although a number of studies do describe psychological differences in older and younger siblings (*e.g.*, Altus, 1965; Brim, 1958; Dittes and Capra, 1962; Hall and Barger, 1964; Koch, 1960; Lasko, 1954; McArthur, 1956; and Sutton-Smith and Rosenberg, 1965). However, some partial explanations can be suggested and supported by anecdotal evidence from the interviews.

Younger children seemed often to emulate older siblings, which can have negative consequences when the older child is handicapped. A Private U man with three younger siblings talked at length about how his being older than his mildly retarded brother, Paul, greatly reduced the impact of Paul's retardation on him and contrasted this situation with that of his still younger brother.

"What do you think the effect has been on you of Paul's retardation?"

"I was old enough by the time that Paul was having an influence on me that I'd really already broken away from the family. I never really came under his influence. I was never restricted in the sense that his interests defined my interests. But Kenny—being younger, he was really for a long time totally dominated by Paul. Not aggressively or anything. Just that Paul chose the things to do, and because Kenny was younger, he'd do the same things, and it took him much longer to get away from this. And even now he's still too much dominated by Paul and his interests."

Another factor that also seemed to operate with mildly retarded children was a strong competitiveness, particularly with younger normal siblings. This competition, and the consequent frustration on the part of the retarded child and guilt and discomfort on the part of the normal brother or sister, seemed strongest when H was older than the normal child and was aware of the usual role of the older sibling. A Private U woman, older sister of a younger mildly retarded boy, described the difficulties that arose between H and a still younger sister, Lori.

"Lori is close enough in age to Stevie (H) to be at times an equal and yet she can dominate him, and I think that he resents this a little bit. She'll boss him around, tell him what to do. And I think that he feels she shouldn't do this because he's older than she is and he's bigger than she is. I think my younger brother has the hardest time because he's about five years younger than Stevie, and yet he's mentally older and more mature. And I think he resents the fact that Stevie is older and is able to do things like stay up later and things like that. It's frustrating for both of them."

On the other hand, older brothers and sisters not only could avoid this kind of competition and guilt, they could more easily step into a parental role toward H and gain considerable satisfaction from it. As the oldest boy in a family of 10 children said of his relationship to his much younger brother with Down's Syndrome, when asked if he had ever wished Butch were not around when his friends were around:

"I never really felt that way, because my friends and I were older than Butch. And so it was always like he was just a little boy around. They might have been kind of curious about him, but I never felt he reflected on me."

The sibling position that appears to maximize difficulties is to be the younger brother of an older mildly retarded brother. (Possibly equally difficult is to be the younger sister of a mildly retarded older girl.) The fact of being the same sex as H, the tendency to model oneself on an older sibling, and the relatively minimal retardation, all increase the likelihood of SibH's tendency to identify with a defective sibling. The following comments from such a younger brother illustrate the problem clearly. SibH described the effect on his father, who left the family shortly after the retardation was identified:

"While you can say the retardation was caused by a medical thing—and very smart people have retarded children—and even though my father was a very intelligent man, he saw it sort of as a reflection of himself. And I guess I'd better say this now. This is something I thought about myself. Whenever I see something in him (H) that reminds me of myself, it really bothers me. That's why I—I suppose, I guess I avoided him at times. Because when I see—when he does something which reminds me of what I did, it just makes me feel worse about what I am. And a lot of people couldn't face up to that at all."

One final factor that also increased the likelihood of older brothers and sisters in our sample making a better adjustment is the fact that their retarded siblings, as a group, were younger at the time of the study than were the retarded siblings of the normal sibling with an older H. Numerous researchers have noted the greater disruption in a family caused by an older retarded child (e.g., Farber, 1964; Kramm, 1963). Further, older SibHs had the chance to grow up in the family when that family was less disrupted by the handicapped child.

All of these factors work in the direction of making it easier for an older brother or sister to cope adaptively with the experience of having a retarded brother or sister, and this ability seems to be one of the few variables influential across social-cultural status levels.

Adaptation, Parent Acceptance, and Liking for H

The Private U students who described their mothers, fathers, and families as accepting H were able to cope adaptively with the experience of having a retarded brother or sister. As one young woman from Private U explained when asked if she had ever wished her younger, severely retarded sister were not around when her friends were around:

"No, I don't think so. She was a member of the family, and we didn't—there was never any feeling that she was different or she was odd. I think it was probably that mother just showed that she loved her so much anyhow. Our parents didn't treat it as being strange, and therefore we didn't either."

This attitude is central to our conception of the family situations and experiences of the Private U students: the feelings and thoughts of their parents played an enormously important role in the normal siblings' own reactions. (Westley and Epstein, 1969, found in their sample of middle-class Canadian college students that the emotional health of the children was greatly affected by the mother's adequacy in her maternal role, which seems closely related to the mother's ability to accept all of her children.)

On the other hand, for the Community U students, their parents' reactions to H seemed little related to their own view of H or their ability to come to terms with H's retardation. In the one significant relationship, Community U men coped better when they described their families as accepting H. This suggests that, for these men, what made a difference was the total family attitude or sometimes only that of the other normal siblings, rather than either their mothers' or fathers' views.

In a related finding, the more the Private U students liked H, the better their adaptation to H and his or her handicap. As with the acceptance scores, few relationships existed for the Community U students, and those that did exist were less important (*i.e.,* the statistical relationships were smaller).

Interestingly, in our data few relationships appeared between the degree of disruption or intactness of the parents' marriages and SibH's health and adaptation.

Parent Acceptance and Liking for H: Comparisons Among Groups

Considering briefly the differences among the groups on acceptance scores, the men students described their mothers as more accepting of H that did the women. Furthermore, Private U students described more family acceptance of H than did Community U students. (On all three acceptance scores—mother, father, and family—Community U women described the least acceptance, Private U men the most, with the other two groups falling in between.)

In part, the men's views of their mothers as comfortably accepting H seemed to stem from their relative unawareness of the stresses and strains on the mother in dealing with H, compared with the perceptions of the women. In addition, however, having a normal boy child can satisfy for many families the need of that family to perpetuate itself.

The greater acceptance described by all Private U students seems to reflect the fewer reality hardships in these families with a retarded child, compared with the Community U families. There also existed in the Private U families an ethos that made them feel they ought to accept and love the child, and this affected how they responded to H and how they communicated to SibH about H, as well as how SibH talked with us about the family's experiences with H. (We have noted before the great difficulty the Private U students had in being critical of, or angry at, H.)

Community U students seemed to like their retarded sibling better than did students from Private U. There were no differences among the groups in the degree of marital intactness or disruption of the SibH's parents.

Parent Acceptance, the Severity of H's Handicap, and Demographic Variables

We wondered to what extent the parent- and family-acceptance scores, which correlated so strongly with the health of the SibHs in both groups of Private U students, themselves simply reflected the family members' responses to such factors as the severity of H's handicap or the size of the family.

In fact, although we did find some relationships between acceptance and the other measures, these connections were in no way large enough or systematic enough to account for all the differences in the SibH's adaptation.

For Community U women, the less H's retardation, the more their fathers seemed to accept H. For Private U men, their mothers' acceptance was stated as greater the less the retardation, but mothers', fathers' and families' acceptance were all greater, the more obvious H's physical handicap or stigmata. (Again, this relationship between acceptance and adaptation and greater physical handicap in H in the sample of Private U men has been found repeatedly.) Farber (1964) reported from his review of the literature that fathers tend to be more affected by such variables as the diagnostic label given the child, while mothers are more affected by variables that directly influence the relationship with the child, such as H's level of social competence. This is not corroborated by our findings, but the fact that our information was obtained from the students alone may explain this discrepancy.

As a group, all of the mothers and fathers were judged more accepting of a retarded daughter than of such a son, though the effect was stronger and more consistent for fathers. Aberle and Naegele (1952), who interviewed fathers of middle-class families, found that because men must be "responsible, show initiative, be competent, be aggressive, be capable of meeting competition," etc., to fit in with our culture's expectations for men, the fathers worried a good deal about their sons' development in these directions. Fathers' views of their daughters' future were much more vague and less concerned. "If she is a sweet little girl, that is enough."

Clinical excerpts from the interviews clearly illustrate the concern of fathers with a retarded son, particularly when they had no normal sons. In the first family, the retarded child was the youngest of three and the only boy. When asked how her father felt about her brother George's handicap, the daughter replied:

"My father always wanted a son, and I've been a tomboy, the tomboy of the family. In fact, on my twenty-first birthday last year they gave me a pocket watch. 'To my favorite son' was engraved on it. And I think he misses the fact that, you know—like you're so happy when a son is born, and especially someone to carry on the name some day. I had a cousin who was killed in Viet Nam, so there's all daughters in the family. The [family] name will not be carried on since my brother's retarded. I think my father is disappointed in this and disappointed that he couldn't go out and play football and baseball and basketball."

In another family with the same sibling constellation, in describing the effect of the retarded boy's handicap on the family as a whole, SibH said that the fact that H is the only boy affected her father in a way that it did not affect anyone else in the family.

"Yes, I think it probably was most difficult for him to accept, out of the whole family, mainly because Irwin is the only boy in the family. I would say he is quickest to react if Irwin does anything wrong or doesn't do it exactly right, or doesn't do it quickly enough. And he has less patience. This might be because it's a father-son relationship, or it might just be his—Father's—personality to begin with."

In contrast, a Private U woman, second of four daughters, described her father's reaction to H, the youngest girl, as follows:

"[Laughs] Well, it's a little bit hard to say. I think that he's very reconciled, very happy, I mean. Not happy *about* it, but happy *with* it. He now has a little girl to love. I think he thinks it's too bad, but also I think he thinks she's the happiest of anyone."

In contrast to much of the literature, the acceptance scores had no relationship to the religion of the family for reasons discussed above. Finally, just as normal siblings older than H were judged to have coped better with him or her, so these older siblings also reported more family acceptance of H than did brothers and sisters younger than the retarded child. (This finding could be partially accounted for by the fact that in this latter group, H was already older and possibly causing more difficulty for the family.)

TENTATIVE CONCLUSIONS

At the beginning of this chapter, we restated one of the questions prompting this research project: was it possible to find brothers and sisters of retarded children who seemed to have benefited from the experience, and, if so, could we identify factors in their lives that might be related to the positive effects of the experience? Our results clearly demonstrate the existence of such young people; a significant proportion of our student-subjects were judged as having apparently benefited over-all from their association with their retarded brother or sister.

Some of the gains we saw included what seemed to be greater tolerance for deviant individuals and more awareness of prejudice and of the damage it can do. Some reflected an unusual degree of understanding of, and compassion for, others. Many described a sense of family closeness and of pride in the family's ability to have been able to cope as a unit; others described a sense of vocational purpose and direction.

On the other hand, almost half of our student subjects—and probably a considerably larger proportion in the total population of college siblings of retarded children—seemed to us to have been harmed. They felt shamed by the association with the retarded child and angry bitterness at their fate. Many felt guilty about their own good health, and even more guilty about their hatred and resentment of H. Some felt that they had been cheated out of the time, love, and attention they needed from their parents because of their parents' preoccupation with H. Some described their families as generally having been disrupted by H and by the family's reactions toward him or her. Some, like Cindy, overidentified with the handicap of H and consequently viewed themselves as also defective in some way.

Thus, we found wide variations from family to family in what it meant to each to have a retarded child. We also were able to identify some factors about the family situations that related to whether the over-all impact on the normal brother or sister was positive or negative.

There were no significant differences in coping-effectiveness among the four samples; a roughly equal proportion of siblings in each group was judged as gaining or losing from the experience. However, great differences existed in the aspects of their situations that made a difference in their ability to cope adaptively. The health and adaptation of the Community U men and women seemed closely related to various real aspects of their experiences with H, such as the degree of H's retardation or physical handicap. For these students, the feelings and reactions of their parents were relatively unimportant, and, in fact, they seemed to have a great deal of freedom and independence from their parents at this stage in their lives.

In contrast, the Private U students seemed enormously responsive to, and influenced by, their view of their parents' feelings toward H. Actual characteristics of H played little role in their ability to cope adaptively with H and his or her handicap, although interpretations attached to these characteristics were extremely important.

One of the few factors that related to coping for all of the students from all groups was the age relationship between the normal brother or sister and H: older siblings had a relatively easier time than those younger than H. All siblings were more embarrassed by a same-sex sibling than by one of the opposite sex. Finally, although the parents' acceptance of H—based, of course, on our clinical judgments from what was told to us by the SibHs—was somewhat related to the severity of H's handicap, this relationship was complex and varied among the different samples, and consequently cannot be said to account entirely either for their acceptance scores or for SibH's adaptation.

Summing up, then, siblings and their families within the same broad cultural context vary greatly in the way they perceive and respond to a retarded child. More strikingly, siblings and families of different "sociocultural status" within this culture are responsive to, and influenced by, very different aspects of family situations.

CHAPTER 10

Information and Curiosity: What's Wrong With Johnny?

INTENSE CURIOSITY about a brother's or sister's retardation, fear of knowing too much, and at times a startling lack of information about the handicap, were central issues for many of the brothers and sisters of retarded children we saw. As Cindy once commented, when her intense curiosity about her retarded older brother was pointed out: "Yes, it's my sickness."

This Community U man described his fascination and puzzlement at the age of 14 when his mother came home from the hospital with a retarded younger brother:

"I remember going to the hospital to pick up Bobby. Coming home she—Mother—was acting funny, and I didn't know what was going on. And I remember this one scene for some reason. It's really clear in my mind. This person living in back of us, in the house behind us, came over to see the baby. You know, like everybody does. And my mother started crying. I was in the room. And they just said: 'Beat it! Get outa here!' I couldn't understand it. I guess I kinda picked up after a couple of days that there was something wrong with Bobby.

"My mother used to say: 'Look at him! Look at him!' And so I sneaked in there a couple of times and I looked at him. I didn't—I couldn't see any difference. He's a kid, he's small, you know. 'What's wrong with being small? He was just born.'"

This sibling's family in fact seemed to have dealt with his curiosity quite openly once the mother recovered from the immediate shock and trauma of discovering Bobby's handicap, and he described himself as having been open and comfortable with questions. As he said, when we asked how his family felt about his asking questions about Bobby:

118

"I guess they were happy that I was smart enough to ask them. They did not get up tight about it."

On the other hand, the inhibition of curiosity and fear of knowing can be seen unusually clearly in this exchange with an extremely bright and intellectual Private U man. He asked us, after describing his younger brother who was diagnosed as having cerebral palsy, what cerebral palsy was. The interviewer responded to the question first by answering it, then by sharing her curiosity about the question with SibH:

"Something which puzzles me, listening to you, is that you've read an enormous amount about a great number of things. Why do you think you haven't read about cerebral palsy?"

"I think that—that I'm incriminating myself now. But I think that another aspect of this is that, you know, although for a long time I've known the disease—the name of it—at times I tried to think of it, and I know I couldn't. Even though I knew that I knew the name, I was just unable to think of it."

"How do you explain that to yourself?"

"I think, being as objective as possible, there are two aspects. One is that I didn't really attribute any importance to it or I attributed very little importance to the disease. Also the fact that it was such a foreign word—it didn't mean anything, and it didn't explain anything. And it was—I don't know—perhaps it was also that retardation is something that you're—you know—ashamed of, or that you don't want to be connected with. Maybe I was forgetting it for that reason."

The following example is a striking illustration of lack of information in an otherwise bright young man. This Private U man was trying to describe his retarded sister, 10 years older than himself.

"What's wrong with Susie?"

"She had pneumonia when she—I believe when she was 12. And it's physically handicapped her. And she's retarded some mentally. Well, she graduated from high school but I believe my parents were told that she would never attain a great mental capacity, not beyond that of a 13-year-old."

"And it's all attributed to—?"

"Yeah, bulbar pneumonia, I think that's what it was."

Later he mentioned telling friends that Susie had polio.
"I thought you said pneumonia."
"I may have. It was polio."
The interviewer asked if he ever questioned his parents about Susie's handicap.
"You mean to my parents? I've asked them and they gave me complete information. This was some years ago, then. I haven't really discussed it since."

Does this lack of accurate information make any difference in the lives of the normal brothers and sisters? Considerable evidence exists to suggest the importance of accurate knowledge, particularly concerning events of great emotional importance, to a child's ability to cope with those events. Berlyne (1954) suggests that knowledge about strange or unusual events makes a child less fearful of them; the child feels less helpless in the face of them. Further, by thinking and rethinking the event, the child has a chance to become accustomed to it and so conquer his fear. "One of the most distressing plights for human beings is not to know or understand a state of affairs, particularly if it is important for their security or contrary to their expectations" (p. 188). Berlyne continues: "If people do not know, they often show a tendency to believe in the most alarming prospect they can imagine. . . ." Emch (1944), discussing clinical material from child psychoanalysis, says that children can deal with tension-producing situations if they can convert the unknown into the known, i.e., if it can be made to seem familiar to them. He believes that when the experience for any reason cannot quickly be assimilated by the child, he will try to cope with it by repeating the situation. Thus, for example, the child frightened by a trip to the dentist will "play dentist" repeatedly when he returns home until he has gained some sense of mastery over the situation. Emch suggests that a common form of this repetition is by identification with the object about which the child is confused or uninformed. "It is almost as if the child were saying, 'If I act like that person—become him—crawl into his skin, I shall know him and be able to predict what he will do and not be surprised—hurt—by him'" (p. 14). The consequences of this identification with a retarded brother or sister can be far-reaching.

Numerous other clinicians and researchers have emphasized the importance of information. Kessler (1966) describes the spreading effect that can occur: when curiosity is inhibited on any subject, the inhibition may affect all subjects. A child comes to feel that all curiosity is bad or dangerous. One consequence, according to Kessler and others (e.g., Brodie and Winterbottom, 1967) is academic underachievement, as the child is too frightened to let himself be curious about the world around him. Sarason (1961) argues similarly that problem-solving begins in the earliest years of development as the child tries to puzzle out such issues as his or her own sexual identification, the relationships between family members, etc. Sarason suggests that the child's experiences as he tries to solve these problems enormously influence that child's subsequent approach to intellectual problem-solving. So that, for example, if a child finds these early problems too complex, confusing, frightening, or incomprehensible, he might come to avoid approaching all intellectual problems. If this is so, then how a young child comes to terms with the problem of understanding a brother's or sister's handicap can have important consequences on his future ability to think.

Although none of these writers addresses himself directly to the problem of a child's understanding a handicapped sibling, the formulations seem highly relevant to this situation. Children who do not have accurate information about a retarded brother or sister often develop elaborate and terrible fantasies about the unknown source of fear and danger, far worse than the realities could ever be. Whether children with less information tend more to identify with their image of the retarded child, as Emch suggests would happen, is unclear from our clinical experiences but is an intriguing hypothesis.

These formulations by Berlyne and Emch are also consistent with the few findings in the literature that knowledgeable adults are better adjusted and better able to cope with the problem of retardation when it occurs in their own child. Stone (1967), for example, reports on an extensive and intensive research project with 103 families having young children with Down's Syndrome. She found that the parents who knew more about the abnormality were significantly more accepting of the child and were less likely to institutionalize their child. Giannini and Goodman (1963), Rapaport (1962), and Slobody and Scanlan (1959) all stress the importance of accurate and adequate information in order to help parents of a retarded child come to terms with the fact and to enable them to make adequate decisions about him or her. Felzen (1970) found that mothers who had a good understanding of their child's Mongolism seemed more realistic in their perception of the child and were also judged to be coping better with the child and his retardation than mothers who had a less adequate understanding. Finally, Wright (1960) reports clinical data showing that an individual, in order to adjust to a physical disability, must first acknowledge it and accept it as part of himself. The first step in such acknowledgment is accurate and relevant information about it. Although none of this research focuses on brothers and sisters, our clinical experiences suggest that knowledge about the handicap of a retarded sibling does make it easier for the normal child to make sense of the situation and consequently to adjust to it.

Yet many of the siblings we had seen before beginning the formal research seemed to have very little accurate information about their retarded brothers or sisters. Several factors might contribute to this lack. We believe that all young children are curious. Further, children have a natural curiosity about anything that is different, including retardation in a family member. What, then, interferes with their obtaining accurate information?

We discovered in our clinical contacts that mental retardation is not a topic many parents can discuss comfortably with the normal children (Chapter 3). Some are ashamed of it and treat the handicap as an awful family secret. Others try to deny the existence of the handicap and consequently cannot discuss it with the other family members. As one parent of an adolescent in the discussion group put it: "Of course we answer their questions [about H]. It's just like the way we always answer their questions about sex." Apparently, concerning retardation, as with sex, the topic is taboo for many families in this culture—one to be clothed in secrecy and shame or mentioned only rarely and with great discomfort.

A related factor, in addition to the taboo nature of the topic, is one described by Becker and Margolin (1967), where parents tended to avoid talking with their children about the death of the other parent, both in the belief that their silence will protect the child and also to protect themselves from the strong emotions the discussion might arouse.

On the other hand, not all families we have known err in the direction of too little information and discussion. Exaggerated or compulsive attention to the handicap also occurs, and also can cause difficulties for the normal children. The following excerpt illustrates what we considered overintellectualization and over-emphasis, resulting from a highly educated and ambitious family's attempts to cope with the shock and grief of learning their youngest son had Down's Syndrome.

"What do you think has been the effect on the family?"

"Yeah, I think the major effect—there was one basic thing I think would be extraordinary in our family. As I mentioned, when we found out that she [Mother] was pregnant, we were in the middle stages of moving. The year before, our dog had died. He'd been an old dog, died of old age, lots of fleas and everything. And mother was going around the house as we were moving, spraying all kinds of insecticides. And she had a backache and was taking some kind of pills for this. Now, after we found out that Donny was a Mongoloid, we—Father realized of course that there are two types, old-age mothers and young mothers, who have Mongoloid children. It was probably just the genes associated with this that caused it, but he didn't know for sure. So he went back and he made up a list of all the kinds of drugs she had been taking, all the insecticides she had been using, plus all kinds of normal things, like lipstick and so forth. And my brother's doing a science experiment on it, to test out if any of these chemicals caused it. And my father's encouraging him, which I truly frankly don't regard as too healthy in the application of it. But it's a good science experiment. He enjoys doing it. He's been scaling the dosages down to rats and then giving them to pregnant mother rats during various stages in development to see what changes come about in the fetus. It's almost as if we're testing what happened. And this is very unusual, I think. I don't know, but it seems to me, looking at it abstractly, this is rather an unusual reaction to something to occur."

This young man began psychotherapy shortly after participating in the research. He told us his counselor had suggested that he seemed overly involved with his retarded brother and it was interfering with his ability to establish relationships at college.

In respect to a related phenomenon, the modern-day parents' attempts to be "open" regardless of their own personal style or comfort with this approach, Tooley (1968) has pointed out that this kind of "openness," which is unnaturally done and often overdone, results in its own kind of psychopathology.

MEASURES OF CURIOSITY

We were particularly interested in the issues of curiosity, the extent to which the family was open to discussion about the handicapped child, and our student-subject's ability as a young adult to think freely and effectively. We asked a series of questions about the normal sibling's memories of how he or she first learned about H's handicap, how comfortable the family seemed to be with questions about it, how curious he or she remembered having been about H, etc. To supplement this retrospective account, we tested each SibH's current knowledge about retardation and brain damage.

As the research evolved, we were impressed repeatedly with the similarity between the way these SibHs described their families' dealings with curiosity about the retardation and the way many families deal with their children's curiosity about sex. Consequently, we added a question about how SibH remembered learning about sex as a child, and how curious he remembered being about it.

We also asked these young adults if they had ever wondered anything in particular about their family, to test their curiosity and their acceptance of that curiosity in areas not necessarily related to handicap.

As soon as we began collecting data we became aware that the responses to this type of question were far from direct and simple reflections of the way these families had dealt with such issues. A host of complicating, albeit fascinating, factors appeared to be operative. The personality style of the student and what role free curiosity or inhibition played in that style, the nearly ubiquitous early repression of sexual curiosity and interest, the differential response to upper middle-class female interviewers, all seemed to influence the final responses of the students. This complexity, although increasing for us the fascination of these data, also made any interpretations of the results highly speculative.

To summarize, we used the following four scores:[1]

1. Openness of discussion about H. This score is made up of five separate subscales, including ratings of the extent to which SibH remembered being curious about H's handicap and the extent to which he or she remembered his or her parents as being willing to discuss the issues openly and comfortably. (Initially, we tried keeping these two general areas separate, but the extremely high intercorrelations between them made it apparent that we were not meaningfully separating out dimensions of the problem.) A high score means open discussion and strong curiosity. [For actual scoring, see Table 10, IV (1).]

2. Information Score. This is a score on a test of the SibH's factual knowledge about mental retardation and brain damage (Appendix D).

3. Curiosity about sex. A composite score of SibH's remembered curiosity about sex and his or her remembrance of how openly and comfortably it was satisfied by the parents. A high

1. Initially, we also used a fifth score, "Concern About Having a Retarded Child," which was our judgment of how much SibH reported feeling concern about the possibility that he or she might one day have a retarded child. [For specific scoring, see Table 10, V (3).] However, because a person's experienced concern about such a topic is so greatly influenced by his or her defensive style, we found we could not interpret the results of this score; consequently, we have eliminated it from further consideration. The correlations between this score and the other curiosity-openness measures can be found in Table 18, a comparison of SibHs and SibNs on this score in Table 19, and the relationship between this score and the severity of H's handicap and demographic characteristics of the family in Table 20.

score means strong curiosity and open discussion [Table 10, IV (2)].

4. Acknowledged curiosity about the family. A scale coding SibH's response to the question, "Have you ever wondered anything about your family?" A high score means acknowledged curiosity [Table 10, IV (3)].

STATISTICAL RESULTS

Initially, we asked questions about the student-subject's curiosity about sex when he was young, and his curiosity about his family, to study the relationships between the way a family dealt with these issues compared with the way they dealt with the normal child's curiosity about H's handicap. As was the case with the adaptation measures (Chapter 8), these items appear to have very different meanings for the SibHs in the four different samples (Table 18). For Private U men, for example, the more they described early curiosity about H and open family discussion about the retardation, the more early curiosity about sex and about the family they reported. And, similarly, for Community U women, curiosity about sex correlated positively with open discussion about H. On the other hand, for Community U men and Private U women, neither curiosity about sex nor curiosity about the family related to open discussion about H, suggesting that, in these samples, either they were dissimilar issues or that the responses they gave to the interviewers had different meanings on the different issues. (For example, response to questions about sexual curiosity asked by an upper middle socioeconomic-class female interviewer is probably quite different for a Community U or Private U student, as well as differing for a male or a female subject.)

Among all of the men, the siblings receiving higher Information scores reported more curiosity and open discussion about H. This was not true for either group of women.

Although the different patterns of relationships are fascinating in their own right, the data suggest that curiosity about sex and curiosity about the family are related to curiosity about a retarded brother or sister in varied and complex ways, and are somewhat tangential to the central focus of this chapter. Hence, these scores are not considered in further analyses.

The siblings of retarded children in each group got higher scores on the Information scale than did the siblings of only normal children (Table 19). (Not surprisingly, given the differences in IQ, students from Private U knew more about retardation than did students from Community U.)

Curiosity, Severity of H's Handicap, and Family Variables

Do such factors as the severity of retardation in a sibling or the social class of the family "predict" (correlate with) how openly a normal sibling describes his parents' comfort in discussing that child, and how much he knows about H?

When we examined these relationships in our data (Table 20), several interesting results appeared. Community U women received higher Information scores, the more retarded—but the less physically handicapped—their sibling. There was some tendency for social class to correlate negatively with open discussion of H in all four groups (although only one of the four was statistically significant).

As discussed in previous chapters, the relationships between the sex of H, the religious orientation of the family, and the age relationship between SibH and H with the curiosity-openness items could best be examined by the analysis-of-variance technique, with only main effects considered and those somewhat tentatively. Brothers and sisters older than H did know more about retardation and brain damage, as reflected in their Information scores, than those younger than H ($F = 2.67$, $p \leqslant 0.05$).

The results of the analysis of variance of curiosity-openness scores by religion showed no significant main effects. In the analysis by the sex of H, siblings of girl retarded children knew less about retardation than siblings of boy Hs ($F = 2.43$, $p \leqslant 0.05$), with the sample heavily weighted toward siblings of male Hs: 27 SibHs had a sister who was retarded; 56, a brother.

Curiosity and Coping

Our initial hypothesis was that siblings who reported open discussions about H in their families would also appear to us at the time of the interview to be better adjusted. Coping-effectiveness did correlate with open discussion about H in all of the samples, and reached statistical significance for Community U men and Private U women (Table 21). Community U women who described more curiosity about H and openness on the part of the parents did better academically and talked more openly to friends about H. All Private U students who described such open discussions also described themselves as less embarrassed by H, and the Private U men in these families talked more openly with friends about H than their peers who reported less open discussion of H in the family.

The Information score correlated highly with embarrassment for Community U men: the more they knew about retardation, the more embarrassment they felt about being seen with H. For Private U men, the higher their Information score, the higher their over-all academic functioning.

Curiosity-Openness and Acceptance of H

As regards Private U students, the more we judged the mother and the family as having accepted H, the more open discussion about H and his handicap they described (Table 21). For these women—but not the men—father acceptance also correlated highly with open discussion. The only relationship between the curiosity-openness items and the acceptance scores for Community U students was one for the men between open discussion and family acceptance of H. On the other hand, mother's and family's acceptance of H did positively correlate with the Information score for Community U women.

DISCUSSION OF THE RESULTS

One major conclusion to be reached from the clinical material as well as the statistical results is that students who described their families as having been more open in permitting and encouraging questions about H, and who described themselves as having been more curious about the handicap, were judged by us on other criteria as having coped better with the fact of H's retardation. In all four samples, coping-effectiveness correlated positively with open discussion about H, although the relationship only reached statistical significance for Community U men and Private U women.

Children are naturally curious. A handicap in a member of the family is a natural object of curiosity, and children seem to be better able to understand and come to terms with the handicap and its implications for the family and for themselves when they can share their thoughts and confusions about it with their parents.

Many of these siblings described their parents as being comfortable about discussing the handicap and as having provided them with as much information as the parents themselves had. Others sensed a discomfort or tension in either mother or father— or both—about discussing it, often despite the parents' specific statements to the contrary.

These normal children who sensed their parents' discomfort quickly learned either to get information from some other source, such as teachers at school or books, or they learned not to think about the problem at all.

A fascinating and complicating aspect of the issue results from the fact that, even for children whose parents attempt to provide complete explanations, retardation and physical handicap or stigmata are difficult to comprehend and often frightening to consider. Further, many children's questions are unanswerable, such as: Why did it happen to *our* family? Consequently, in our samples, both in families in which the parents did discuss the issues openly and in the others (and independently of the level of the normal sibling's eventual adaptation and understanding), many of them described a long process of gradually coming to understand and to cope with the idea of a sibling's handicap. At the time of the study, some still had not reached any comfortable resolution. (This is similar to a result obtained by Wood, Friedman, and Steisel, 1967, who found that parents of children with phenylketonuria had surprisingly little accurate knowledge and some misinformation about this condition, despite the fact that all were given accurate information by their physician when the disease was first recognized in their child.)

The following excerpt is from the interview of a Community U man, one of nine children, who was seven when his retarded brother was born. (He received a relatively high score for open discussion about H, and a relatively high coping score.) It illustrates the intense curiosity and also the difficulty in appeasing it, despite some attempts by his parents to explain. It also illustrates one major aspect children seem to focus on: the sometimes strange physical appearance of the handicapped child.

"When did you first learn about John's handicap?"

"The day he came home from the hospital. Let's see, he's seven years younger than I, so that was when I was seven years old."

"How did you first learn about it, do you remember?"

"Yeah, I remember my mother and father were coming in. My mother was crying and my father was very upset. And they were talking about it. And my grandmother came over and they had a lot of talk about it for several months—and I overheard all this."

"Did you used to wonder about it often?"

"Yeah, quite a lot. I really didn't understand it at all at the time, so—."

"What were some of the things you didn't understand about?"

"I was completely bewildered. I really didn't understand the situation. And my father I think said: 'He's not normal, he'll never be any good.' My father used to say that: 'He'll never be any good.' I used to wonder what this meant. And then I remember he just didn't seem to be able to learn to do things. My father got very upset over it, and I wished I could understand why. I didn't know why. He didn't look particularly different. He had an empty glassy stare, and I remember when I was about 10 years old. I got a camera for my birthday and I remember taking pictures of Johnnie. I wanted to take pictures of that stare. It was just an unbelievable one and it's such an empty glassy stare that it fascinated me."

"What did you do when you didn't understand something?"

"I used to ask questions, but they didn't have too—too many answers. They used to answer the questions with the statement that I didn't understand. So it wasn't until I found out through a little reading on my own, or a little question from some of my teachers, that I understood. Not that my parents didn't explain it, but I just didn't understand what they were saying too much."

"Do you remember what questions you asked?"

"Yeah: 'Why won't he be any good?' 'What's wrong with him?' And I heard—they used to use the term Mongolism—and I said, 'What's Mongolism?' And I didn't understand the answer for that. And: 'Why can't he walk and why won't he talk?' Things like that."

"How did your parents feel about questions about John?"

"Before—at the beginning—they were very, very self-conscious. It took a lot of time for them to get used to it. That's important. Plus that he has so much more control over himself now. They feel very much more comfortable with the situation. They just didn't seem to want to talk very much about anything, let alone John."

A Community U woman also received a high score for open discussion. The interview segment presented here illustrates the process, in what appears to be a rather open family, of a young child gradually coming to understand a sibling's handicap.

"Do you remember when you first learned about Betsy's handicap?"

"It's kinda funny, since she's older than I am. It was always there. But I think when I was three, I can remember Mom kinda helping her with walking or spending time with her, you know, helping her with her speech. This kind of thing I think I can remember a little bit from when I was pretty young."

"Did you ask questions about it?"

"No, I think as far as that's concerned, I think it was explained to me. Maybe I did. I was always kinda inquisitive. I may have asked, 'What does CP mean?' Maybe when I was a little bit older, maybe six or seven, maybe I asked more definite questions. And I think Mom just said it was—you know—it's brain damage. I think I have had other explanations since then. I've talked more with my mother about it. But I was quite young, you know, and Betsy was always just part of our family unit."

"Do you remember wondering about it?"

"I remember wondering whether it was fatal, you know, and I remember wondering if it was completely curable—put it that way."

"What did you do when you wondered?"

"Well, I usually asked questions. Mom was always quite frank with me, I think. Whatever the question may have been—these different ages—I think she tried to explain it to me."

"Does your family feel comfortable about questions about Betsy?"

"Yeah, I think they do. And as well my dad—he's kinda been 'way up in the organization for CP children, and he's always giving talks about it. And I think it's quite open, you know—easily discussed, if it comes up."

The following two excerpts reflect the responses of siblings who felt their parents would not be comfortable about responding to questions. The first is from an interview with a much younger brother (Private U) of an institutionalized retarded boy. The young man seemed to deal with his parents' discomfort by inhibiting his own curiosity, and was judged by us to have been harmed by his experience as a sibling of a retarded child:

"When did you first learn about Albert's handicap?"

"Hm, I don't know—very young, I imagine. Probably when he was still around. And I guess there were questions asked when he left. I don't know how many questions a three-year-old could ask. Yeah, that's right, my nephew's about three, now, and he asks about things and can understand things, so I guess I knew, you know."

"Do you remember when you first realized he was retarded?"

"No."

"Do you remember when he left?"

"No."

"Have you ever wondered anything about him?"

"What do you mean, wondered?"

"What your parents' decisions were, what was wrong with him, things like that."

"Hm, yeah, not too much thought. No, not really. I did fairly little thinking about it. And I know there was once—you know—my mother explained something about a premature birth—I don't know whether that had any effect or not."

"Was he premature?"

"I think so."

"Do you remember asking questions about him?"

"Hm, if I did, it was years ago, and I don't really recall anything."

"How does your family feel about discussing Albert?"

"I know they don't like to. I'm sure my parents don't like it brought to their minds. It's very galling or hurting for them. They don't like to talk about it."

An interesting question—although one for which we have no answer—is how this young man would have responded had his parents been more open to discussion about Albert.

Another Community U woman was the oldest of three children. H, a boy, was 11 years younger, and was retarded from birth. Her parents also were uncomfortable about questions but her response, unlike that of the last-mentioned student, was to seek information elsewhere; over-all, we were impressed with her effectiveness in coming to terms with H's retardation and its meaning to her.

"Do you remember wondering about it when you were little?"

"Yes, in fact, I did wonder about it. It used to upset me. Like my girlfriend's mother had a baby not too long before, and her little sister was doing so many more things. And I wondered, you know—'why isn't my brother doing the same?'"

"What did you do when you wondered?"

"Really just wondered. I think my sister and I both learned very fast that we didn't ask questions about this because, you know, it was like Mom would get upset—miserably upset. And if she got upset, things would go wrong, and we'd get into trouble, and we'd get punished. So, you know, it's like cause and effect. So we would just wonder, talk among ourselves."

Later in the interview, she was asked how she feels now about questions about Casey.

"Right now, going through my courses and everything [in the Special Education program], I ask questions of professors—everybody I can get hold of. I'm really curious, especially about his seizures. I've gone as far as—I've often wondered if I couldn't just have one myself, just to understand what it's like. Because he whimpers the whole time. I don't know if it's because of fever or pain or what."

The difference in consequences for these two siblings of their responses to parental inhibition seems extremely important. The first, the young man from Private U, seemed depressed and inhibited; we gave him a low score on coping. In contrast, the Community U woman seemed to us to have come to manageable terms with her brother's handicap despite her mother's inability to discuss it with her.

A critical issue is what factors lead a sibling to respond in one way or another. A final excerpt, also from an interview with a Community U woman, illustrates the complexity of the issue, and the problem of making judgments for scoring. She described her parents as having been comfortable about questions, but herself as relatively incurious. Later, however, she was asked if she ever wondered anything about her family:

"Oh, yes. [Said in a surprised tone, as if she had just remembered it.] Quite interesting. My father has a sister who is mentally retarded, and is living in a mental—in an institution for the mentally retarded. And I always wondered when I was younger if there was some relationship in our family—was someone meant to be retarded in each generation or something; this used to bother me, I think."

"Did you ever ask about it?"

"No, I didn't."

Several other related results appeared in all samples except that of the Community U men. The Community U women and Private U men talked more with friends about H, the more the family talked about H at home. That is, if the parents did not view the handicap as a source of shame to be ignored and hidden within the family, then these brothers and sisters also seemed comfortable in taking the same stance outside of the family. Similarly, both Private U samples described themselves as being less embarrassed by H, the more open discussion about H occurred in the family.

We had predicted one further step in the relationship between open discussion and curiosity about H and the health and flexibility of these normal young adults. Our hypothesis was that children in a family free to be curious about this important family matter would also remain free to be curious about other issues, and consequently would be more open to learning about the world. However, only for Community U women did the relationship between open discussion about H and academic functioning hold true. Private U students were probably functioning at too high an academic level to be influenced by this factor, and Community U men, as we have mentioned in different contexts, seemed insufficiently involved in the issue for it to have had a major impact on their functioning.

The Information score was a measure more closely related to retardation and handicap, designed to assess the students' current functioning and knowledge in this area. Only for Private U men was there a relationship between their knowledge about handicap and their academic performance. SibHs who described frequent family discussions about H in fact knew more about retardation and brain damage than SibHs who reported less openness and less curiosity on their part about H. (That this relationship did not hold up for the women seems in part due to the fact that an extremely high proportion of women students in these samples participated in a Special Education program at college. This seemed to have a leveling effect on their knowledge about handicap, regardless of the family backgrounds.)

Factors Relating to Curiosity: Severity of H's Handicap and Demographic Variables

The relationship between coping and open discussion in the family is an important one. It raises the question: what factors— either concerning the severity of H's handicap, demographic variables, or psychological ones—relate to, and possibly influence, the extent to which families do talk openly about a retarded child? Neither the severity of H's handicap nor demographic variables seemed to make a difference in affecting open discussion about H in these four samples, although, for Community U women, the higher the social class of the family, the *less* open discussion about H occurred. (This is reminiscent of the finding that the higher the social class of Community U men, the fewer friends SibH spoke to about H.) And, for Private U men, the more children in the family, the less open discussion that occurred, possibly because of the sheer logistics of the situation. Siblings older than H, and SibHs of retarded brothers, knew significantly more about retardation and brain damage than SibHs younger than H and those of retarded sisters. (The fact that the four samples had many more siblings of retarded brothers who were also more knowledgeable about retardation is not fortuitous. Rather, it is one more reflection of the sample bias that brought the better adjusted and better informed to participate in the research.)

In toto, however, the paucity of significant results and the lack of relationships between open discussion about H and *any* characteristic of the retarded child are startling, and again leave us with the question: what factors do influence individual differences in the way that families come to deal with the issues?

Other Factors Relating to Curiosity: Parent Acceptance of H

In the two Private U groups, those whose descriptions led us to rate their mothers, fathers, and families as highly accepting of H also described open discussions about H in the family. (The only acceptance score not related to open discussion in these two samples was father's acceptance in the Private U men's group. These fathers seemed to be sufficiently isolated from the day-to-day activities within the home, partly by virtue of their long working hours and career orientations, to be uninvolved in discussions about H with the normal children.) To tie together several relationships, SibHs more adaptively came to terms with

H's retardation in those Private U families in which the mother and family (and for Private U women, the father as well) were more accepting of H, and in which the families also discussed H openly among themselves.

On the other hand, for Community U students, parents who accepted H did not necessarily talk openly about H. (Although the women from this group whose mothers and families seemed to accept H did get higher Information scores.) One might speculate that, in Community U families, open discussion and curiosity about H was neither highly valued nor encouraged, and consequently was less related to feelings about H. In contrast, Private U parents believed in such discussion and openness, but could only manage it comfortably when they were themselves comfortable with H's retardation. (Felzen [1970] found higher SES mothers more encouraging of open discussion about a young Mongoloid sibling than were lower SES mothers.)

In order that young men and women may come to terms with the idea and fact of having a retarded sibling, they must acknowledge and deal with its impact on their own lives. We asked: "Have you ever thought about the possibility that you might have a retarded child?" Although, as we have said earlier in this chapter, we did not include this score in our analyses because of the difficulty interpreting the results, some of the SibHs' responses to the question are worthy of note. Virtually all said they had thought about it, with the SibHs expressing more frequent and intense awareness of the issue than the SibNs.

When asked how they felt about it, many said they felt better equipped to deal with such a child because of their experience with a sibling. Some said they would be doubly traumatized. A number commented on what they would do the same or differently from their parents *vis-à-vis* a handicapped child in the family.

We asked the SibHs when they first considered the possibility that they might have a retarded child. Their answers ranged in time from the period when they first started dating (early adolescence) to that in the most common reply, when they first considered getting married. Recently (in a clinical contact outside the study) the mother of a 5-year-old normal girl and an 11-year-old, severely retarded girl reported the following conversation. The younger girl said to her mother:

"Judy can't go to the bathroom by herself because she's 'tarded." Her mother agreed. After a pause, the little girl mused: "When I grow up, I might have a 'tarded child, too," and went on to talk with her mother about how she would help this hypothetical child.

These and other clinical examples make it clear that children do think actively about such issues at a very young age when confronted with a retarded brother or sister. The fact that young adults do not remember that early curiosity is a reflection of the general repression of early childhood thoughts, feelings, and wishes, as well as the frequent avoidance of such anxiety-arousing thoughts as the possibility of having a retarded child.

TENTATIVE CONCLUSIONS

Cindy and the young adolescents described in Chapter 3 had difficulties in understanding their brothers' and sisters' handicaps. They tended to be confused, misinformed, and sometimes afraid to even try to think about it or understand. They and their parents highlighted for us the often taboo nature of the topic by the difficulties they had in discussing it together.

These and other clinical experiences with families with normal and retarded children led us to believe that normal children in such families are better off when the parents can discuss the retarded child's handicap openly and comfortably, and when the young people have a realistic understanding of it.

The data from our college-student siblings support these clinical impressions: the more open discussion about H the normal brother or sister remembered occurring in the family, and the more curiosity about it they recalled expressing, the better their effectiveness in coping with the impact of H's handicap on their own lives. Further, for some but not all of the students, the more open discussion and curiosity about H they described, the better they were doing academically, the more they knew about mental retardation and brain damage, and the less embarrassed by H they described themselves as being.

We wondered: in what ways does this open discussion and uninhibited curiosity help siblings to adapt? Although we cannot as yet prove the correctness of our view, our clinical impressions suggest that children who are able to talk over their puzzlement, as well as their fears and fantasies, seem better able to master both their confusion and fright. Successful mastery of this potentially difficult and complex issue seems to give a child confidence in his or her ability to come to terms with other complex issues. Finally, children's ways of explaining to themselves things that seem inexplicable are nearly always more horrifying than are the realistic answers; e.g., Cindy's conviction that someone had hit her brother on the head and caused his retardation, or the young adolescent boy's explanation of his sister's handicap as stemming from a "lump on the back of her head which secretes poison."

One intriguing and puzzling issue we found was that some of our college-student siblings appeared not to have followed their families' leads in terms of either expression or inhibition of their curiosity about H. Some who described their families as quite comfortable about questions and discussions of H themselves seemed to us to be reticent and uncomfortable about it—as if at least for some young people, at certain ages, the topic itself can be inherently disturbing and/or embarrassing. (Our general impression is that this is most true for young adolescents and, further, that it occurs not only with respect to topics like retardation but also in a host of other potentially sensitive areas.)

More frequently they described a situation in which the parents seemed willing to explain and discuss but in which they, as young children, had great difficulty in understanding their sibling's handicap. Again this is reminiscent of the course of events as young children come to understand sex. Their view of this matter often involves distortions and misunderstandings, regardless of their parents' ease and clarity in trying to explain it.

Finally, some siblings whose parents were not comfortable with the topic nonetheless themselves had strong curiosity and actively sought out information from other sources. Unfortunately, we cannot determine from our experiences under what conditions normal children are able to maintain their curiosity and freedom to think in the face of strong parental inhibition. In the few instances in which we saw this clearly, the children viewed their parents' difficulty in talking about retardation as their parents' problem rather than viewing retardation itself as a taboo topic.

These data on curiosity and open discussion further support our formulations about the centrality of psychological and social characteristics of the situation in determining any given family's response to a retarded child. First of all, we found marked differences between the Private U and Community U families on these dimensions. The parents of Private U students seemed to believe in the value of discussing things openly with their children and of trying to encourage their curiosity. Consequently, those Private U parents who accepted H believed in the value of open discussion, were able comfortably to participate in such discussions, and were described as openly discussing H and encouraging questions about him or her. Those who had not come to terms with H's handicap were unable to discuss the topic easily with the normal children despite an ethos encouraging openness. For the Community U families, this positive value placed on curiosity and understanding in children was less evident in the students' reports, and for these families there was no relationship between a given family's acceptance of H and the extent to which open curiosity and discussion about H were encouraged.

Even more impressively in support of our social-psychological orientation, no personal characteristics of H related strongly in any group to the amount or kind of open discussion and curiosity about H. Thus, it was not anything specific about H's handicap or person that determined the degree and kind of openness, but rather aspects of the family and of the subculture.

CHAPTER 11

They Have Feelings, Too

SOME of the young men and women we talked with described their handicapped brothers and sisters as three-dimensional, complex, feeling human beings. These siblings saw many similarities between themselves and the retarded child. They emphasized their likenesses as members of the same family and as people. As one Private U student said, when asked if he minded his resemblance to his retarded sister: "Why shouldn't we look alike? We're brother and sister!"

On the other hand, some of the college students seemed to view the handicapped children more in terms of categories; as "retards," for example, and, in their descriptions, portrayed these children as having little personality or complexity—as having few feelings. They seemed to see the children as "alien," and emphasized their differences from themselves.

These contrasts in the way the siblings described their retarded brothers or sisters seem important to us, with implications beyond the families directly involved. Some of the most serious social problems we face today involve groups of people perceiving other groups as different from themselves and consequently as dangerous and frightening. The fear of people who are different seems ubiquitous (e.g., Ackerman, 1967), and frequently is dealt with by the translation: if he is unlike me, then he is of less value that I. Anecdotal evidence—often from soldiers—repeatedly confirms that one way people enable themselves to hurt others is by dehumanizing the others in their own minds: they are not real people with feelings but only "Gooks," or "Niggers," or "Charlie." More generally, people seem able to behave badly or callously toward others when they see them as less human than themselves, and consequently experience less guilt

141

and less identification with the victim. It is more difficult to hurt others in the face of a full awareness of their humanity.

In closer relation to the material on siblings of retarded children, we have noted repeatedly our culture's manner of dealing with "differentness" by segregating the deviants from the rest of the "normal" people. Aside from its obvious costs to the ones so isolated (e.g., Braginsky and Braginsky, 1971; Farber, 1968), this segregation possibly causes problems for the rest of the culture as well. When individuals who are in some way different are segregated from the rest of the culture, one lesson drawn from it is that differences in fact are dangerous, and so it is important constantly to be wary for signs of differentness in others. Possibly, also, this emphasis on differentness keeps alive in us the fear that we too may be seen as different and so excluded from the dominant culture, much as normal siblings of children who are institutionalized fear that they may be the next to go, as did Cindy or the 10-year-old who feared "the boogey man" would get her and take her to the institution.

Given this concern with the meaning of difference, it seemed to us that the concrete experiences of a child growing up with someone who was different—someone who was retarded—might teach that child something about differentness in general. Specifically, we wondered if a normal child who came to view his or her retarded sibling as a person with feelings might also tend to see others who were different as human. Conversely, a sibling who comes to view a retarded child as subhuman, without feelings, and valueless, might also generalize such an attitude toward all who were "different."

This formulation is speculative and cannot be proved or disproved by the available data. Our clinical impression was that learning their retarded siblings were persons taught many of these students in very real and meaningful ways that other people who were different from themselves were also human beings, and hence of value. Thus, a Private U student described the effect on him of having a retarded brother:

"... it's taught me to be tolerant. I mean from a very early age I've learned people are different, and you have to make exceptions, and you have responsibilities to other people. And being aware of prejudice and misconception—. James (H) is different but he's not *that* different. That's one thing it's undoubtedly taught me—that there are not only normal people and crazy people, but there are shades, and it's just getting used to that fact."

A Community U man, one of six boys and the older brother of a young boy with Down's Syndrome, put it this way:

"Would you say you liked him?"

"Yeah. We used to share a bed, and—I don't know. Like when we were all growing up, my parents used to say, 'He is different but he is human. And he is just like any other brother and sister.' "

"What would you say are some of the effects on you?"

"I think it opened me up more. When I was a kid, all the other kids would laugh. And I don't know what it is with a kid—I guess they just don't know—but they'd laugh at a cripple. It made me aware that people can't always help the way they are. It's not even like the way they are is wrong. It's different, and they can't do anything about it. And to laugh at him didn't make any sense. So I guess when I was a kid it stopped me from making fun of other kids. I guess this has affected all of my brothers the same way. I know people laugh at Biafra and about what's going on there. I suppose they don't think about it, and so it doesn't bother them. But, if you start to think about it, if you sort of put yourself out, you can start to feel uncomfortable while you are trying to understand it."

"How would you describe the effects on your brothers?"

"I guess it was pretty much like they all became responsible for Dan in some ways, and they became more aware of handicap or differences. I can remember we lived in a nice lower middle-class or middle-class housing project, and everybody had prejudices. And I can remember a lot of people getting up tight because they [his brothers] used to hang around with these four black kids. They lived about a mile away. I knew them in school and I used to bring them over to the house, and, you know, it didn't bother me a bit. But I guess it used to put the neighbors up tight. And that was like part of the prejudice that was broken down in the family because of Dan."

In addition to this general formulation about the relationship between the way a sibling comes to view a retarded brother and sister and his or her own response to differentness on a larger and less personal scale, we were also interested in the specific effects on the sibling of how he or she viewed H. Two conflicting alternatives presented themselves. Possibly, siblings who perceived and described the humanness of H would be better able to cope with H's retardation. On the other hand, seeing the humanness of a retarded child might make the perception of that child's defect more painful and frightening, much as the Community U student quoted above described the discomfort that can come from trying to understand a Biafra, and perhaps might also increase a sibling's tendency to identify with that child and his or her defect.

Despite these potential problems, we feel that if growing up with a handicapped child can sometimes teach lessons in humaneness and tolerance, it has important and intriguing implications for such seemingly diverse issues as the integration of schools along racial lines, homogeneous versus heterogeneous grouping in classrooms in respect to academic ability, and, most broadly, for teaching tolerance and understanding of people who are different from oneself.

Others also have noted that intimate experience with "difference" can lead to greater positive feelings and respect. Jaffe (1966), for example, found that high school seniors who had had contact with a retarded person evaluated the label "MR" more favorably than did those with no such experience. Begab (1970) notes that the social-work students he studied who had a retarded brother or sister rated retarded people more favorably than those with more distant retarded relatives (e.g., cousins), and all with a retarded relative of any sort rated retarded people more highly than did students without such contacts.

Sometimes, though, intimate experiences seem to lead to other interpretations of differences. Ackerman (1967) has commented on the meaning of differences within some families. In his view, symbolic meanings often become attached to such irrelevant differences as various character traits, or even hair color, and the difference is then seen as a source of danger and threat to the family. Our clinical impression from this research was that families who felt less threatened by H's handicap, who saw it less as a major reflection of their intellectual and personal integrity, were better able to see H for what he or she was, including the humanness of the child.

We were interested in trying to isolate those characteristics of the family, the normal sibling, and/or of the retarded child that related to—and possibly influenced—the SibHs' views of the humanness of H. We considered family factors such as the degree of acceptance by members of the family of H, as well as the severity of H's handicap. We also wondered to what extent the degree and kind of direct contact between the normal child and the retarded related to the extent to which the sibling described H as a person with feelings.

SCORING ITEMS

We wanted to develop a way to score the extent to which the normal sibling seemed to us to describe and respond to H as a *person*, in contrast to a nonhuman *thing*, and developed rating scales for that aspect.

1. *Views H as human.* This is made up of the sum of scores on two scales. The first rated the extent to which SibH seemed aware in his descriptions of H that H had feelings and was in fact a person (regardless of the degree of H's handicap). The second scale rated the extent to which SibH described H's feelings with any subtlety or awareness. (This last was judged within the framework of H's degree of intellectual and social development.) High scores show more awareness of H as human. [For details of scoring, see Table 10, II (2a & b).]

2. *Sees H as similar.* This second score is the rating of a SibH's response to the question: Is there any way in which you and ————(H) are similar? SibHs who comfortably accepted that possibility and were able to describe similar attributes were given high scores [Table 10, II (2)].

This latter item seemed to be another important reflection of the extent to which SibH saw the child as human, and was comfortable identifying with that humanness, as well as with the family-relatedness of the child.

In our search for other variables that might be related to, or influence, the extent to which SibH viewed H as human, we developed several other scores, reflecting aspects of the degree or kind of actual relationship between SibH and H.

3. *Feelings toward H.* This reflects the extent to which SibH seemed to us to like H, be ambivalent toward H, or primarily dislike H. High scores were given for more positive feelings [Table 10, II (3)].

4. *Spent time as playmate.* This score is the sum of scores on two subscales, one reflecting the proportion of possible time SibH spent with H as a playmate, the other the approximate amount of absolute time per week they spent together during their childhood days. High scores were given for more time spent together [Table 10, II (4a & b)].

5. *Time responsible for H.* Also the sum of two subscales, one reflects the actual amount of time in a week SibH was responsible for H during the time they were both living at home. The other reflects the extent to which SibH felt the family urged him or her to spend time with H, and/or take responsibility for H. High scores reflect more time together when SibH was responsible for H [Table 10, II (5a & b)].

Statistical Results

While there was no statistically significant relationship between the items, "Views H as a person" and "Sees H as similar" (with the degree of handicap statistically controlled) for either Community U sample, large and significant positive correlations occurred among Private U women ($r = 0.50$, $p \leqslant 0.05$) and Private U men ($r = 0.59$, $p \leqslant 0.01$) samples. Thus, at least for Private U students, the two items seem to reflect related, if not identical, issues.

An analysis of variance (Table 22) showed no differences among the samples in the extent to which they viewed H as a person, but Community U students saw H as more similar to themselves than did Private U students.

The "Humanness" of H, Severity of H's Handicap, and Demographic Variables

Table 23 shows the relationship between the two "Humanness of H" items and the degree of mental and physical handicap of H. Although there was no relationship between the degree of physical or mental handicap (in each case with the other statistically partialed out) and the extent to which the normal siblings described the retarded child as similar to themselves, there were relationships with the extent to which they viewed H as a person. For all but Community U men, the less the degree of mental retardation, the more they described H as a person with feelings. (Also, for Private U men, the greater the physical handicap, the more they described H as a person.) Thus, to some extent the degree of mental impairment did affect the normal brothers' and sisters' views of retarded siblings as human. However, in no case did the correlation account for as much as half of the variance, leaving considerable variation along this dimension still unexplained.

An analysis of variance comparing siblings younger and older than the retarded child showed one significant main effect: SibHs younger than H described H as a person with feelings more than did SibHs older than H, and described themselves as more similar to H. No differences appeared in an analysis of variance by religion or by the sex of H.

How Much Were They Together?

An analysis of variance between the scores of the Community U and Private U students showed important differences in SibH's liking for H, spending time as a playmate of H, and spending time responsible for H (Table 24). Community U students liked H more and spent more time both as a playmate and when responsible for H. Furthermore, although the amount of time spent was unrelated to the degree of handicap (Table 25), to the sex of H, or to the age relationship between SibH and H, significant differences did appear by religious groups ($F = 3.53$, $p \leqslant 0.01$) such that Protestant SibHs spent more time as playmates and less time responsible ($F = 2.13$, $p \leqslant 0.05$) than Catholic students. (Again, the small sample size makes it impossible to draw conclusions about Jewish students.)

The relationships between liking for H, spending time with H as a playmate or when responsible for him or her, and the two "humanness" items are complex (Table 26). For Community U students, neither their liking for or dislike of H, nor the time they spent with H as children, either as playmates or babysitting, related to their view of the humanness of H. (There was one exception. The more Community U men spent time responsible for H, the more they described H as a human with feelings.) On the other hand, the results for Private U students show that the more they liked H and the more they spent time with him or her as a playmate and when responsible, the more they viewed the retarded child as human and as having feelings. The relationships of these three items with "Sees H as similar" for the Private U students were all positive, but only three of the possible six reached statistical significance. So for these Private U siblings, the nature and degree of contact they had with H as a child had at least as much to do with the extent to which they viewed H as a person with feelings as did the degree of H's handicap.

"Humanness" of H and Parent Acceptance

A fascinating difference appeared in the relationships with mother's acceptance (Table 27). The more Private U students described their mothers as accepting H, the more they themselves liked H and saw H as a human with feelings. For Private U men, mother's acceptance also correlated positively with the extent to which they spent time with H as a playmate. On the other hand, mother's acceptance had no positive relationship with these items for Community U students. Further, the less mother accepted H, the more time female students from Community U had to spend taking care of H.

These women from Community U did like H more, the greater their fathers' and families' acceptance of H. Family's acceptance for the Community U men correlated negatively with the extent to which SibH saw H as a person with feelings.

For Private U SibHs, father's and family's acceptance both tended to correlate positively with liking H and seeing H as a person with feelings. For Private U men, these scores also related to the extent to which SibH saw H as similar to himself, and family's acceptance related to the amount of time he spent with H as a playmate.

Seeing H as Human and Coping-Effectiveness

Only for Community U women was there no relationship between aspects of the interaction between SibH and H and their scores on coping-effectiveness. For all three other samples (although not reaching statistical significance for Private U men), the more they liked H, the higher their judged coping. For Private U students, higher coping scores also correlated with viewing H as a person (Table 27). For both groups of men, coping correlated significantly with seeing H as similar and spending time with H as a playmate. Finally, for Community U men, the more SibH reported some responsibility for H, the higher the coping scores.

Discussion of Results

We began by suggesting that the way a normal brother or sister came to view H—the extent to which he or she saw H as a full-fledged human being, as a person similar to him- or herself—might have some broader ramifications for the way that sibling came to see any person who is different. Although our data were not designed to prove or disprove that conjecture, in our clinical judgment (as well as in the estimation of some of our student-subjects) such a generalization did occur with some siblings. As the young man quoted earlier told us:

"James (H) is different, but he's not that different. That's one thing it's undoubtedly taught me, that there are not only normal people and crazy people, but there are shades, and it's just getting used to that fact."

We also wondered about the effects on SibH's coping-effectiveness of seeing H as human. It was unclear whether being aware of the humanness of H would relate to better coping in the normal sibling or possibly make the perception of H's handicap more painful and consequently more disruptive to SibH. For the Private U students, high coping-effectiveness and a view of H as a person with feelings and as similar to themselves went together; for Community U students, they did not. (Just as many of the Community U siblings described H as a person as did the Private U students, and more Community U students saw H as similar to themselves. However, among the Community U young people, these dimensions were unrelated to their over-all adaptation to H and his or her handicap.)

The possibility that seeing too clearly the humanness of H might make some SibHs' adaptation to H's handicap more difficult received partial support in our findings. Brothers and sisters younger than H tended more often to describe H as a person with feelings, and saw themselves as more similar to H than did SibHs older than their handicapped siblings. We know from results presented earlier (Chapter 9) that younger SibHs tended to have coped less well with H's retardation. Possibly these younger siblings did see H as human and consequently had less of a defensive shield to protect them from their guilt and pity.

In order to better understand these results, we explored those characteristics of the retarded child and of the family that might relate to the SibH's view of H. In particular, it seemed that the severity of H's retardation would affect this view, and, in fact, for all but the Community U men, the more H was retarded the less complexity of feeling and personality the SibH attributed to him or her. However, this relationship was not strong enough to explain entirely why some SibHs saw their retarded brother or sister as more human than did others. Furthermore, and somewhat surprisingly, no relationships appeared between the severity of H's retardation and the SibH's view of the similarity between him- or herself and H.

For the Private U students, nearly all of the variables we explored were interrelated. As was mentioned, those students saw H as more human the less he or she was retarded. Furthermore, those Private U students who spent more time with H liked H better, saw their parents as accepting H, and themselves saw H more as a person with feelings and more similar to themselves. Those students who spent less time with H liked H less, described their parents as less accepting of H, and tended to dehumanize H in their descriptions of him or her.

One Private U student, one of four children and sister of a moderately retarded younger brother who was institutionalized at age six, seemed actively to attempt to avoid seeing H as a person with feelings (probably to avoid guilt), received low scores on this measure, and low scores on the amount of time she had spent with H and on coping-effectiveness.

"How do you think George feels toward you?"

"He doesn't feel anything any more. I don't think—he used to know all of us by name, sort of—. Now he doesn't know us at all, I don't think."

"Because you've not been around him much?"

"Yeah, probably. I don't really know."

"How do you feel toward George?"

"Well, that's a hard question, 'cause—you know—you like to go and play with him when he's there. But like when he's not there you are just sorta unconcerned with him, because there's no kind of relationship between you. Because he hasn't really a personality."

She talked of her grandparents visiting George and taking him out on trips.

"Does George recognize your grandmother and grandfather?"

"Yeah, he knows them best. I guess it's because they saw him more, and he lived with them when he was older. It sounds kinda like we deserted him, but it's hard. Like me—I don't have time to go over there all the time. I see him when he comes. And I don't know what else to do."

Later in the interview, she was asked:

"What do you think has been the effect on your mother?"

"It made her a little harder, I think. I think she is more likely to just, you know, say all handicapped kids are alike now. And nothing can be done to them. It's sad." [She laughs.]

In contrast is the response of a Private U student, also with a moderately retarded brother who was institutionalized in early childhood, who described H as a human being and as similar to himself in some ways, who liked H and had coped well with H's retardation.

"How do you think William sees himself?"

"I might be able to give a partial answer. I know he sees himself as being isolated from the rest of the children his own age. I notice when other children are outside playing, William doesn't seem to mix with them. He wants to be friendly with them, but I don't think he knows how. He just can't get along with them, and I think he realizes that. And sometimes he'll just sit on the porch and watch them play. He looks real sad because he knows he just can't play with them; he doesn't know how to."

"Are there any ways William is like you?"

"Physically, yes, he's almost identical to what I looked like when I was his age. I was also very big, blue eyes and rosy cheeks, and blond hair. Other than that, I guess there's no way I can compare us."

Finally, another Private U student spelled out how important it was for him to have spent "growing up time" together with H. He also went on in an intriguing and revealing way to discuss explicitly the struggles he had in viewing his mildly retarded, slightly older sister as a person. He illustrated this by describing the difference in his own attitude toward Diana from that of his younger brother.

"He's five years younger—that's seven years younger than Diana is. The thing is, he never—he just never sees the problem—that this is somebody who is perfectly natural but who will never grow up, which is sort of the way I feel about her. Because, I remember times when we were both little and when it didn't really matter, particularly. There were some very pleasant experiences."

He described his younger brother's frustration with Diana and his own when he was younger:

"The thing is, I wanted to treat her as a person, and yet, you couldn't. I sort of found it frustrating. And my little brother, who didn't really know her as somebody who seemed pretty much as you were when you were a small child, I'm sure doesn't think of her as a person. I'm sure he never has. He's had a very short experience with her constantly around, and so when she comes back for a short period, there was something that didn't seem to him to fit in."

Later, we asked: "Is there any way you and Diana are similar?"

He responded immediately that they look very much alike.

"How do you feel about looking like her?"

"It doesn't bother me at all. It seems perfectly natural that I look like her. She's my sister, I mean."

On the other hand, for Community U students, none of the further dimensions explored—such as the time they spent with H, their liking for H, their mother's acceptance of H—related to their view of H. The major dimension we found affecting these SibHs' perceptions of H was the degree of H's retardation.

Several other incidental findings possibly are relevant to this point. Community U students liked H better than did Private U students and saw H as more similar to themselves. As a group, Community U students spent much more time, both as playmates and as caretakers, with the retarded sibling. Both the later and less frequent institutionalization of H in the Community U sample (Table 2), and the reliance on normal children in the family to help out around the house and particularly to care for younger siblings, normal or handicapped, greatly increased the amount of time both men and women SibHs from Community U spent with H. (All girls spent more time as a playmate of H, although not necessarily in a position of responsibility.) Farber and his colleagues have noted in several studies (Farber, 1960; Farber and Jenné, 1963) the central importance of how much time the normal sibling has to spend in a position of responsibility for H. Girls in particular are negatively affected when they must spend inordinate amounts of time taking care of H. In these data we were impressed not so much by the damage caused to SibHs by this time as by the extent to which the important factors affecting these girls were the aspects of H's handicap rather than psychological processes and reactions occurring in the family.

Although we cannot entirely explain these findings, they are consistent with the picture we have been developing of the life styles of the Private and Community U families. In some respects, in the Community U families, H seemed to be more part of the family. He or she was better liked by the normal children, kept home longer and more often, and seen by SibH as similar to the normal sibling. Although, psychologically, H was viewed less as a threat, he or she could be disruptive if great amounts of time and effort were required for his or her care. Further, mother's acceptance of H seemed to have consequences not because of any subtle psychological implications, but concretely; if mother was nonaccepting of H she spent less time with H, and the normal siblings—particularly the daughters—had to assume more responsibility.

In Private U families, in contrast, great concern existed with all sorts of psychological nuances. The thoughts and feelings of the parents about H greatly influenced SibH's views of H and the extent to which he or she viewed H as a person. Those Private U students who were more aware of the humanness of H and who saw H as similar to themselves also were judged as coping better.

TENTATIVE CONCLUSIONS

With these data on brothers' and sisters' views of the humanness of a retarded sibling, and with our speculations about how this view relates to a broader response to differentness in others, we have raised more questions than we have been able to answer.

Brothers and sisters of retarded children do vary greatly in the extent to which they attribute human complexity and feelings to H. Roughly half of this difference can be accounted for by the degree of H's retardation; most see more complexity and subtlety of feelings in a less retarded person than in a more handicapped one. However, at least half of the differences among the student-siblings is not attributable to any characteristics of H's handicap and needs further explication. Private U students tended to see H as human if they saw their parents as liking and accepting H. As is consistent with all of our data, reactions to H by parents of Community U students had little to do with the students' own view of H.

We cannot say with any certainty that the way these young people came to see their retarded siblings affected the way they came to see others who are different. However, our impression is that responses to mental retardation in this culture have more in common with responses to all other kinds of deviance than they are unique and wholly unrelated to anything else. Given this, it seems to us unlikely that a sibling's response to the deviance of his brother or sister has no relationship to, or effects on, his response to other forms of deviance.

CHAPTER 12

A View on Institutionalization

IF, WHEN, AND HOW a retarded child is institutionalized is of enormous importance to the rest of the family, as well as to that child. Most retarded people in this country do not live in residential facilities; the usual figure given is 4 percent of the approximately 5.5 million retarded people (*e.g.*, Farber, 1968; Wolfensberger and Kurtz, 1969). However, for the several hundred thousand children and their families who use such facilities and for the hundreds of thousands of others who at one time or another consider the possibility, the decision of whether or not to institutionalize is extremely difficult and often traumatic.

For many years and until quite recently, institutionalization was the major resource for families with retarded children and was viewed by professionals and laymen alike as the treatment of choice for such people. (The only factor limiting the number of children placed in institutions was the lack of adequate bed space.) This approach to the "problem" of retardation reflects directly the "change-the-child" view discussed in Chapter 1, as well as our culture's practice of isolating deviants from so-called normal people in institutions such as mental hospitals, training schools for the mentally retarded, prisons, etc. (Chapter 11). The problem is seen as contained in the handicapped child's head. Consequently, the solution is to try to bring about some change in the child or, failing that, to prevent the child from disrupting and contaminating the rest of the family and community.

An alternative view, as we have said, is to see the problem as existing in the entire family, community, and culture, and as consisting of the difficulties these social units have—as they are now constituted—in making a place for deviant and/or less capable individuals. The practice of segregating people who are different has led until recently to a disregard of the need to develop other forms of assistance to families with deviant members. For families with retarded children, these can include extensive day-care and educational programs within the community, adequate parental guidance, concrete aid in managing a handicapped individual at home, recreational programs, etc.

It is clear that for some families the availability of major assistance, whether it be residential care or some other form of aid, is essential to their survival. Carver's study (1956) of families waiting for space for their retarded child in the state training school documents in brutal detail the devastating effects on families in our culture of hyperactive and/or otherwise disruptive children when they do not get adequate assistance (also Kaplan, 1970). However, it is also clear that this group represents a small proportion of all families with retarded children.

Several factors have caused the shift away from institutionalization for most retarded people. One is the cost: it is financially unfeasible to provide residential care for all retarded children. Second, following a series of studies on the negative effects of institutionalization on young children (see Sarason and Doris, 1969) and, more recently, some exposés of the realities of life in many institutions (e.g., Blatt and Kaplan, 1966), questions have been raised about the effects on the child of being segregated from nonretarded people in separate residential facilities.

Questions about the efficacy of this form of treatment have come finally to focus not only on the effect on the retarded child but also on the effects on the family and community. While in the past institutionalization of the child was seen at times as essential to the well-being of the parents and normal children, examples of the negative effects on the family of the segregation of a family member have proliferated in the literature. As Wolfensberger and Kurtz point out (1969):

> In a society which places great value on children as a means of family actualization, and which emphasizes cohesiveness and togetherness in family interaction, the removal of one member must be seen as a highly significant event for all members. . . . This entire process of surrendering the family's socializing role

to another agent stands in sharp contrast to the American value system. It is no wonder that such family decision-making problems are highly emotionally charged. (pp. 453–54)

Some of the negative and dehumanizing effects on both normal and retarded children of the institutionalization of H are apparent in interviews cited in Chapter 11. A number of other writers have documented and discussed the problems created in a family by inappropriate or badly handled residential placement (e.g., Farrell, 1956; Kramm, 1963; Slobody and Scanlon, 1959; Yannet, 1963). For a family to place a member outside of the home can and often does exacerbate strong guilt reactions in the family members. Further, the tendency of some families to "close out" the excluded family member arouses fears in the others that if one person can be eliminated from the family circle they, too, are vulnerable. Neither immediate and automatic institutionalization of a child as soon as a serious mental defect is identified nor a commitment to keep a retarded child at home, regardless of circumstances, seems to us to do justice to the complexities of the issues involved.

As we have suggested, one reason often given for placing a child is "for the sake of the other children." Yet our clinical experiences do not entirely support the assumption that the normal children are better off when the retarded child is out of the house. Cindy seemed traumatized by her brother's institutionalization, and lived in constant fear that she would be the next to be forced to go. Similarly, the 10-year-old whose older sister was placed in a residential institution feared that she also would be sent away. Among the young adolescents in the discussion group, those with siblings in residence struggled with their fear and guilt.

Given these experiences, we wondered about this frequently made assumption that a normal brother or sister of a retarded child is better off with that child placed outside of the home, and decided to explore the issue in our four groups.

First, we were interested in determining the number of retarded children, as represented by our students, who were in residential facilities. Knowing this, we went on to explore the factors that related to, and possibly influenced, the degree to which residential care was used by any given family. Finally, the most intriguing question for us was the effects on the normal siblings of home care or institutionalization of the retarded child: did placement influence SibH's adaptation to H, or feelings and thoughts about H?

SCORING ITEMS

The only score used in this chapter and not previously discussed is that reflecting the extent to which the retarded children represented in this study were institutionalized.

Extent of institutionalization: A scale reflecting both the age at which H was first placed in a residential setting and the degree to which he or she lived there exclusively once placed, in contrast to spending some or all of his or her time at home. High scores indicate minimal residential care. [For exact scoring, see Table 10, I (3).]

STATISTICAL FINDINGS

Who Lived in Institutions?

The families of Private U students made significantly greater use of residential facilities than did families of Community U students (Table 28). A breakdown of these data (Table 29) emphasizes the differences. While only 3 of 33 retarded children from the Community U samples spent most of their time in an institution, half the siblings of both the Private U women and men were in residential facilities for a large part of their early and adolescent years. In contrast, 26, or 75 percent, of Community U families' retarded children were never away overnight, while only 16, or 33 percent, of Private U retarded siblings remained home.

Does the Severity of H's Handicap Make a Difference?

For the families of Community U students, who generally made little use of residential facilities for H, there were no statistically significant relationships between that use and either the severity of H's handicap or demographic characteristics of the family (Table 30). On the other hand, Private U women's families made more use of residential facilities the more H was retarded and physically handicapped and the fewer the children in the family. For families represented by Private U men students, the greater H's retardation, the more H was institutionalized. Analyses of variance of the age-of-institutionalization score by the sex of H, the age relationship between SibH and H, and the religion of the families showed no significant main effects related to these dimensions.

When the Family Accepts H

Although keeping a retarded child at home might seem by definition to be more accepting of that child than institutionalization, "acceptance" was scored independently of residential placement on quite different data, making it possible to examine the relationship between these variables (Table 31).

Only two correlations reached statistical significance. For Community U men, the more they described their mothers as accepting H, the less often and early the family placed H. For Private U men, families who scored higher on family acceptance of H tended to keep H home.

Institutionalization and Coping

For Community U students, in the context of minimal use of residential placement for H, no relationships existed between measures of their health and adaptation and the extent to which residential facilities were used (Table 32). On the other hand, for Private U women, the later and less total the institutionalization of H, regardless of the severity of H's handicap, the better their coping scores, the less embarrassment they described about H, and the lower their test anxiety scores. For Private U men, the relationship between extent of institutionalization and coping was in the same direction as for Private U women, but did not reach statistical significance. These men described themselves as somewhat *more* embarrassed by H the more H was home.

Institutionalization: Did it Affect SibH's Impression of the Humanness of H?

Again, no significant relationships appeared for Community U men or women (Table 33). For Private U students, the less H was in residential care—with the degree of defect held constant—the more the SibHs viewed H as a person with feelings, the more he or she liked H, and, for Private U men, the more similarly he viewed himself and H.

Discussion of Results

Who in These Samples Used Residential Facilities for H?

In these groups, the differences in the use of institutionalization are striking. The Private U families placed their children in residential facilities much more often, earlier, and more completely than did the Community U families.

These results are discrepant from those reported by Farber (1964) who found, in his summary of the relevant literature, that higher SES families tend to institutionalize retarded children less often than lower SES families. Similarly, Stone (1967) studied 103 families with children with Down's Syndrome, approximately half of which applied for institutional care and half did not. She found that those families who sought residential care and accepted it when it became available had the least adequate socioeconomic situations, as well as the poorest family relationships. Those families not interested in placement had, among other attributes, greater economic stability. Saenger (1960), Farber, Jenné, and Toigo (1960), and Farber himself in his more recent publication (1968), report complex interactions between a family's educational and economic situation and their readiness to institutionalize a retarded child.

A number of factors could account for the results found among our subjects' families. Not all of the families in our sample had access to residential care if they wanted it. In particular, while all families represented in the Private U samples could afford private residential care for H, and many utilized this circumstance, few of the Community U families could afford such care, and none had children in private facilities.

Second, and more speculatively, all Community U students came from an area known to have unusually good day-care programs for retarded children, and many of their retarded brothers or sisters were participating in these programs. In contrast, Private U students came from all over the country, and many described a lack of any available day-care program, which made residential placement the only service available.

Given these factors, it seems more reasonable to assume that the differential rate of institutionalization between the Private and Community U families was as much an artifact of who participated in the research as anything intrinsic to their class status.

Institutionalization, Severity of Handicap, and Demographic Variables

Given the minimal use of institutional placement of H among Community U families, it is hardly surprising that virtually no results appeared in these two groups relating institutionalization to other variables, including the severity of H's handicap or demographic characteristics of the family.

For the Private U families in this study, as has often been reported in the literature (e.g., Saenger, 1960; Stone, 1967), the more severely H was retarded, the earlier and more completely he or she was placed in a residential facility. Further, for Private U women, the greater H's physical handicap, the greater the extent of institutionalization. (Saenger, 1960, found no relationship between institutionalization and physical handicap associated with retardation.)

However, in these Private U families, neither the sex of the retarded child nor the age relationships between the normal brother or sister and H related to the family's use of residential facilities. This is in marked contrast to the reports in the literature. For example, Farber (1964) reported from his review that generally girls are institutionalized less than boys. (Also Stone, 1967.) Stone also found that parents were more willing to institutionalize older retarded children than younger; but our indirect measure of this—the age relationship between SibH and H—showed no differences in extent of institutionalization.

Institutionalization and Family Acceptance

Fewer relationships than we expected appeared between our judgment of the parents' and the family's acceptance of the handicapped child and the degree to which the family tended to institutionalize him or her. In the only two significant results, families of Private U men who were more accepting tended less often to institutionalize H, and Community U men whose mothers seemed to accept H more also placed H in residential settings less often.

However, in these Private U families, institutionalization did not necessarily mean the child was forgotten or totally rejected. Some families in this sample who institutionalized the retarded child at an early age maintained close and meaningful contact with him or her; others who kept H at home showed what seemed to us to be massive rejection.

These data are in contrast to some reported by Farber (1964), who stated that when higher SES families institutionalize a child, they tend to do it early and then "forget" the child, *i.e.*, relinquish all but legal responsibility. Possibly, siblings from Private U families who do try to "forget" the retarded child tended not to volunteer to participate in the research, for fear it might remind them of the existence of the excluded family member.

The following excerpt is an example of a situation in which the family did seem to have maintained some ties with H, despite his having been institutionalized at a young age. Our subject, a Private U student, was the second child of four, and one of three boys.

"Tell us about Adam."

"O.K. First, of all, he's always gone away to school. I mean, he's never been—. I've heard of people and known families who have had them at home, and dealt with them liberally. And some who have tried to hide them and things like this. But Adam has always gone to school. So he's always been—sort of—always a visitor. And looking back, I never thought of him naturally as a brother. He was special, not only because he was different, but because you saw him not quite so often. And because of this—like a guest—we didn't knock him around much and things like that."

Later, he told about his mother's handling of Adam:

"But she's always been a very, very concerned person, and so consequently there was never any time we had to take care of him. There was no question he was always being taken care of. She was always ready to know what he was doing. Mom was so responsible for him that we didn't really—never had any real problems, as such. And being not around so much. I have good memories of him from back then—'cause he was something special and so seldom around, he couldn't get on your nerves or anything.

"I get a kick out of of him, I really do. He's a lot of fun. He's got a real temper that comes out sometimes, but—. Anyway, I don't know—maybe it's because I have all the privileges of him without the real responsibility."

He went on to talk of Adam's being home only for several weeks at a time.

"I mean, I guess it's just not a good thing to have them home for too long. For one thing, at ——, you pay for the whole year, whether you're there or not, so it's sort of silly to have a place and not use it. Besides, the school has better facilities for him, so it's silly to have him at home. And the best you can do is send him off for a few hours every day, whereas —— has got every-thing—classes, swimming pool—practically a country club."

We judged this young man to have made a relatively good adjustment to Adam, and to Adam's residential placement, al-though his view of his handicapped brother was somewhat "gilded" and the defensive quality was evident, for example, in his explanations of why they did not have Adam home more. But despite this sign of some discomfort and guilt, he seemed to us to have come to adequate terms with Adam and his institutional placement. He also seemed to have some sense of Adam as a person with feelings.

Institutionalization and the Effects on the Normal Siblings

With regard to the Private U women, the earlier and the more total the institutionalization of their retarded sibling, regardless of the degree of H's handicap, the less well we independently judged their coping with the fact and idea of having a retarded brother or sister. Further, the earlier and more total the institutionalization of H, the more embarrassment these young women felt about H. The same relationship between the extent of institutionalization and coping approached, but did not reach, statistical significance for Private U men. (No such relationships existed in either Community U group.)

Similarly, for Private U students, the more H was home, the more he or she was viewed as a person with feelings, the more the normal sibling liked H, and, for Private U men students, the more the retarded child was seen by SibH as similar to himself. In other words, the more time these young men and women spent growing up with H, the more humanly they perceived him or her. (Again, there were no such relationships for the Community U students.)

The following excerpt is from the interview with a Private U student, fifth child in a family of 11 and brother of a younger girl with Down's Syndrome who was institutionalized from the hospital at birth. This interview, although far from typical, does illustrate unusually clearly the enormous guilt, discomfort, rationalization, and rejection that can be aroused in a child by the institutionalization of a retarded sibling, as well as the resulting dehumanization of that child in the normal child's eyes. This young man began the interview by justifying H's placement.

"What is important for us to understand about Gail?"

"Uh, I think the retarded sibling has been institutionalized since birth, a few days after she was born or something, and she's never been home, which I think is very good. Especially because there are other kids her age. If I were the youngest one, and then she had been born 10 years younger, it wouldn't matter. But with lots of other kids, it would just be impossible for her to have any self-esteem when she reached the stage where she should have any. I didn't see how it could possibly be sensible to have somebody who is definitely handicapped and could not possibly keep pace with someone a year younger around the house."

"What is Gail like?"

"Well, she's Mongoloid."

"How do you feel about her?"

"Uh, rather uninterested. I mean—you know—I'm interested in her progress, but I don't enjoy going to see her. I don't enjoy it. Obviously, it's not very pleasant."

He was asked why he continued to visit if he did not enjoy it.

"Well, the thing is, she—it doesn't give her any great joy to see me—it's just like the delivery man who comes and goes again. She can say 'hi,' and 'bye bye.' "

"What do you think has been the effect on you?"

"I don't think she's affected me except, uh, you run into the question of euthanasia. And just arguing about justified abortion—such as, if you know a kid is going to be Mongoloid, is it right to have her exist like that for as long as she lives? I mean it's—it's certain she won't live very long; she's six now, but that's rather old for a Mongoloid, actually. She'll never really turn into anything. It's just a certain—a certain bother, with everyone involved. But just in terms of herself, is it worth bringing someone into the world and sticking them with that?"

"Do you remember what you first thought or felt when you learned Gail was retarded?"

"I was kind of surprised, but I don't know if it really destroyed anything."

Later, very defensively, he added:

"I feel, I feel definitely that it's the only solution—unless it's an only child, it's not feasible to have her at home, at all."

"Do you ever talk to friends about Gail?"

"Well, I have, but it's not exactly my favorite topic."

"Have you ever told a girlfriend?"

"Oh, come on! On a date?!"

The defensive quality of his efforts to rationalize Gail's residential placement needs no further comment. His characterization of Gail ("Well, she's a Mongoloid") indicates that he felt the phrase totally explained or described her. He further dehumanized and disassociated her by himself referring to her as "the retarded sibling." From his further comments, as well as from the fact of his participation in the research, it was clear that he could not help but have greater interest in her than he professed to have, but also desperately wished she had never been born, or, since she existed, would either die quickly or could be eliminated by some socially acceptable method. We judged him to have been harmed by the experience.

This next student was a twin, younger by eight years than the retarded boy. He began, before we asked him any questions, by volunteering:

"I think I made it clear on the thing I sent in—the form responding to the letter—I never really knew him. I never remember seeing him or living with him, because after I was about—I don't know—five or six, he was sent away. Because he was definitely retarded, and there was nothing to do with him at home. So that the experiences I had with him weren't so much those I personally had, but I suppose would be the effects of his presence on the actions of my parents, somewhat indirectly."

"Would you describe Joe for us."

"There isn't much I can say."

He went on to say he did not know the cause of Joe's retardation; it was not clear to us if his parents knew the exact diagnosis.

"He's been in a state school I guess for the last 15–16 years, I guess, now."

"Where is that?"

"Right now, I guess, he's in a New York State school, I'm not sure of the name. My parents visit him on occasion—I haven't seen him myself in probably two years, but he doesn't know me anyhow right now."

"What is wrong with him?"

"I don't know. His intellectual level is about that of a four- or five-year-old. I mean, he does not have enough intelligence to be a normal member of society; there is nothing you can do with him."

"How do you think Joe sees himself?"

"That I have no idea. I really have no understanding of his complete condition, whether he has a conception of himself consciously, and if he does, what it would be. I just can't say."

"How do you feel toward him?"

"Well, I never actually really—I mean, the blood relation is there, but other than that I never considered him a brother or anything. Because I never see him or lived with him and I never will."

"If you had to say, would you say you like or dislike him?"

"I don't know. I never really considered that because I didn't consider him the same as anyone else—just wouldn't make any sense. I just don't consider him a normal person."

"Can you think of any ways you two are alike?"

"Not that I'm aware of."

In contrast is this excerpt from the interview of a somewhat unreflective Private U woman student. She had a sister with Down's Syndrome but who was never institutionalized.

"How do you think Carol sees herself?"

"That's hard to say, I don't know. She's lots and lots of fun. She's always happy, so I guess, she sees herself as whatever she wants to. I mean, I think like little children say—you know—they're going to be somebody some day—that's the way she thinks of herself."

"How do you think she thinks about her handicap?"

"I don't think she knows."

"How do you think she feels toward you?"

"I think she really loves everybody."

"And how do you feel toward her?"

"Oh, well, I just love her."

"Is there any way Carol is like you?"

"Well, we both have blue eyes, if you mean characteristics, traits, or something; we both eat a lot."

She went on to describe how the family considered placing Carol in a residential setting when she was first born.

"Then, I think, she came home, sort of on a trial basis to see how everything worked out. But now nothing more has been said other than just the only possible thought is maybe placing her years and years from now."

She said she felt Carol's retardation seemed to have made the family more of a unit, and said in response to our question that she assumed one of the normal children would take Carol to live with them when something happened to one of their parents.

These results of the close relationship between institutionalization and the normal siblings' adaptation are in partial contrast to those previously reported by others. Farber and Jenné (1963) did find that adolescent brothers of moderately and severely retarded younger siblings functioned better when their retarded brother or sister was at home, but noted the opposite effect among girls. They found that an adolescent sister of a moderately retarded younger sibling did less well when that child was home because of the demands placed on the sibling's time and energy to help care for the handicapped child. Similarly, Fowle (1968), who compared 35 lower middle- and upper lower-class families who had institutionalized their severely retarded child with 35 matched families who kept the child at home, found that the role tensions of the oldest girl in the family were much higher when the child was at home, and were reduced when the child was institutionalized. Fowle found no differences in role tension among the oldest male children in these families.

A possible way to resolve these differences lies in the awareness of different social class and SCS populations involved. The important dimension added by *these* data is that in those families where the direct care of H is *not* a major problem because of the variety of resources available to the family, the normal children seem to be better off with the retarded child at home. In those families in our study in which having H at home or away *would* make a major difference in the amount of time and effort demanded of SibH, *i.e.*, in the Community U group, too few families used residential care to make meaningful comparisons. (That is why virtually no statistically significant result appeared in the data.) These families were probably similar to those studied by Farber and Fowle, and might well have shown similar effects had residential care been available to them.

For example, this excerpt is from the interview with a Community U woman, oldest of five children, with a moderately retarded youngest sister. The family, in a situation all too familiar to people involved with retarded children and their families, had been waiting for a residential bed for Barbie (H) for some time.

"Let me describe her. She's big for her age, a big girl. And, of course, she just lies around, you know, sucking her thumb. And she eats so much, and then she just sits around, so she gets fat. And she was always very good-natured, very agreeable. Of course, everyone has their moments when you can't get along with them, but she was always very agreeable. We just thought she was an adorable little girl. And now that she's gotten older, her eyes do look far away and she has a terrible acne problem."

"What kinds of things can she do?"

"Honestly, I think she's improved a lot. Because she went to ——— for six weeks this fall—she was supposed to stay there but they didn't have room for her. Apparently she's better off, you know, than a lot of others. And we feel very fortunate that a lot of other kids are worse off. And we feel very fortunate. But this last fall, about September, when I went away to school—I guess that maybe it was the change in the family situation—that I wasn't there—maybe it was just a little shock to her—but she turned very nasty. She had a terrible few months where we just couldn't control her. Like I was really scared of her, because she's bigger than me. And she could—she had a lot more strength than I did. And she hurt, you know. She bit her arm, she bit her clothes, and she bit her arm to the point where it would bleed. And it was just terrible—it was frightening, you know. If she ever hit one of the little children playing at our house, it would really be awful. We just couldn't handle her—my mother couldn't leave us alone with her. I just couldn't handle her. It took two of us to hold her down because she was so strong. So we—she was sent to ——— for six weeks, and she came back and she was like a completely different girl. Oh, I forgot to tell you, she has seizures, and she used to fall, when she was young. We're all upset, we didn't know what's best for her, whether we should put her in ——— to protect the family or whether we should give her a normal family life. But yet it isn't really normal, because she was just disrupting our family. And of course we didn't want to send her away—you know, put her in an institution somewhere—but we'd like to do what is best for her. And she seemed to be happy at ——."

She then described an earlier period when she and Barbie attended the same public school:

"Because I was also in that school—I was in the same elementary school. And the principal happened to—we happened to know him quite well, and Mother happened to substitute-teach at that time. And, uh, quite often I'd be called out of class and had to go down to be with Barbie, because she'd had a seizure or something. And there was nothing I could do. [She laughs.] No more than anybody else—but I was always taken out of class to go help Barbara. Which really didn't bother me. It's just that there was nothing I could do. I felt helpless. Because there was nothing I could do to help her. So as long as I was with her then the teacher could quiet her own class, I guess."

"What do you think has been the effect on the family?"

"I really think it has limited us in what we can do, because my parents think twice before they go out. You can't have a babysitter for Barbara. When she was younger, you know, what high-school girl would want to come in and babysit for Barbara? So my parents didn't go out that much. I wished they could. And when I was 13 or 14, of course mother used to leave me with the kids, and even before this, I guess I kind of took to being mother for the kids—you know, they had two mothers."

"How would you describe the effects on your mother?"

"Well, I was going to write a book about her. [Laughs.] My mother lives a really rough life. Because she works midnight to morning—because she can't work during the day, because if anything happened to Barbie at school, she'd have to be there or even if something happened to one of the other children. So she can't work during the day because of Barbie. She can't work evenings, because she'd never see the kids. And she does have to work, so she works midnights. And she just doesn't get enough rest. I don't know how she does it; I really don't know. Four hours sleep a night, a day. But she—I give my mother a lot of credit, because I really think she's a marvelous mother, and she's done an awful lot to educate other people about Barbie. And yet she tries to do too much, you know—she's housemother for little Rhena, and she's Cub Scout mother for Ronny. My mother never misses a school play for anything, even though she hasn't had any sleep. I think it has affected her, you know—it's a terrible heartache that Barbie is as she is."

In contrast to the situation in most of the Private U families, this family seemed desperately to need help in dealing with Barbie. Further, SibH as the oldest girl seemed to share much of the burden with her mother and was at least in part limited and harmed by this task.

In this last excerpt, a Private U woman described the reality hardships created by her hyperactive, severely retarded younger brother:

"I remember I used to get so frustrated, because he's terribly hyperactive. And he would throw anything off the bookcase and everything. And I was probably embarrassed if somebody else was there, because I felt that I should be able to control him. But it was impossible to do, 'cause he just ran around and would throw things and rip up magazines and stuff. And I don't remember being upset about the amount of attention he got at the time. He had to be watched for 24 hours a day because he's so hyperactive, and by the time he left for school, his bedroom was just a mattress on the floor and nothing else. And all the windows were boarded up because he used to love to break glass."

These last two excerpts make it clear that our data do not indict all institutional placements of a retarded child, at least as long as other resources are unavailable to these families. There are families in which the retarded child needs great amounts of care, and neither the family nor community facilities can provide this help while keeping the child in the family. Our clinical evidence confirms the findings of other researchers that, for these families, at least the girl siblings seem better off when the retarded child is institutionalized.

One might argue that, since no causality can be inferred from these correlational relationships, perhaps some third factor, such as the family's over-all acceptance of H, affected both the normal sibling's coping and the degree to which the retarded child was institutionalized. However, the lack of more than a few relationships between acceptance and institutionalization, and the strong relationships between coping and institutionalization, suggested that the effects on SibH were not mediated primarily by the degree of acceptance of the parents or family.

SUMMARY

In summary, the decision as to whether or not to institutionalize a retarded child is a complex and difficult one, and can only be made after consideration of the specific situation of each family, as well as the community and cultural context in which the family functions. One of the factors to be considered is the effect on the normal children in the family. The results of our research in no way contradict the findings in the literature that, when a girl must spend inordinate amounts of time helping care for a retarded brother or sister, the experience often can have harmful consequences for her by restricting her freedom to participate in more usual peer group activities.

However, when the family resources—financial and other—are sufficient to cope with the care-demands of a handicapped child without placing an undue realistic hardship on the normal siblings, our data suggest that the normal siblings often cope more adaptively with H's retardation and experience less guilt and discomfort when H is at home.

Further, our findings suggest to us that—for virtually all families—were more adequate help available within the community for the care of a handicapped family member, the negative consequences for all involved would be less if that member could be kept at home.

While we cannot prove with these data that keeping the retarded child at home causes a better adjustment in the normal siblings, we can present our clinical understanding of the situation in these families that suggests this is sometimes the case. In those families for whom the retarded child does not present major care problems, or who have adequate assistance with these problems, the major stress of institutionalizing H comes from psychological reactions to the exclusion from the family. In these instances, the guilt, the overidentification with the handicapped child and consequent fear of being eliminated from the family, and the elaborate fantasies about that child that build up in the absence of day-to-day contact with him or her all seem heightened, and play a major role in the normal sibling's adjustment to the situation.

CHAPTER 13

The Total Picture

A PSYCHO-SOCIAL ORIENTATION toward mental retardation first led us to inquire about the life experiences and situations of brothers and sisters and continued to guide us in formulating the research project. Looking back over the clinical and research experiences presented here, we can now ask whether this orientation led to any important contributions to our understanding of mental retardation and its consequences.

The fallacies and limitations of the "change-the-child" approach that focuses exclusively on the child and his or her defect were illustrated most starkly in the case of Cindy. Born into a family already seriously disrupted by the experiences with a severely retarded older brother, the parents' strong expectations that Cindy also would be defective resulted in her behaving as if she were in fact damaged. Although it was these expectations, and the underlying despair and hopelessness of these parents in conjunction with the neurological "equipment" Cindy was born with that caused Cindy's pathology, mental health professionals and others had treated the problem as if it were confined entirely in Cindy. They had provided special education, for example, and repeated psychological assessments, without substantially improving the situation. When a broader orientation that included the interaction between Cindy and her parents was taken, the core of the psychopathology was highlighted, although it turned out to be too complex to undo with present techniques the years of distorted development that had affected Cindy and her parents.

In a different way, the young adolescent group also demonstrated the necessity for a psycho-social orientation toward mental retardation. Our interest in these young people grew from our concern as to the importance of the social systems surrounding a retarded child; without such a focus, the group would not have

175

been assembled. Yet, the comments and questions of the adolescents showed unmistakably their need for some opportunity to talk over their thoughts and feelings about their retarded brothers and sisters. It also demonstrated the necessity of taking siblings into account in trying to understand and influence the functioning of these families *vis-à-vis* the retarded child.

The extended research project with college siblings reaffirmed for us that the reactions of a family to a retarded child are not inevitably defined by the nature of the handicap. The college students and the families they described varied enormously in how they felt toward, and responded to, a handicapped member of the family, depending on a variety of cultural, social, and psychological factors. Beyond providing further support for the value of the social-psychological perspective on mental retardation, a great deal of specific information about brothers and sisters emerged.

What We Found

We found a surprising number of brothers and sisters of retarded children who appeared to us to have benefited in some way from the experiences of growing up with a handicapped sibling. These students seemed to us more tolerant, more compassionate, more aware of prejudice and its consequences; sometimes more focused, both occupationally and personally, than comparable young adults without such experiences. We also found many students who seemed damaged: students who were bitterly resentful of the family's situation, guilty about their rage at their parents and at the retarded sibling, fearful that they themselves might be defective or tainted; sometimes truly deprived of the time and resources they needed to develop because every support the family had to give was used in the care of the handicapped child.

Although, in our study, about as many students seemed to have benefited as were harmed, we suspect we would find many more in the latter category in any unselected group of college-age brothers and sisters of handicapped children; our sample was almost unavoidably heavily biased toward those who had coped

to some extent with the retardation and its meaning and consequence for themselves and for their families. In addition to these
findings of siblings who seemed to us to have benefited from
growing up with a retarded child, the most obvious findings of the
entire study were the ways the differences in life situations between Private and Community U students affected their experiences and descriptions of a retarded brother or sister.

Private U Students

One of the most striking features of these young people was
their close and intense involvement with their parents, and the
consequences of this involvement for their reactions to a retarded
brother or sister. For both the men and women siblings in these
families, the extent to which their mothers and fathers were seen
as accepting the retarded child and his or her handicap related
most strongly to the young people's own ability to deal adaptively
with the meaning of the handicap to themselves and their own
lives.

In those well-to-do families which had sufficient resources
to purchase services for H, and for which the growth and development of each normal child was often of paramount importance, both the men and women SibHs seemed to have been
protected from experiencing many of the direct consequences of
H's retardation, such as the amount of care required by H. Often,
the retarded child lived most of his or her life outside the home.
Further, the young men were frequently exempt from intensive
caretaking responsibility for H, even when both were home together.

Given this limited and protected contact with H, few characteristics of the retarded child seemed to influence either the
young men's or women's capacity to cope adaptively with H's
retardation. An interesting exception among the Private U men's
group was the influence of the degree of H's physical handicap; in
virtually all of the research findings, the more H was physically
handicapped or had physical stigmata, the better adjusted the

SibH was to the handicap. This result seemed closely tied to the entire family's greater clarity about, and comfort with, a visible defect in the child, in contrast to their discomfort and uncertainty with retarded children who showed no visible evidence of defects.

These Private U men and women knew quite a lot about mental retardation and brain damage—more than either their college peers who did not have a retarded sibling or the Community U students. For these young men and women—so involved with, and responsive to, nuances of feelings and reactions in their parents—the more open and comfortable the parents seemed to have been in talking about H's handicap, the better able the normal sibling was to deal with it. And generally, the more these families, and particularly the mothers, accepted H—regardless of the severity of the retardation or physical handicap—the more openly the family members seemed to have talked about his or her difficulties.

The severity of H's retardation did influence these students' views of the humanness of H, although not the extent to which they saw H as in some ways like themselves. However, of equal importance in their view of H was the extent to which the mother seemed to have accepted H, and the amount of time they themselves spent with H as a babysitter and playmate. Those students who saw the humanness of H also saw H as in some ways like themselves, liked H, and were better able to come to terms with H's retardation. (We were not able to determine whether they coped better because they liked H and acknowledged H's feelings or whether they liked H better and saw him or her as a human being because they were better adjusted to H's handicap.)

Last, for both groups of Private U students, and most notably for the women, their retarded brothers or sisters were most often in residential facilities. The more severe the retardation, the more often and the more completely he or she was institutionalized. However, for these young adults (and regardless of how retarded or handicapped H was), the more H was at home growing up with the other children, the better able the SibHs were to deal adaptively with H's retardation, the more they liked H, and the more they saw H as a human being with feelings—as a person much like themselves.

Community U Students

These groups of young men and women differed in their experiences with a retarded brother or sister, as well as differing from the Private U students. Both the men and women seemed relatively uninvolved with their parents by the time they were in college, the men in particular having achieved a level of financial as well as psychological independence from their parents. Consequently they tended to be less influenced by subtle aspects of their parents' thoughts and feelings than were the Private U students, and their parents' reactions to the retarded child seemed to have had much less impact on their own thoughts and feelings about their sibling's retardation.

These families lacked the financial resources to pay for assistance in dealing with H's retardation; they either received services through the local community program or they did without them. Further, the role-expectations they had for a son or daughter in a family were very different; the girls were expected to take a major share of the responsibility in caring for the other children, including a retarded one, while the boys were not expected to provide such help. When they were younger, these women spent far more time than the men with their retarded siblings, both as playmates and as babysitters.

The women consequently were greatly influenced by characteristics of H that directly affected their relationship with that child. Most strongly, the less the child was *physically* impaired, and presumably the less his or her physical dependence, the better the Community U women were able to cope adaptively with the child and the handicap. On the other hand, for these women, the more H's *retardation*, the better their coping. The pain of seeing a mildly retarded brother or sister struggling with an awareness of his or her handicap seemed to make this most difficult for these young women.

Those Community U women who coped well also acknowledged experiencing more anxiety, suggesting the adaptive value of greater freedom to acknowledge and express their fears and concerns. Within this group of women, those from larger families coped better, possibly protected from overinvolvement in the day-to-day care of H by the presence of other siblings to help out.

The Community U men, on the other hand, appeared to be the least involved of any of the four groups with H's handicap, as well as with other aspects of their family of origin. (Some had already established families of their own.) They were the hardest to recruit for the research, and those who came seemed to us generally the most reticent of all the students participating in the study. Possibly, being asked to verbalize personal feelings to unfamiliar upper-middle class women researchers was a more difficult and unprecedented task for these young men than for the other subjects. Whatever the explanation, in this context the reactions of the Community U men to H's handicap were relatively unrelated to the dimensions we considered, including aspects of H's handicap. We know little more than we did before about what factors in the situation made a difference to these young men.

As with the Private U students, the Community U students as a group knew more about mental retardation than did their peers without a retarded sibling. And as in the Private U groups, the more openly and comfortably they remembered their family as having discussed H's retardation, the better the adjustment made by SibH. For the men, as with the Private U men, the more openly the parents were described as discussing H and encouraging the SibH's curiosity about the handicap, the more SibH knew about retardation and brain damage at the time of the research interview. However, unlike the Private U students, the extent to which their parents accepted H was unrelated for either Community U group to their remembrance of open discussions about H.

As a group, the Community U students liked H better, and saw H as more similar to themselves, and spent more time with H than did the Private U students. However, none of these factors related to their view of H's humanness, nor did their parents' reactions to H. (In fact, the less their mothers accepted H, the more time the Community U girls spent caring for H.) These students also saw H as more human, the less H's mental retardation.

Very few of the Community U families had a residential placement for H, although many sought it and some certainly would have benefited from it. In this context, no relationships appeared in our data between SibH's adaptation and the extent to which H was institutionalized.

Several important results can best be presented independently of a discussion of the differences between the Private and Community U students. These factors described here are mentioned either because of their apparent centrality to the problem of retardation—such as the severity of H's handicap—or because they seemed to have an impact regardless of the socio-cultural class or other dimensions of the students and their families.

Severity of H's Mental and Physical Handicap

The severity of the retarded child's handicap in and of itself was not a significant factor in affecting most aspects of the normal brothers' and sisters' responses to H, although, for all groups, the less H's retardation, the more he or she was regarded as a person with complexity and feelings by SibH. No other relationships appeared consistently in all the groups as affected by the severity of H's mental or physical handicap.

This lack of results confirms most strongly that it is not the handicap itself, but the way in which it is interpreted and responded to, that determines its impact on the involved individuals.

Sex of H and of SibH

More siblings of retarded brothers volunteered to participate in the research, described themselves as talking more about H to friends, and knew more about mental retardation than did brothers and sisters of retarded sisters. On the other hand, all students described their mothers, and particularly their fathers, as more accepting of a girl than of a boy retarded child. All four groups of college student men and women described themselves as being more embarrassed by a retarded sibling of the same sex.

The normal sisters in our groups described themselves as being more anxious than did the men, reported a greater willingness to talk about H with friends, and seemed less embarrassed about being seen with H in public. In one other possibly related finding, the women students described their mothers as less accepting of H than did the men students.

If H is Older or Younger Than the Normal Brother or Sister

To a marked extent, older brothers and sisters of younger retarded children came more often to the research, knew more about mental retardation, described more family acceptance of H, and were judged as having coped more adaptively with H's handicap than younger brothers and sisters of an older retarded sibling. On the other hand, SibHs younger than H described H as a person with feelings more than did SibHs older than H, and saw H as more similar to themselves.

Big Family—Little Family

Community U women from larger families coped better with H's handicap than women from smaller families. Although this result did not appear in the other samples, our impression is that it would have done so had we gotten more student-siblings from smaller families. That is, the sampling bias that resulted in our getting fewer volunteers from small families probably influenced these results. The clinical material strongly suggests that the normal brother or sister in a two-child family feels a great deal of pressure to achieve or more generally to make up to the parents for their disappointment over the retarded child. This effect seems strongest when the retarded child is a son.

Smaller families of the women students from Private U institutionalized H more than did larger families, possibly indicating greater disruption and unhappiness about H in these small family units.

Religion: Does it Help?

We found few differences in the impact of H on a sibling or on the parents in Catholic and Protestant families, despite the literature that reports numerous differences. (Too few Jewish students participated in the study to draw conclusions about this group.) A number of the families did emphasize religious explanations in their understanding of the hows and whys of H's handicap, but we found no clear relationships between the use of such explanations and the sibling's ability to adapt to H's handicap.

TO WHOM CAN WE GENERALIZE?

To whom can we generalize our conclusions? Have we reason to believe that other groups of brothers and sisters are similar to the ones we spoke with and hence that we can describe and predict aspects of their experiences with a retarded sibling?

For the Private U men and women, our answer is an unequivocal affirmative: we can generalize safely at least to the better adjusted half of upper sociocultural-status college student siblings, and with a lesser degree of certainty to all upper SCS college-student siblings. We know with some assurance the nature of the sampling bias; it reduced the proportion of less well-adapted students, those from smaller families and those with the most severely retarded brothers and sisters. It is also important to keep in mind the fact that all of these young people were in highly competitive colleges and hence, by preselection, were functioning at a high level; we can only generalize from them to other upper SCS young adults who are attending comparable colleges.

The problem is more complex for the Community U groups, since we know less about the specific sampling biases that were operating. It is probable that a much smaller proportion of all of the siblings of retarded children in these colleges volunteered to participate. That is, the Community U students who did come are probably much less representative of all Community U student siblings than the Private U students were of their comparable college group. Our impression is that, as with the Private U students, the subjects we did get to talk with us were much better adjusted to their retarded siblings than those college siblings comparable in background to the Community U sample who did not come. Our student-subjects are probably even more discrepant from other college-*age* siblings of retarded children from comparable socioeconomic-class families. So we can generalize our results to rather well-adjusted college siblings of comparable SCS families, but not to the entire group. In addition, certain kinds of findings—such as the relative independence of these young people from their parents' reactions to H—are more likely generally valid than such quantitative observations as the proportion of well versus badly adjusted siblings or the amount of information about mental retardation and brain damage demonstrated by our subjects.

Are the Results Valid?

Before going on to consider the clinical implications of our results, one final question must be considered. Given the interview format and the type of data we obtained, can we believe in the validity of the results? We arrived at conclusions about the siblings and their families on the basis of descriptions and responses from the students alone, and at times on the basis of the students' reports of their remembrance of the way things used to be.

We presented in Chapter 6 some of the kinds of evidence that convinced us that the data were reliable, and not primarily the result of artifactual biases introduced by the interview situation. What do we believe the data reflect about a sibling and his or her family?

Scientific proof of the validity of what the students told us and its relationship to their earlier family experiences is not available as yet, and each reader must arrive at his or her own decisions and conclusions about the meaning of the results. We ourselves find encouraging the psychological coherence of the results and the internal consistency of many related findings. The fact that much of what we found is consistent with, or can be understood in relation to, the relevant literature, both about mental retardation and about social class and its impact, is also reassuring to us. Finally, the experiences described by our sibling-subjects as having occurred in their families when they were younger are entirely consistent with our clinical experiences and with other research (*e.g.*, Felzen, 1971) into what does, in fact, happen in families with young retarded and normal children.

SOME CLINICAL IMPLICATIONS

What, then, are the clinical implications of the findings we summarized here? What do these results suggest for clinical practice?

We have noted repeatedly the markedly different patterns of responsiveness to parental thoughts and feelings in the upper and lower SCS groups; to upper SCS college students, their parents' reactions are of vital importance and centrality, while for lower SCS students this is not the case. Clinical interventions intended to help siblings of retarded children from upper SCS families then might best be directed primarily toward the parents, and focus on helping these parents come to terms with this retarded child and the meaning of the handicap for themselves.

When these parents themselves accept H and H's handicap, they tend to be able to help their normal children deal with H and, furthermore, they do this with some sophistication. For example, many of these parents—and particularly the mothers—make a point of talking openly with the normal children about H, encourage their questions, and answer to the best of their ability. These parents often help the siblings see and respond to the humanness of H.

On the other hand, the upper SCS parents who are unable to come to terms with H's retardation—Cindy's parents are an extreme example—largely are unable to help their children with this issue, not because they do not *know* what might be helpful to the normal children but because their emotional involvement in the situation makes them unable to implement what they do know. For such parents, the advice by professionals to talk openly and comfortably with their children about H is less than helpful; if they were able psychologically to do that, they would have done so without being told. An attempt to carry out this advice in the face of personal discomfort and trauma is unlikely to be seen by the normal children as a genuine opportunity to raise questions and problems.

We have evidence that upper SCS parents of retarded children with no demonstrable physical handicap or stigmata need particular assistance in acknowledging and accepting the reality of H's handicap. Without such help, many tend to "blame" H's difficulties on his or her lack of motivation or on some other potentially remediable factor, and consequently never reconcile themselves to the fact of the handicap. As with all their reactions toward it, they convey this discomfort and frustration to the normal children in the family, who then have difficulty in accepting H's limitations and the disruptions these limitations cause for the family.

In contrast to this approach to upper SCS siblings through their parents, serious attempts to be helpful to lower SCS siblings must first ensure that the family is receiving adequate medical, educational, recreational, and allied services for H. Heavy reality burdens caused by H's handicap and borne by the family are often detrimental to the health and well-being of the normal children (particularly the daughters) in these families, since they assume a large share of the responsibilities for the retarded child. Adequate help to the family frees these young people from having to commit inordinate amounts of time and effort to H, allowing them the time to engage in normal peer friendships and dating relationships, and the freedom to develop generally during these important adolescent years.

Second, given the relative independence of the lower SCS students from their parents' responses toward H, some direct professional contact with these siblings—focused on their feelings, thoughts, and fantasies about H—can help them deal with their reactions and gain some perspective on their family situation. Discussion groups—similar to the group described in Chapter 3, but not necessarily composed of young adolescents—to allow them to share their concerns with their peers seem to offer one of the best adaptational situations for these young people. One particular focus of such a group, or of individual meetings with siblings, should be to encourage them to express curiosity about the handicap and to provide some concrete answers to their questions.

The young adolescents in the sibling group were enormously enthusiastic about the opportunity we provided for them to do volunteer work with retarded children. Similarly, many of the Community U students in our study expressed satisfaction about their participation as volunteers in working with retarded children in various community programs. This type of contact is valuable to them for several reasons. It provides siblings with a much broader perspective on mental retardation, concretely demonstrating to them that they and their families alone have not been singled out to cope with such a child, and that there exists a community of people involved with the associated problems. Many develop a sense of belonging to that community and of contributing actively to it, which helps to offset their frequent sense of being isolated and different from others because of their retarded sibling. The volunteer work itself gives the siblings an opportunity to counteract their sense of helplessness and impotence about their own retarded brother or sister, as they find they can help some of the children to grow and develop. It also allows many to work through some of their ambivalence and confusion about their own handicapped brother or sister, but in a less threatening context than dealing directly with their own sibling.

Finally, and despite the relatively smaller amount of involvement between these lower SCS children and their parents, several concrete recommendations can be helpful to the parents and through them to the normal siblings. These parents do not always encourage curiosity and open discussion in their offspring, in part because they are unaware of the importance of such openness for the cognitive and psychological development of the children. Yet children in these families whose parents give them an opportunity for sharing and discussing problems about

H, benefit from it. Many of these parents can benefit from the recommendation to encourage and value open curiosity about the handicap in their normal children. When they are made aware that even very young children wonder about such things and cope more adequately when they can express and satisfy their curiosity about it, many are able to permit more curiosity and respond more openly to their children's questions.

Recommendations About Residential Placement

Any decisions about the institutionalization of a retarded child must involve consideration of numerous aspects of the child, the family, and the community. Our results lead to some tentative recommendations about residential placement insofar as the effect on the normal sibling is concerned. For upper SCS families, when adequate services for the retarded child and the family are available in the community, the normal brothers and sisters seem to cope better with their sibling's handicap when they grow up together with H in the home. When this is not possible, or does not seem for other reasons to be the best arrangement for the family, it is important that parents, as well as professionals, make a particular effort to help the normal children deal with their guilt, fears, and fantasies about the institutionalization of H. Young children especially need repeated discussions about where H is, why he was sent there, and reassurance that they themselves will not be sent away.

On the other hand, more services, residential and otherwise, than are now available are clearly needed by many lower SCS families. When the task of maintaining H at home and providing adequate care for him or her creates an inordinate burden on the normal children, particularly the girls in the family, our data and that reported in the literature suggest the siblings are better off when H is out of the house. At the very least, families and professionals need to be aware of the hazards to the normal children when they commit a large part of their time and energy to the care of a retarded brother or sister.

This recommendation does not imply that the normal siblings

in these lower SCS families are not involved with H and do not share with the upper SCS siblings strong and complex reactions to institutionalization. It only reflects the fact that, on balance, it is the reality burdens rather than the fears and fantasies that have the major impact on this group. In retardation, as in other mental health fields, when reality presents serious and persisting problems, more subtle psychological reactions take a secondary role in their impact on the individual or group involved.

Several other findings have consequences for clinical practice. The sex of the normal sibling, in relation to the sex of the retarded child, makes a difference to all brothers and sisters. All other things being equal, the presence of a retarded boy generally has more impact on a family than the presence of a retarded girl. Normal college children are more aware of a handicapped brother, know more and talk more about his handicap, and see more unhappiness and disruption in their parents than college siblings of a retarded girl. On the other hand, although boy siblings are more embarrassed by their retarded brothers, normal girls are more embarrassed by a retarded sister.

It is clear that both parents and normal children need help in dealing with their feelings about their own identifications with a retarded child of the same sex as themselves. Boy siblings, for example, need more assistance in seeing themselves as different from, and not defective like, a retarded brother. Additionally, a retarded child's handicap conflicts with the fantasy-expectations held by family members of a normal boy or girl child in that family. If a girl expects a sister to be pretty and slender, she will be especially disappointed by a chubby and unattractive retarded sister; similarly, brothers and sisters respond to a handicapped brother in part in terms of their expectations of what a brother is like. All family members, including the siblings, need help in acknowledging and accepting their disappointment at the discrepancies between their expectations and the actuality of H.

Normal siblings older than H tend to cope more adaptively and understand more clearly what is going on in relation to the handicap than siblings younger than H. Older siblings seem to take on a parental stance toward a retarded brother or sister that gives them an acceptable and comfortable way to relate to H.

Helping and teaching H in concrete ways gives them some sense of mastery over their situation, reducing their sense of helpless impotence and frustration. Disciplining and controlling H allows an acceptable outlet for their aggression. Younger siblings, in contrast, less often have this avenue open to them. Some get caught up in competition with H, especially when H is only mildly retarded, and struggle with such issues as who should be the boss of whom and who should have the privileges of the older child, such as later bedtime and a larger allowance. These younger brothers and sisters seem to identify more with H and H's defect, as exemplified in the extreme by Cindy. Parents seem able to be more accepting of a retarded child when there are already normal children in the family; they communicate this acceptance to the normal siblings.

In terms of clinical intervention, it is important to alert parents to the potential problems of younger siblings, and to give such children special opportunities to clarify their confusions and work out an identity separate from H.

Finally, adjusting to a retarded child is easier for parents and normal children when that child is one member of a large family than when he or she is one of two or three children. More broadly, the data suggest that the presence of a retarded child in the home is most traumatic when that child carries a major part of the hopes, wishes, and aspirations of the parents. Any shift in the family involvements and dynamics that provides other outlets for these needs reduces the pressure on the normal children to fulfill both their own and their retarded sibling's role in the eyes of their parents.

A FINAL THOUGHT

This book, and the clinical work and research that led up to it, focused on brothers and sisters of retarded children, and we have learned a great deal about this group. Even more significant, from our vantage point, is what we have learned about the importance of familial and cultural responses to an event such as retardation in determining the total impact of the event. In particular, in our culture and in our time, the sociocultural status of young people has an enormous effect on their experiences and development. That difference has consequences for the effects of having a retarded sibling that go far beyond that specific experience.

In the face of strong cultural pressures on families and siblings to respond to a retarded child in certain ways, we were impressed with the capacity of many of the siblings and their families to learn and grow from the presence of a retarded child in the family.

Appendix A

TABLE 1

COLLEGE STUDENTS' RESPONSES TO INITIAL LETTER OF INQUIRY

	Letters Delivered	Responses No.	Responses %	Siblings of Normal (SibNs)		Siblings of Retarded (SibHs)	
				Respondents	Agreed to Participate	Respondents	Agreed to Participate
Private U, men	3,097	929	30	889	353	40	37
Private U, women	1,414	910	36	481	230	29	25
Community U1	1,885	136	7	128	57	8	7
Community U2	3,664	461	13	433	273	28	22

TABLE 2

CHARACTERISTICS OF SIBHS AND HS

FAMILY CHARACTERISTICS			CHARACTERISTICS OF H		
SibH	Religion	Number of Children	Diagnosis[a]	Sex	Age Relationship to SibH[b]
			Community U: Female SibHs		
1.	Jewish	4	Growth problem, no MR	m	—5
2.	Catholic	2	Birth injury, moderate MR	m	—7
3.	Protestant	3	Birth injury, mild MR	f	—2
4.	Protestant	3	Autistic, moderate MR	m	—9
5.	Protestant	5	Moderate MR	f	—3
6.	Catholic	2	CP, severe MR	f	—2
7.	Catholic	3	Birth injury, mild MR	m	—6
8.	Catholic	2	Epilepsy, profound MR	f	—3
9.	Catholic	4	Mild–moderate MR	m	7
10.	Catholic	2	Albinism, blind	m	—7
11.	Protestant	3	Mild–moderate MR	m	—9
12.	Catholic	2	Petit mal, no MR	f	2
13.	Catholic	5	Down's Syndrome, moderate MR	m	—9
14.	Protestant	3	Birth injury, moderate MR	m	—11
15.	Jewish	3	Accident, profound MR	m	4
16.	Catholic	6	Down's Syndrome, moderate MR	m	—12
17.	Jewish	3	Brain damage, no MR	m	—11
18.	Catholic	6	Down's Syndrome, mild–moderate MR	m	—13
19.	Catholic	3	CP, severe MR	f	—10
20.	Catholic	7	Paraplegic, accident	m	1
			Community U: Male SibHs		
1.	Catholic	8	Down's Syndrome, moderate MR	m	—12
2.	Catholic	9	Down's Syndrome, moderate MR	m	—7
3.	Catholic	5	Down's Syndrome, moderate MR	m	10
4.	Catholic	4	Emotional disturbance, mild MR	m	—4
5.	Protestant	6	CP, severe MR	f	—8
6.	Protestant	3	Mild MR	m	—9
7.	Protestant	3	Down's Syndrome, moderate MR	f	—4

FAMILY CHARACTERISTICS			CHARACTERISTICS OF H		
SibH	Religion	Number of Children	Diagnosis[a]	Sex	Age Relationship to SibH[b]
8.	Catholic	5	Moderate MR	f	−12
9.	Catholic	6	CP, moderate MR	m	−14
10.	Catholic	5	Down's Syndrome, moderate MR	m	−8
11.	Catholic	3	CP, mild–moderate MR	m	−3
12.	Jewish	3	Mild MR	m	−4
13.	Protestant	3	Birth injury, mild MR	m	3
14.	Protestant	2	Congenital amyotonia, no MR	m	2
		Private U: Female SibHs			
1.	Protestant	3	Down's Syndrome, moderate MR	m	−9
2.	Protestant	3	Down's Syndrome, moderate MR	f	−3
3.	Protestant	8	Down's Syndrome, moderate MR	m	−19
4.	Protestant	4	Down's Syndrome, moderate MR	f	−14
5.	Protestant	4	Down's Syndrome, moderate MR	m	−4
6.	Protestant	6	Emotional disturbance, moderate MR	m	−10
7.	Protestant	4	Severe CP, moderate–severe MR	m	−6
8.	Protestant	4	PKU, severe MR, autistic	m	−6
9.	Protestant	4	Severe CP, moderate MR	f	−6
10.	Protestant	5	CP, mild MR	m	−2
11.	Protestant	3	CP, moderate MR	m	−6
12.	Protestant	3	CP, moderate MR	m	−2
13.	Catholic	4	Mild–moderate MR	m	−2
14.	Protestant	2	Mild MR	f	−3
15.	Protestant	3	Mild CP, mild MR	m	3
16.	Protestant	4	Mild MR	f	3
17.	Protestant	3	Mild CP, no MR	f	4
18.	Protestant	3	Mild CP, mild MR	m	−4
19.	Catholic	7	Emotional disturbance, mild MR	f	1
20.	Protestant	4	Mild MR	f	2
21.	Protestant	4	Brain damage (birth), no MR	m	3

[a] Mild, IQ level between 50 and 85; moderate, between 25 and 50; severe, between 0 and 25.

[b] A minus number means H is that many years younger than SibH.

TABLE 2 (Cont.)

CHARACTERISTICS OF SIBHS AND HS

FAMILY CHARACTERISTICS			CHARACTERISTICS OF H		
SibH	Religion	Number of Children	Diagnosis[a]	Sex	Age Relationship to SibH[b]
			Private U: Male SibHs		
1.	Protestant	4	Down's Syndrome, moderate MR	m	−14
2.	Catholic	11	Down's Syndrome, moderate MR	f	−12
3.	Catholic	10	Down's Syndrome, moderate MR	m	−12
4.	Jewish	6	Down's Syndrome, moderate MR	f	−18
5.	Protestant	4	Down's Syndrome, moderate MR	m	−9
6.	Catholic	9	Down's Syndrome, moderate MR	m	1½
7.	Protestant	4	Down's Syndrome, moderate MR	m	−4
8.	Catholic	3	CP, mild MR	m	1½
9.	Catholic	5	Moderate MR	m	−13
10.	Jewish	2	Emotional disturbance, mild MR	m	3
11.	Catholic	4	Severe MR, seizures	m	10
12.	Protestant	4	Moderate MR	m	4
13.	Catholic	2	Mild MR	m	2
14.	Protestant	3	CP, mild MR	f	2
15.	—	8	Mild MR	f	11
16.	Jewish	2	Mild MR	m	−3
17.	Protestant	3	Moderate MR	f	3
18.	Protestant	2	CP, mild MR	f	−1
19.	Protestant	4	Mild MR	m	−3
20.	—	4	CP, mild MR	m	−2
21.	Protestant	4	CP, no MR	m	0[c]
22.	Catholic	4	CP, no MR	f	−10
23.	Jewish	4	CP, no MR	m	−1
24.	Jewish	3	Severe epilepsy, mild MR	m	4,9[d]
25.	Protestant	3	Moderate MR, autistic	m	−9
26.	Protestant	6	Emotional disturbance, mild MR	m	−5
27.	Protestant	5	Polio, mild MR	f	12
28.	Protestant	2	Brain injury	f	6

[c] Twins.

[d] Two older brothers with the same difficulty, probably an unusual form of Tay-Sachs that develops in adolescence.

TABLE 2 TOTALS

	RELIGION			NO. OF CHILDREN			SEX OF H	
	Catholic	Protestant	Jewish	2	3–4	5+	f	m
Community U, women (N = 20)	12	5	3	5	10	5	6	14
Community U, men (N = 14)	8	5	1	1	6	7	3	11
Private U, women (N = 21)	2	19	–	1	16	4	8	13
Private U, men° (N = 28)	8	13	5	5	15	8	9	19

° Families of 2 students had no religious affiliation.

TABLE 3

ANALYSIS OF VARIANCE OF DEMOGRAPHIC VARIABLES
BY COLLEGE AND SEX OF SIBH

(For details of scoring, see Table 10.)

	Social Class	Religious Orientation	Number of Children	Sibling Position of SibH
Community U, women (N = 20)	2.95	3.45	3.55	1.50
Community U, men (N = 14)	2.79	3.50	4.64	1.93
Private U, women (N = 21)	4.33	3.00	4.05	1.76
Private U, men (N = 28)	4.43	2.75	4.50	2.46
F				
College	49.88†	10.75†	0.17	0.29
Sex of SibH	0.03	0.67	0.54	2.49
College × sex	0.37	0.30	3.15°	5.00†

° $p \leq 0.05$ † $p \leq 0.01$

TABLE 4

INTERCORRELATIONS AMONG SCORES REFLECTING THE DEGREE OF H'S
HANDICAP AND DEMOGRAPHIC VARIABLES IN THE FOUR SAMPLES

	1	2	3	4	5	6	7
Community U, Women (N = 20)							
1. Degree of mental retardation	–	–	–	–	–	–	–
2. Degree of physical handicap	0.56†	–	–	–	–	–	–
3. Age of institution-alization	0.56†	0.45*	–	–	–	–	–
4. Sex of H	0.34	0.06	0.10	–	–	–	–
5. Religion	−0.10	−0.03	0.22	−0.26	–	–	–
6. Number of children	0.25	−0.32	0.07	0.13	0.09	–	–
7. Age relationship	0.11	0.17	0.38*	0.09	0.02	0.01	–
8. Social class	−0.29	−0.50*	−0.03	0.19	−0.11	−0.05	0.44*
Community U, Men (N = 14)							
1. Degree of mental retardation	–	–	–	–	–	–	–
2. Degree of physical handicap	0.33	–	–	–	–	–	–
3. Age of institution-alization	0.18	0.15	–	–	–	–	–
4. Sex of H	0.40	0.24	−0.17	–	–	–	–
5. Religion	−0.51*	−0.29	−0.41	0.14	–	–	–
6. Number of children	−0.60*	−0.30	−0.19	−0.01	0.55*	–	–
7. Age relationship	−0.38	0.06	0.15	−0.32	0.14	0.48*	–
8. Social class	0.04	−0.06	0.24	−0.30	−0.55*	0.07	0.25

TABLE 4 (Cont.)

INTERCORRELATIONS AMONG SCORES REFLECTING THE DEGREE OF H's
HANDICAP AND DEMOGRAPHIC VARIABLES IN THE FOUR SAMPLES

	1	2	3	4	5	6	7
Private U, Women $(N = 21)$							
1. Degree of mental retardation	–	–	–	–	–	–	–
2. Degree of physical handicap	0.57†	–	–	–	–	–	–
3. Age of institution- alization	0.56†	0.32	–	–	–	–	–
4. Sex of H	−0.25	0.03	−0.22	–	–	–	–
5. Religion	0.35	0.14	0.22	−0.18	–	–	–
6. Number of children	−0.11	−0.24	0.28	0.10	0.19	–	–
7. Age relationship	0.79†	−0.63†	−0.19	0.34	−0.23	0.18	–
8. Social class	0.14	0.40*	−0.01	0.18	0.00	−0.51*	−0.07
Private U, Men $(N = 28)$							
1. Degree of mental retardation	–	–	–	–	–	–	–
2. Degree of physical handicap	0.29	–	–	–	–	–	–
3. Age of institution- alization	0.38*	0.17	–	–	–	–	–
4. Sex of H	0.04	0.14	0.16	–	–	–	–
5. Religion	−0.21	0.14	−0.14	−0.09	–	–	–
6. Number or children	−0.29	−0.46†	−0.21	−0.11	−0.10	–	–
7. Age relationship	−0.51†	−0.40*	0.20	0.14	0.02	0.26	–
8. Social class	0.07	−0.07	0.14	−0.26	−0.22	0.11	−0.02

* $p \leqq 0.05$ † $p \leqq 0.01$

TABLE 5

SOCIAL CLASS OF SIBHS IN EACH SAMPLE BY EDUCATION AND
OCCUPATION OF HEAD OF HOUSEHOLD

	Community U women (N = 20)	Community U men (N = 14)	Private U women (N = 21)	Private U men (N = 28)
SOCIAL CLASS				
1. Lower (manual labor)				
2. Upper lower class (semi-skilled labor)	7	7	–	2
3. Lower middle class (white collar, less than college education)	9	4	5	2
4. Middle class (semi-professional, small business, college education)	2	2	5	7
5. Upper middle class (professional, business)	2	1	10	16
6. Upper class (inherited wealth, high-level executive in large company)	–	–	1	1

TABLE 6

ANALYSIS OF VARIANCE OF SCORES REFLECTING CHARACTERISTICS
OF H BY COLLEGE AND SEX OF SIBH

	Degree of MR	Degree of Physical Handicap	Extent of Institution-alization
Community U, women	3.95	3.85	5.55
Community U, men	3.86	3.64	5.36
Private U, women	4.00	4.05	4.05
Private U, men	4.43	4.39	4.46
F			
College	0.79	2.00	15.36†
Sex of SibH	0.23	0.04	0.13
College × sex	0.56	0.68	1.81

† $p \leq 0.01$

TABLE 7

Degree of Mental and Physical Handicap of H by College and Sex of SibH

	Community U women (N = 20)		Community U men (N = 14)		Private U women (N = 21)		Private U men (N = 28)		Total (N = 83)	
	No.	%	No.	%	No.	%	No.	%	No.	%
Degree of Mental Retardation*										
Severe or profound, IQ 25 or below	4	20	1	7	5	23	4	14	14	17
Moderate, IQ 25–50	9	45	7	50	6	29	7	25	29	35
Mild or nonexistent, IQ 50 or higher	7	35	6	43	10	48	17	61	40	48
Degree of Physical Handicap or Stigmata										
Severe	5	25	2	14	1	5	2	7	10	12
Moderate	9	45	8	57	13	62	12	43	42	51
Mild or nonexistent	6	30	4	29	7	33	14	50	31	37
Down's Syndrome (Mongolism)	3	15	5	36	6	29	7	25	21	25

* Mild, IQ level between 50 and 85; moderate, between 25 and 50; severe, less than 25.

TABLE 8

DISTRIBUTION OF ALL RESEARCH SUBJECTS

	SibH	SibN	
Community U, women	20	11	
Community U, men	14	9	
Private U, women	21	20	
Private U, men	28	26	
Total *N*	83	66	149

TABLE 9

Comparisons of Characteristics of SibHs From the Private Women's College and the Ivy League College With Representative Samples from These Two College Populations

	Ivy League College					Private Women's College				
	SibH (N = 28)		Survey (N = 288)		X^2	SibH (N = 21)		Survey (N = 133)		X^2
	No.	%	No.	%		No.	%	No.	%	
Number of Children										
5 or more	8	29	36	13	17.00	4	19	20	15	35.3
4	11	39	49	17	$p \le 0.001$	10	48	14	10	$p \le 0.01$
3	4	14	80	28		6	29	40	30	
2	5	18	123	42		1	5	50	38	
only	—	—	—	—		—	—	9	7	
Religion*						(N = 131)				
Nonpracticing	4	14	13	5	NS	1	5	12	9	11.1
Jewish	4	14	59	21		—	—	28	21	$p \le 0.02$
Protestant	12	43	161	58		18	86	66	50	
Catholic	8	29	46	16		2	10	25	19	

* Thirteen subjects did not report their religion. Hence, the N for the total college survey is 279.

TABLE 10—SCORING

(Nearly all items were scored on a 6-point scale.)

I. Characteristics of the handicapped child (H)
- (1) Degree of mental retardation
  1. Profound (no speech, IQ below 15, few self-help skills)
  2. Severe (little speech, IQ 15–25, can feed self, dress)
  3. Moderate (trainable, adequate speech, IQ 25–50, minimal academic skills)
  4. Mild to moderate
  5. Mild (educable, IQ 50–75, academic skills up to 3rd-grade level)
  6. Minimal, if present (IQ 75 or above)
- (2) Degree of physical handicap or stigmata
  1. Severe
  2. Moderate
  3. Noticeable, e.g., features of Down's Syndrome, if no other physical handicap involved
  4. Somewhat noticeable, but not so much as in Down's Syndrome
  5. Very mild, e.g., slight limp
  6. Nonexistent
- (3) Extent of institutionalization
  1. Total, at birth
  2. Total, by or before age 3
  3. Generally away at school, home for frequent vacations, but after age 3
  4. Institutionalized at some point for at least several years, but after age 3
  5. Not institutionalized, may spend some nights at school
  6. Not institutionalized, never at school overnight
- (4) Age relationship of SibH to H
  1. H over 6 when SibH born, other sibs in between
  2. H over 6 when SibH born, no sibs in between
  3. H between 2 and 6 when SibH born, other sibs in between
  4. H between 2 and 6 when SibH born, no sibs in between
  5. H less than 2 when SibH born
  6. SibH less than 2 when H born
  7. SibH between 2 and 6 when H was born, no sibs in between
  8. SibH between 2 and 6 when H was born, other sibs in between
  9. SibH 6 or older when H was born, no sibs in between
  10. SibH 6 or older when H was born, other sibs in between
- (5) Sex of H and SibH
  1. Both females
  2. H is female, SibH is male
  3. H is male, SibH is female
  4. Both males

II. Relationship between SibH and H
   (1) Perceived similarity between SibH and H
      1. SibH sees them as very different; no perceived similarity
      2. SibH sees them as different, little perceived similarity
      3. Ambivalent, emphasis on differences
      4. Ambivalent, emphasis on similarities
      5. SibH sees them as similar, but not as much as in #6
      6. SibH sees them as very similar, marked perceived similarity
   (2a) Extent to which SibH sees H as a person
      1. SibH sees H as completely dehumanized, as defective
      2. General emphasis on aspects of H's being defective, some awareness of H as having feelings
      3. Views H as having some feelings, still seen largely as a defective
      4. Views H as having some feelings, sees H as highly limited
      5. Views H largely as a person with feelings, little emphasis on handicap
      6. Views H entirely as a person with feelings
   (2b) Extent to which SibH can describe H's feelings about self
      1. SibH surprised at idea that H has ideas or feelings about self
      2. Minimal idea that H has feelings, no idea what they are
      3. Some acceptance of idea that H has feelings, little ability to describe in any detail
      4. Believes H has some feelings, still sees them as highly limited, cannot describe in great detail
      5. Discusses H's feelings about self almost as would about any other family member
      6. Discusses H's feelings about self as would about any other family member
   (3) SibH's feelings toward H
      1. Strong dislike
      2. Quite negative, but occasional praise of H
      3. Ambivalence, emphasis on negative
      4. Ambivalence, emphasis on positive
      5. Quite positive, but occasional criticism of H
      6. Glorification
   (4) Amount of time SibH spent with H. (This score the sum of 2 scores.)
   (4a) Time as playmate or companion
      1. Never spent any time
      2. Spent small amount of time on weekends (*e.g.*, if H away), very occasionally with H
      3. Spent several hours a week
      4. Between #3 and #5
      5. Spent some time (less than 1 hour) every day over period of at least 3 years
      6. Much time every day over period of at least 5 years
   (4b) Time SibH spent with H relative to the amount of time possible, *i.e.*, amount of time when both were living in the family
      1. No time together
      2. Very small fraction of possible time

TABLE 10–SCORING (Cont.)

3. Less than ½ of possible time
4. More than ½ of possible time
5. Great proportion of possible time
6. All of possible time

(5) Time SibH had responsibility for H. (This score the sum of scores on following scales.)

(5a) Time responsible for H
   1. Little or no time
   2. Occasionally, e.g., once a week
   3. At least several times a week for brief periods
   4. Small amounts of time daily, or nearly daily
   5. Moderate amount of time, more than #4
   6. Great deal of time

(5b) Extent to which parents encouraged—or insisted—that SibH spend time with H
   1. Parents put no pressure on SibH, or discouraged them from being together
   2. Parents put no pressure on SibH but had no objections to their being together
   3. Parents had mild appreciation for SibH being with H, not a big issue
   4. Parents indicated they liked SibH to spend some time with H
   5. Parents encouraged SibH to spend time with H
   6. Parents strongly encouraged SibH to spend time with H and/or take responsibility for H

III. Family Characteristics
   (1) SibH's feelings toward parents
      1. Strong dislike
      2. Quite negative, but occasional praise
      3. Ambivalence, emphasis on negative
      4. Ambivalence, emphasis on positive
      5. Quite positive, but occasional criticism
      6. Glorification
   (2) Sib's feelings toward normal siblings
      1. Strong dislike
      2. Quite negative, but occasional praise
      3. Ambivalence, with emphasis on negative
      4. Ambivalence, with emphasis on positive
      5. Quite positive, but occasional criticism
      6. Glorification
   (3) Father's acceptance of H and of H's condition
      1. Complete disruption, continued mourning, driven behavior
      2. Notable disruption, grief
      3. Some unhappiness, some drivenness, not extreme
      4. Relative comfort, some unhappiness and/or drivenness, generally adaptive response

5. Minimal disruption, relative acceptance
6. Near complete acceptance, comfort

(4) Mother's acceptance of H and of H's condition
1. Complete disruption, continued mourning, driven behavior
2. Notable disruption, grief
3. Some unhappiness, some drivenness, not extreme
4. Relative comfort, some unhappiness and/or drivenness, generally adaptive response
5. Minimal disruption, relative acceptance
6. Near complete acceptance, comfort

(5) Family's acceptance of H and of H's condition
1. Complete disruption, continued mourning, driven behavior
2. Notable disruption, grief
3. Some unhappiness, some drivenness, not extreme
4. Relative comfort, some unhappiness and/or drivenness, generally adaptive response
5. Minimal disruption, relative acceptance
6. Near complete acceptance, comfort

(6) Religious orientation of family
1. Nonpracticing
2. Practicing Jewish
3. Practicing Protestant
4. Practicing Catholic

(7) Social class of family, by father's occupation
1. Lower—manual labor, unskilled.
2. Upper lower—semiskilled
3. Lower middle—white collar, e.g., salesman, clerical
4. Middle—semiprofessional, owner of independent small business
5. Upper middle class—professional, business
6. Upper class

(8) Marital intactness
1. No disruption
2. Some disruption, not until Sib 12 or older
3. Divorce, Sib age 12 or older
4. Divorce, Sib younger than 12
5. Desertion of one parent

(9) Number of children in the family

IV. Psychological Variables—Curiosity

(1) Open discussion and expressed curiosity about the handicap. (This score the sum of scores on the following 5 items)

(1a) Over-all judgment of extent to which the family was open with respect to the handicap and SibH did ask questions about it
1. Family very restricted, SibH did not ask questions
2. Quite restricted, minimal curiosity
3. Some openness about information or some remembered curiosity
4. Some openness and some curiosity, or a great deal of one or the other

TABLE 10–SCORING (Cont.)

    5. Quite open, noticeable curiosity
    6. Very open, considerable curiosity

(1b) Amount of remembered interest and curiosity about H by SibH
    1. No remembered curiosity
    2. Little remembered curiosity, *e.g.*, remembers asking one question
    3. Some curiosity, remembers several questions
    4. Generally curious, asked some questions or wondered about it
    5. Curious, asked many questions and wondered about it
    6. Very curious, asked many questions and wondered about it

(1c) Extent to which parents permitted and encouraged questions about the handicap and answered satisfactorily. (This is inferred from the interview and not taken directly from SibH's reply to the question about this.)
    1. Did not seem to welcome questions
    2. Grudgingly permitted questions
    3. Answered some questions, were not too comfortable about it
    4. Answered some questions, no special issue was made of it
    5. Answered questions, not as welcoming of questions as in #6
    6. Made it clear, explicitly and implicitly, that they would consider and welcome all questions

(1d) SibH's factual knowledge about the handicap (compared with our estimate of the parents' information)
    1. Minimal information, unclear about diagnosis
    2. Minimal information, diagnosis only
    3. Knows something about it, many things does not know
    4. Knows quite a bit, noticeably lacking some information parents probably have
    5. Knows nearly as much as parents
    6. Knows as much as parents, knows a good deal

(1e) Extent to which handicap was openly discussed among members of the family
    1. Family never discussed it
    2. Family "discussed" it once, *e.g.*, when handicap was identified
    3. Occasional family discussions, rare
    4. Some family discussions, not too often (*e.g.*, once a year)
    5. Fairly frequent family discussions
    6. Great deal of family discussion

(2) Open curiosity and discussion about sex. (This score the sum of scores on the following 2 items.)

(2a) Extent to which Sib remembers being curious about sex
    1. No remembered curiosity
    2. Minimal remembered curiosity, *e.g.*, remembers one question
    3. Some remembered curiosity, *e.g.*, wondered occasionally
    4. Fairly curious, not remembered as pressing issue
    5. Quite curious
    6. Very curious, many questions remembered

(2b) Extent to which Sib describes parents as permitting and encouraging questions about sex

1. Did not seem to welcome questions or forbade them
2. Grudgingly permitted questions
3. Answered some questions, were not too comfortable about it
4. Answered some questions, no special issue made of it
5. Answered questions, not as welcoming of them as in #6
6. Made it clear, explicitly or implicitly, that they would answer all questions and welcomed them

(3) Extent to which Sib acknowledges and is comfortable about remembered curiosity about things concerning family

1. No remembered curiosity, or repeated denials of such curiosity
2. Minimal remembered curiosity, e.g., one question, or an uncertain denial of such curiosity
3. Some remembered curiosity, wondered occasionally
4. Fairly curious, not remembered as pressing issue
5. Quite curious
6. Very curious, many questions

V. Mental Health

(1) Over-all adjustment at college. (This score the sum of the following 5 scores)

(1a) Academic adjustment at college

1. Failing
2. Probation, possibly failing
3. Borderline
4. Doing adequately, average between 70–79
5. Doing quite well, average between 80–89
6. Doing extremely well academically, honors list, average 90 or above

(1b) Social adjustment at college—extent to which Sib has friends

1. Few friends—some difficulty about this clearly evident in interview
2. Few friends, indicates not very satisfactory relationships but better than #1
3. Several friends, fairly satisfactory relationships
4. Several friends, evidently considered good friends and mostly satisfactory relationships

(1c) Social adjustment at college—dating

1. No dating; if freshman, no dating last year
2. Occasional dating, attendance at mixer or on date once or twice during past month
3. Some dating, at least once every 6 or 7 weeks, some satisfaction about it
4. Dates regularly, at least once a week, expressed satisfaction about it

(1d) Social adjustment at college—participation in school activities

1. No activities; if freshman, no activities last year
2. One activity, participated in occasionally
3. Several activities, participated in fairly regularly
4. Several activities, active participation and feels part of

TABLE 10—SCORING (Cont.)

(1e) Social adjustment at college—participation in sports
1. No sports other than required physical education
2. One sport participated in fairly often
3. Two sports participated in fairly regularly
4. Heavy investment in sports

(2) SibH's effectiveness in coping with the fact of H's handicap *vis-à-vis* the external world (clinical judgment of interviewer)
1. Markedly ineffective, handles extremely badly
2. Strong disruption
3. Some disruption *vis-à-vis* the world, relatively mild
4. No discernible effect
5. Some enhancement of personality
6. Has enhanced personality development markedly

(3) Sib's concern about the possibility of having a handicapped child
1. Enormous expressed concern
2. Strong concern
3. Definite concern, not overwhelmingly strong
4. Mild concern, *e.g.*, occasionally thought about it
5. Very mild concern, *e.g.*, thought about it once
6. No discernible concern, no remembrance of having thought about it

(4) Extent to which SibH talked with close friends about H
1. Never mentions H
2. Has mentioned H to a close friend, very reticent
3. Discusses occasionally, only with close friends
4. Will discuss when directly relevant, all best friends know
5. Talks about it sometimes, no particular hesitation about mentioning it
6. Talks freely whenever topic may arise, enjoys discussing it

(5) Extent to which SibH feels (felt) embarrassed when H around and outsiders present
1. No discomfort reported or evident in behavior as described
2. Slight suggestion of mild discomfort, generally comfortable
3. Mild discomfort, tolerates situation readily
4. Noticeable discomfort, prefers to avoid situation but can tolerate
5. Strong discomfort
6. Great embarrassment, avoids situation at all costs

(6) Lateness—extent to which Sib came on time and reliably to research appointments
1. On time or early
2. Late at least once, but no more than 15 minutes
3. More than 15 minutes late at least once
4. More than 15 minutes late, one canceled or missed appointment
5. Did not come or call at least twice, or other serious problems about keeping appointments

TABLE 11

INTERCORRELATIONS AMONG MEASURES OF HEALTH AND
FUNCTIONING FOR THE FOUR SAMPLES OF SIBHs

	Coping	Embar-rassed	Talks	Academic Function	Over-all Function	IQ
Community U, Women (N = 20)						
Coping	–	–	–	–	–	–
Embarrassed	−0.27	–	–	–	–	–
Talks to friends	0.52†	−0.06	–	–	–	–
Academic functioning	0.03	0.47*	0.28	–	–	–
Over-all functioning	0.14	0.22	0.05	0.17	–	–
IQ	−0.06	0.52*	0.26	0.69†	0.26	–
TAQ	0.15	−0.19	0.23	0.36	−0.21	0.24
Community U, Men (N = 14)						
Coping	–	–	–	–	–	–
Embarrassed	0.01	–	–	–	–	–
Talks to friends	0.18	−0.46*	–	–	–	–
Academic functioning	0.04	0.27	0.01	–	–	–
Over-all functioning	0.16	0.21	0.03	0.11	–	–
IQ	0.00	0.30	0.12	0.20	0.27	–
TAQ	−0.11	−0.01	−0.26	−0.47*	0.03	0.06
Private U, Women (N = 21)						
Coping	–	–	–	–	–	–
Embarrassed	−0.72†	–	–	–	–	–
Talks to friends	0.17	−0.07	–	–	–	–
Academic functioning	0.29	−0.11	−0.16	–	–	–
Over-all functioning	0.42*	−0.17	0.24	0.39*	–	–
IQ	−0.39*	0.32	0.17	−0.26	0.02	–
TAQ	−0.37*	0.28	−0.37*	0.40*	−0.03	−0.04
Private U, Men (N = 28)						
Coping	–	–	–	–	–	–
Embarrassed	−0.67†	–	–	–	–	–
Talks to friends	0.35*	−0.29	–	–	–	–
Academic functioning	−0.08	0.12	−0.17	–	–	–
Over-all functioning	−0.24	0.07	−0.46*	0.06	–	–
IQ	0.47†	−0.25	0.10	0.03	0.06	–
TAQ	−0.03	−0.06	0.08	0.15	0.05	−0.31

* $p \leq 0.05$ † $p \leq 0.01$

TABLE 12

ANALYSIS OF VARIANCE OF SCORES ON MEASURES OF ADAPTATION
OF SIBHs AND SIBNs ($N = 149$)

	Academic Functioning	Over-all College Functioning	IQ	TAQ
SibHs				
Community U, women (*N* = 20)	3.42	14.85	117.35	14.21
Community U, men (*N* = 14)	3.61	14.32	120.36	10.77
Private U, women (*N* = 21)	3.81	15.05	126.24	15.81
Private U, men (*N* = 28)	3.66	14.70	136.04	12.07
SibNs				
Community U, women (*N* = 11)	3.30	13.50	118.18	14.55
Community U, men (*N* = 9)	3.06	13.33	115.75	9.22
Private U, women (*N* = 20)	3.92	16.47	129.00	15.00
Private U, men (*N* = 26)	3.73	13.90	135.08	14.31
F				
SibH × SibN	1.59	4.32†	.73	4.43
Private U × Community U	19.93†	4.02†	94.38†	2.55*
Sex of Sib	1.04	3.20†	8.53†	6.23†
Condition × college	4.81†	0.15	0.26	0.59
Condition × sex	1.47	1.65	2.65*	0.42
College × sex	0.52	5.38†	7.38*	0.65
Condition × college × sex	1.00	0.12	0.41	1.30

* $p \leqslant 0.05$, $F = 2.08$ † $p \leqslant 0.01$, $F = 2.29$

TABLE 13

Two-Way Analysis of Variance Scores on Measures of Adaptation Among SibH Groups ($N = 83$)

	Coping	Embar-rassed	Talks to Friends	Academic Functioning	Over-all Functioning	IQ	TAQ
Community U, women ($N = 20$)	4.03	2.00	4.95	3.43	14.85	117.35	13.50
Community U, men ($N = 14$)	4.25	3.29	4.07	3.61	14.32	120.36	10.00
Private U, women ($N = 21$)	3.93	2.58	3.98	3.81	15.05	126.24	15.81
Private U, men ($N = 28$)	4.09	3.36	3.79	3.66	14.70	136.04	11.64
F							
Private U × Community U	0.23	1.20	4.57†	3.02*	0.26	12.14†	1.50
Sex of Sib	0.53	12.25†	3.30*	0.02	0.62	44.67†	5.66†
College × sex	0.02	0.73	1.37	1.72	0.03	3.41*	0.04

* $p \leq 0.05$, $F = 2.74$ † $p \leq 0.01$, $F = 4.08$

TABLE 14

PARTIAL CORRELATIONS BETWEEN SCORES REFLECTING SEVERITY OF H'S
HANDICAP, DEMOGRAPHIC VARIABLES, AND MEASURES OF ADAPTATION

(In each correlation, all six other variables, including those reflecting severity of
H's handicap and demographic variables, were statistically controlled.)

	Degree Mental Retardation	Degree Physical Handicap	Number of Children	Social Class
Community U, Women (N = 20)				
Coping	−0.11	0.58*	0.75†	0.45
Embarrassed	−0.18	0.25	0.08	0.30
Talks to friends	−0.39	0.33	0.44	−0.02
Academic functioning	−0.23	0.22	0.09	−0.02
Over-all functioning	−0.57*	0.41	0.32	0.43
TAQ	−0.56*	0.48*	0.47*	−0.27
Community U, Men (N = 14)				
Coping	−0.06	0.07	0.06	−0.31
Embarrassed	−0.20	0.43	−0.20	0.54
Talks to friends	0.76*	−0.54	0.56	−0.85†
Academic functioning	0.06	−0.20	0.09	0.37
Over-all functioning	−0.44	−0.34	−0.28	−0.02
TAQ	−0.17	−0.20	−0.19	0.09
Private U, Women (N = 21)				
Coping	0.13	0.10	−0.15	−0.19
Embarrassed	0.10	−0.28	0.19	0.12
Talks to friends	0.25	−0.17	−0.41	−0.07
Academic functioning	−0.34	−0.27	0.32	0.45*
Over-all functioning	−0.11	−0.35	0.16	0.25
TAQ	−0.63†	−0.23	0.33	0.34
Private U, Men (N = 28)				
Coping	0.06	−0.61†	0.07	0.07
Embarrassed	−0.24	−0.02	−0.11	−0.04
Talks to friends	0.14	−0.37*	0.14	0.09
Academic functioning	−0.10	0.06	−0.09	−0.17
Over-all functioning	0.05	0.04	−0.07	−0.12
TAQ	−0.04	−0.02	0.06	0.04

* $p \leqslant 0.05$ † $p \leqslant 0.01$

TABLE 15

ANALYSIS OF VARIANCE OF PSYCHOLOGICAL VARIABLES BY
COLLEGE AND SEX OF SIBH ($N = 83$)

	Mother's Acceptance of H	Father's Acceptance of H	Family's Acceptance of H	Feeling Toward H	Marital Integration
Community U, women ($N = 20$)	2.98	3.22	3.30	4.30	1.35
Community U, men ($N = 14$)	3.43	3.61	3.46	4.50	1.57
Private U, women ($N = 21$)	3.33	3.83	3.91	3.64	1.52
Private U, men ($N = 28$)	3.88	3.84	4.07	3.61	1.46
F					
College	2.59	2.24	4.86†	6.77†	0.02
Sex of SibH	3.95*	0.48	0.36	0.08	0.38
College × sex of SibH	0.03	0.45	0.00	0.16	0.13

* $p \leqq 0.05$, $F = 2.74$ † $p \leqq 0.01$, $F = 4.08$

TABLE 16

CORRELATIONS BETWEEN MEASURES OF ADAPTATION AND
SELECTED PSYCHOLOGICAL VARIABLES

(In all correlations, degree of mental retardation and physical handicap were statistically controlled, as well as any demographic variables that related significantly to either variable in the correlation.)

	Mother's Acceptance of H	Father's Acceptance of H	Family's Acceptance of H	Feeling Toward H	Marital Integration
Community U, Women (N = 20)					
Coping	−0.05	−0.06	0.20	0.05	0.00
Embarrassed	0.10	−0.08	−0.14	−0.41*	−0.25
Talks to friends	−0.04	−0.06	0.37	0.28	−0.13
Academic functioning	0.04	−0.32	−0.02	−0.29	−0.07
Over-all functioning	0.04	0.21	0.34	0.26	−0.35
TAQ	0.13	−0.14	0.22	0.00	0.32
Community U, Men (N = 14)					
Coping	0.31	0.20	0.73†	0.43	−0.08
Embarrassed	0.35	0.00	−0.01	0.01	0.03
Talks to friends	0.41	0.22	0.17	0.53*	−0.66*
Academic functioning	−0.10	−0.03	0.13	0.20	−0.12
Over-all functioning	0.37	−0.31	0.08	0.48*	−0.22
TAQ	0.03	−0.27	0.22	−0.57*	0.38
Private U, Women (N = 21)					
Coping	0.63†	0.66†	0.64†	0.88†	0.10
Embarrassed	−0.45*	−0.44*	−0.46*	−0.85†	−0.22
Talks to friends	−0.02	0.31	0.34	0.22	−0.09
Academic functioning	0.31	−0.13	0.12	0.18	0.08
Over-all functioning	0.23	0.10	0.17	0.40*	0.15
TAQ	−0.08	−0.35	−0.34	−0.41*	0.32
Private U, Men (N = 28)					
Coping	0.61†	0.42*	0.74†	0.65†	0.01
Embarrassed	−0.48†	−0.36*	−0.56†	−0.73†	0.00
Talks to friends	0.21	0.11	0.28	0.08	0.19
Academic functioning	−0.12	−0.31	−0.18	0.02	−0.09
Over-all functioning	−0.20	−0.36*	−0.35*	−0.21	0.12
TAQ	0.04	−0.01	−0.01	0.08	0.37*

* $p \leq 0.05$ † $p \leq 0.01$

TABLE 17

Partial Correlations Between Severity of H's Handicap,
Demographic Variables, and Psychological Factors

(In each correlation, the other six such variables were statistically controlled.)

	Degree of Mental Retardation	Degree of Physical Handicap	Social Class	Number of Children
Community U, Women $(N = 20)$				
Mother's acceptance of H	0.10	−0.27	0.25	0.33
Father's acceptance of H	0.49*	−0.22	−0.09	0.06
Family's acceptance of H	0.14	0.21	0.08	0.38
Community U, Men $(N = 14)$				
Mother's acceptance of H	0.03	−0.35	−0.39	0.57
Father's acceptance of H	0.28	0.57	0.24	0.19
Family's acceptance of H	−0.48	0.24	0.03	0.02
Private U, Women $(N = 21)$				
Mother's acceptance of H	0.09	0.19	−0.31	−0.27
Father's acceptance of H	0.21	0.14	−0.26	−0.45*
Family's acceptance of H	0.20	0.07	−0.13	−0.30
Private U, Men $(N = 28)$				
Mother's acceptance of H	0.37*	−0.69†	0.00	−0.16
Father's acceptance of H	0.32	−0.45*	0.25	−0.16
Family's acceptance of H	0.32	−0.57†	−0.06	−0.10

* $p \leqslant 0.05$ † $p \leqslant 0.01$

TABLE 18

INTERRELATIONSHIPS AMONG THE CURIOSITY-OPENNESS VARIABLES

(In all correlations, degree of mental retardation and physical handicap were statistically controlled. Any other demographic variable that correlated significantly with either variable in the relationship was also partialled out and the significance level changed accordingly.)

	Open Discussion H	Information	Curiosity-Sex	Curiosity-Family
Community U, Women (N = 20)				
Open discussion about H	–	–	–	–
Information score	0.09	–	–	–
Curiosity about sex	0.56*	–0.05	–	–
Curiosity about family	0.13	0.47*	–0.17	–
Concern about an MR child	0.18	–0.18	0.40*	0.08
Community U, Men (N = 14)				
Open discussion about H	–	–	–	–
Information score	0.70†	–	–	–
Curiosity about sex	0.47	0.34	–	–
Curiosity about family	–0.01	0.25	0.58*	–
Concern about an MR child	–0.11	0.31	–0.24	0.11
Private U, Women (N = 21)				
Open discussion about H	–	–	–	–
Information score	0.03	–	–	–
Curiosity about sex	0.11	0.37	–	–
Curiosity about family	–0.11	0.19	0.49*	–
Concern about an MR child	–0.02	–0.36	–0.15	–0.09
Private U, Men (N = 28)				
Open discussion about H	–	–	–	–
Information score	0.36*	–	–	–
Curiosity about sex	0.48†	0.20	–	–
Curiosity about family	0.33*	0.30	0.34	–
Concern about an MR child	–0.26	–0.43*	–0.03	–0.30

* $p \leq 0.05$ † $p \leq 0.01$

TABLE 19

ANALYSIS OF VARIANCE OF CURIOSITY-OPENNESS SCORES
COMPARING SIBHs AND SIBNs ($N = 149$) AS WELL
AS AMONG THE FOUR SIBH GROUPS ($N = 83$)

	Open Discussion About H	Information Score	Concern About Having Own MR Child
SIBHs			
Community U, women ($N = 20$)	19.79	15.50	2.98
Community U, men ($N = 14$)	20.48	13.71	3.18
Private U, women ($N = 21$)	19.52	18.05	3.58
Private U, men ($N = 28$)	20.61	19.11	3.59
SIBNs			
Community U, women ($N = 11$)	—	15.45	4.70
Community U, men ($N = 9$)	—	11.33	3.78
Private U, women ($N = 20$)	—	16.95	3.75
Private U, men ($N = 26$)	—	16.65	4.12
[a]F (Comparing SibHs and SibNs)			
SibH × SibN		4.32†	12.17†
College		26.32†	0.21
Sex of SibH		3.20	0.15
College × sex		5.38†	1.60
College × condition		0.15	3.50†
Sex × condition		1.65	0.80
Sex × college × condition		0.12	2.90†
[b]F (Among SibH Groups)			
College	0.01	17.71†	2.14
Sex of SibH	0.34	0.15	0.46
College × sex	0.08	2.27	0.00

[a]$* p \leq 0.05$, $F = 2.08$ [b]$* p \leq 0.05$, $F = 2.74$
† $p \leq 0.01$, $F = 2.79$ † $p \leq 0.01$, $F = 4.08$

TABLE 20

RELATIONSHIPS BETWEEN CURIOSITY-OPENNESS ITEMS, SEVERITY OF
H's HANDICAP, AND DEMOGRAPHIC FACTORS

(In all correlations, degree of handicap and all other demographic variables were
statistically controlled.)

	Degree MR	Degree Physical Handicap	Number of Children	Social Class
Community U, Women $(N = 20)$				
Open discussion about H	0.25	−0.28	0.17	−0.48*
Information score	−0.61†	0.55*	0.46*	0.38
Concern about having MR child	0.56*	−0.24	−0.33	0.08
Community U, Men $(N = 14)$				
Open discussion about H	0.11	−0.61	−0.10	−0.34
Information score	−0.46	−0.06	0.20	−0.08
Concern about having MR child	−0.30	0.13	−0.21	0.21
Private U, Women $(N = 21)$				
Open discussion about H	0.32	−0.12	−0.20	−0.40
Information score	−0.16	−0.41	−0.37	−0.22
Concern about having MR child	−0.12	−0.20	−0.43	−0.30
Private U, Men $(N = 28)$				
Open discussion about H	0.08	−0.16	−0.36*	−0.27
Information score	0.05	−0.25	−0.17	0.01
Concern about having MR child	0.05	−0.37*	−0.41*	0.20

* $p \leq 0.05$ † $p \leq 0.01$

TABLE 21

CORRELATIONS BETWEEN OPENNESS-CURIOSITY, ADAPTATION,
AND PARENTAL ACCEPTANCE

(In all analyses, the degree of retardation and of physical handicap were statistically controlled. Any demographic variable that correlated significantly with either of the two items in a correlation was also statistically controlled.)

	Open Discussion About H	Information
Community U, Women (N = 20)		
Academic functioning	0.44*	−0.01
Coping	0.27	0.32
Talks to friends	0.56†	0.37
Embarrassed	0.07	0.25
Mother's acceptance of H	−0.12	0.41*
Father's acceptance of H	0.21	0.14
Family's acceptance of H	0.37	0.54†
Community U, Men (N = 14)		
Academic functioning	0.03	0.16
Coping	0.50*	0.19
Talks to friends	0.17	−0.14
Embarrassed	0.52*	0.70†
Mother's acceptance of H	0.08	0.27
Father's acceptance of H	0.17	−0.11
Family's acceptance of H	0.74†	0.17
Private U, Women (N = 21)		
Academic functioning	0.24	0.25
Coping	0.52*	0.23
Talks to friends	−0.01	0.18
Embarrassed	−0.45*	0.18
Mother's acceptance of H	0.63†	0.17
Father's acceptance of H	0.54†	−0.03
Family's acceptance of H	0.50*	−0.11
Private U, Men (N = 28)		
Academic functioning	0.17	0.46†
Coping	0.28	0.09
Talks to friends	0.43*	0.28
Embarrassed	−0.35*	−0.02
Mother's acceptance of H	0.38*	0.10
Father's acceptance of H	−0.01	−0.21
Family's acceptance of H	0.42*	0.07

* $p \leq 0.05$　　　† $p \leq 0.01$

TABLE 22

ANALYSIS OF VARIANCE OF SCORES REFLECTING SIBH's VIEW OF H's
HUMANNESS BY COLLEGE AND SEX OF SIBH ($N = 83$)

	Sees H as Person	Sees H as Similar
Community U, women ($N = 20$)	7.82	3.58
Community U, men ($N = 14$)	7.14	3.39
Private U, women ($N = 21$)	7.95	3.05
Private U, men ($N = 28$)	8.39	2.68
F		
College	1.41	3.43*
Sex of SibH	0.04	0.68
College × Sex	0.93	0.08

* $p \leqq 0.05$, $F = 2.14$ † $p \leqq 0.01$, $F = 2.91$

TABLE 23

CORRELATIONS BETWEEN "HUMANNESS OF H" ITEMS AND DEGREE OF
PHYSICAL AND MENTAL HANDICAP OF H

(In all analyses, either the degree of mental retardation or of physical handicap,
as well as all demographic variables correlating significantly with either variable
in the analysis, was statistically controlled.)

	Degree of Retardation	Degree of Physical Handicap
Community U, Women ($N = 20$)		
Views H as person	0.67†	−0.11
Sees H as similar	−0.01	0.30
Community U, Men ($N = 14$)		
Views H as person	0.17	−0.07
Sees H as similar	0.38	0.22
Private U, Women ($N = 21$)		
Views H as person	0.62†	0.09
Sees H as similar	0.21	0.27
Private U, Men ($N = 28$)		
Views H as person	0.49*	0.33*
Sees H as similar	0.24	0.11

* $p \leqq 0.05$ † $p \leqq 0.01$

TABLE 24

ANALYSIS OF VARIANCE OF SCORES REFLECTING THE RELATIONSHIP BETWEEN
SIBH AND H BY COLLEGE AND SEX OF SIBH ($N = 83$)

	Feels Toward H	Spent Time as Playmate	Spent Time Responsible
Community U, women ($N = 20$)	4.30	9.43	7.30
Community U, men ($N = 14$)	4.50	7.89	8.21
Private U, women ($N = 21$)	3.64	7.86	6.12
Private U, men ($N = 28$)	3.61	6.91	5.89
F			
College	6.77†	6.23†	7.35†
Sex of SibH	0.08	5.89†	0.29
College × sex	0.16	0.33	0.78

* $p \leqq 0.05$, $F = 2.14$ † $p \leqq 0.01$, $F = 2.91$

TABLE 25

CORRELATIONS BETWEEN MEASURES REFLECTING ASPECTS OF
SIBH's RELATIONSHIP TO H AND DEGREE OF
PHYSICAL AND MENTAL HANDICAP

(In all analyses, either the degree of mental retardation or of physical handicap, as well as all demographic variables correlating significantly with either variable in the analysis, was statistically controlled.)

	Degree of Mental Retardation	Degree of Physical Handicap
Community U, Women ($N = 20$)		
Feels toward H	0.13	−0.40*
Spent time as playmate	−0.07	−0.03
Spent time responsible	−0.09	0.14
Community U, Men ($N = 14$)		
Feels toward H	0.04	−0.37
Spent time as playmate	−0.33	0.31
Spent time responsible	−0.20	−0.44
Private U, Women ($N = 21$)		
Feels toward H	0.03	0.04
Spent time as playmate	−0.01	0.30
Spent time responsible	0.06	−0.23
Private U, Men ($N = 28$)		
Feels toward H	0.15	−0.46†
Spent time as playmate	0.33	−0.20
Spent time responsible	−0.26	−0.26

* $p \leqq 0.05$ † $p \leqq 0.01$

TABLE 26

CORRELATIONS BETWEEN MEASURES REFLECTING EXTENT TO WHICH SIBH
VIEWS H AS HUMAN AND MEASURES REFLECTING DEGREE AND
KIND OF DIRECT CONTACT BETWEEN SIBH AND H

(In all correlations, severity of physical and mental handicap were statistically controlled. Any demographic variable that related significantly with either variable in the correlation was also statistically controlled.)

	Feels Toward H	Spent Time as Playmate	Spent Time Responsible
Community U, Women ($N = 20$)			
Views H as person	−0.02	0.16	−0.36
Sees H as similar	−0.26	0.07	−0.08
Community U, Men ($N = 14$)			
Views H as person	0.15	0.18	0.58*
Sees H as similar	0.13	−0.10	0.24
Private U, Women ($N = 21$)			
Views H as person	0.49*	0.73†	0.63†
Sees H as similar	0.35	0.43*	0.23
Private U, Men ($N = 28$)			
Views H as person	0.82†	0.38*	0.41
Sees H as similar	0.57†	0.47†	0.27

* $p \leq 0.05$ † $p \leq 0.01$

TABLE 27

CORRELATIONS BETWEEN SCORES REFLECTING SIBH's VIEW OF H's HUMANNESS,
ACCEPTANCE SCORES, AND COPING SCORES

(In all analyses, severity of mental and physical handicap, as well as all demographic variables correlating significantly with either variable in the analysis, were statistically controlled.)

	Mother's Acceptance of H	Father's Acceptance of H	Family's Acceptance of H	Coping-Effectiveness
Community U, Women (N = 20)				
Views H as person	0.35	0.20	−0.04	0.15
Sees H as similar	0.07	0.18	0.10	0.16
Community U, Men (N = 14)				
Views H as person	0.31	−0.54	−0.55*	−0.28
Sees H as similar	−0.12	0.04	0.42	0.58*
Private U, Women (N = 21)				
Views H as person	0.44*	0.45*	0.36	0.54†
Sees H as similar	−0.01	0.27	0.17	0.35
Private U, Men (N = 28)				
Views H as person	0.39*	0.51†	0.62†	0.60†
Sees H as similar	0.28	0.58†	0.53†	0.36*

* $p \leq 0.05$ † $p \leq 0.01$

TABLE 28

ANALYSIS OF VARIANCE OF THE EXTENT OF INSTITUTIONALIZATION
OF H BY COLLEGE AND SEX OF SIBH ($N = 83$)

	Extent of Institutionalization
Community U, women ($N = 20$)	5.55
Community U, men ($N = 14$)	5.36
Private U, women ($N = 21$)	4.05
Private U, men ($N = 28$)	4.46
F	
College	15.36†
Sex of SibH	0.13
College × Sex	1.81

* $p \leq 0.05$, $F = 2.74$ † $p \leq 0.01$, $F = 4.08$

TABLE 29

EXTENT OF INSTITUTIONALIZATION OF H BY COLLEGE AND SEX OF SIBH

Extent of Institutionalization	Community U		Private U		Total
	Women ($N = 20$)	Men ($N = 14$)	Women ($N = 21$)	Men ($N = 28$)	($N = 83$)
Total, by age 3	0	0	3	2	5
Total, after age 3	1	2	8	12	23
Not institutionalized, spends some nights at a school	3	2	5	3	13
Not institutionalized, never at school overnight	16	10	5	11	42

TABLE 30

INTERCORRELATIONS BETWEEN EXTENT OF INSTITUTIONALIZATION OF H,
SEVERITY OF HANDICAP, AND DEMOGRAPHIC VARIABLES

(In all analyses, severity of handicap and all other demographic variables statistically corrected with either variable in the analysis, were statistically controlled.)

	Degree of Mental Retardation	Degree of Physical Handicap	Number of Children	Social Class
Community U, women $(N = 20)$	0.41	0.19	0.03	0.18
Community U, men $(N = 14)$	0.05	−0.01	−0.02	−0.05
Private U, women $(N = 21)$	0.75†	0.46*	0.49*	−0.01
Private U, men $(N = 28)$	0.55†	0.14	−0.14	−0.22

* $p \leqslant 0.05$ † $p \leqslant 0.01$

TABLE 31

EXTENT OF INSTITUTIONALIZATION AND ACCEPTANCE SCORES

(In all analyses, degree of handicap and any demographic variable statistically correlated with either variable in the analysis, were statistically controlled.)

	Mother's Acceptance of H	Father's Acceptance of H	Family's Acceptance of H
Community U, women $(N = 20)$	−0.39	0.08	−0.14
Community U, men $(N = 14)$	0.67*	−0.09	−0.10
Private U, women $(N = 21)$	0.14	0.33	0.25
Private U, men $(N = 28)$	0.27	0.17	0.48†

* $p \leqslant 0.05$ † $p \leqslant 0.01$

TABLE 32

CORRELATIONS BETWEEN EXTENT OF INSTITUTIONALIZATION
OF H AND SIBH'S ADAPTATION

(In all analyses, severity of handicap was statistically partialed out, as were all demographic variables that related significantly to either variable in the analysis.)

	Coping-Effec-tiveness	Embar-rassed	Talks to Friends	Academic Func-tioning	Over-all Func-tioning	TAQ
Community U, women (N = 20)	0.00	0.05	−0.15	0.01	0.07	0.10
Community U, men (N = 14)	−0.15	0.25	0.27	−0.10	0.45	−0.05
Private U, women (N = 21)	0.48*	−0.47*	0.04	0.02	−0.05	−0.39*
Private U, men (N = 28)	0.29	0.36*	−0.11	0.12	−0.02	0.03

* $p \leq 0.05$ † $p \leq 0.01$

TABLE 33

CORRELATIONS BETWEEN SCORE OF EXTENT OF INSTITUTIONALIZATION AND
MEASURES OF SIBH'S VIEW OF THE HUMANNESS OF H

(In all analyses, severity of handicap was statistically partialed out, as were all demographic variables that related significantly to either variable in the analysis.)

	Views H as Person	Views H as Similar	Feels Toward H
Community U, women (N = 20)	0.32	−0.28	0.19
Community U, men (N = 14)	0.20	−0.35	0.40
Private U, women (N = 21)	0.56†	0.18	0.48†
Private U, men (N = 28)	0.53†	0.46†	0.58†

* $p \leq 0.05$ † $p \leq 0.01$

Appendix B

Dear College Student:

We are interested in how brothers and sisters influence each other and for the past several years we have been talking to college students who have a mentally retarded or seriously handicapped brother or sister and a comparable group of students whose siblings are not handicapped. We very much need your help and would appreciate your taking the time to fill in the enclosed slip.

First of all, please each student check the appropriate box and drop the envelope in the box in the college post office. You do not have to sign your name. It is most important, however, for each student to indicate whether he has siblings or not and whether any sibling is handicapped.

We are especially interested in talking with those of you who have a brother or sister who is mentally retarded and/or seriously physically handicapped. If you want to meet with us, please sign your name and phone or address. We would like to get some idea how you think having a handicapped sibling has affected you. Please check the correct box, however, whether you want to participate or not.

If any of you would like to know more about the research and/or participate in it, please sign your name and phone number or address. List first names and ages of siblings and family religious orientation. We may want to talk with you concerning how you think and feel about being a sibling.

The research procedure takes two to three hours and you will be paid $1.50 an hour. If you have any questions, please call Dr. Kaplan or Mrs. Louis at ——— ————.

Your cooperation will aid greatly our research and we would appreciate your taking the time to give us the needed information.

Sincerely,

FRANCES KAPLAN, Ph.D. MRS. PATRICIA LOUIS
Clinical Psychologist *Research Assistant*

Appendix C

Introductory Comments

Before we begin, let me tell you a little about the research project. In our work with families, we have realized increasingly how little we know about the effects of a handicapped or retarded child on his brothers and sisters. We know they often influence each other, yet we know very little about the specific effects, either positive or negative.

The first part of the research was with young adolescent siblings of retarded children. However, we needed to find people who would be better able to describe their own thoughts and feelings than 13- or 14-year-olds can; so we started talking with college fellows. Last year we met with a number of undergraduates and this year we plan to see more.

Our interest is to learn as much as possible about what it is like to have a retarded or handicapped brother or sister.

Let me just mention that there are no secrets about this research, and we will be glad to talk with you about any aspect of it. Just save your questions until the end of the interview—which we will begin now—or wait until after you have completed the tests.

Interview for College SibHs of Handicapped

I Biographical Data

    Name   Date   Interviewer

    Birthdate   Class   Grade Point

    Father's occupation

    Mother's occupation, if any

    Religious orientation

    Siblings—names and birthdates

II Characteristics of H

    A. Would you describe ——— (H)? (Physical appearance, handicap.)

        1. What does H look like?

        2. What is wrong with H? (Degree of retardation, degree of

231

physical handicap and stigmata; if SibH does not know diagnosis, ask him to find out from parents.)

B. How does H see himself? How, if at all, does H think about his handicap? How does H feel toward you? (Sees H as person, as having feelings, etc.)

C. How do you feel toward H? (Like or dislike him?)

D. Is there any way H is like you? How? Is there any way you are like him? How?

E. What services have been provided for H? (Age of institutionalization when applicable; if SibH does not know, ask him to find out from parents.)

F. How has H affected you? Has H's handicap made a difference in your life? (As a person functioning in the outside world; in your own personality.)

G. How much time did you spend with H and what activities did you do together when you were younger? (Time as playmate, companion, and specific amount of general time.)

1. How much time did you spend with H when you were responsible for him?

2. Did your parents like for you to spend time with H, or did they leave it up to you?

3. Did your parents encourage or discourage your taking care of H?

H. Do you ever talk with your friends about H?

1. What do you tell them?

2. How many friends at ——— (college name), for example, know about H's handicap? (If SibH says no one, ask why.)

3. When you were younger, did you ever wish that H were not around when your friends were around? (If SibH says he was uncomfortable or embarrassed, ask why.)

4. Did you ever wish your other brothers and sisters were not around when your friends were around?

5. How do you feel now when your friends meet H?

I. What do you think about the future of H?

1. What will H do? What will happen to H? (If SibH says he is responsible for H, ask when he first started thinking about that.)

2. How does this fit in with your future? What is your role, if any, in H's future?

3. What is the role of the other children in H's future? (If

SibH says they have no part and/or if he is the only one who has a part or only one who does not have part, ask why.)

III Family Characteristics

A. Has having a handicapped child affected the family as a whole? Give some examples.
   1. Has H's handicap changed the family? If so, in what way?
   2. What effect, if any, has it had on your father? How does he feel about H's handicap?
   3. What effect, if any, has it had on your mother? How does she feel about H's handicap?
   4. What effect, if any, has it had on your brothers and sisters?
B. How do you feel toward your parents? (Like or dislike them?)
   1. What are your parents like?
   2. How do you feel toward your brothers and sisters? (Like or dislike them?)
   3. How do the other children feel toward H?
C. Would you say that you were close to your family?
   1. Would you say that your family is a close one?
   2. How much time do you spend with them—vacations, weekends?
D. How important is religion to your family?
   1. How often did or does your family attend services or observe traditional holidays and customs?
   2. Have they ever used religion to help explain or understand the fact of H's handicap? (Get example. If SibH says religion was a help, ask: How important was this to your parents? How important to you? To the other SibHs?)
   3. Has religion affected your view of H? How?
   4. Has H's handicap in any way affected your view of religion?

IV Curiosity

A. When did you first learn about H's handicap?
   1. Did you used to wonder about it very often? What would be an example of something you wondered? What did you do when you wondered?
   2. Do you remember asking questions at any time about H? For example?

3. Whom did you ask?

4. Were they answered to your satisfaction?

5. How does your family feel about questions about H? (Are they comfortable with questions?)

6. How did and do you feel about asking questions about H?

7. Do you know as much as your parents about H's handicap? What might they know that you do not know?

8. Does your family often discuss H's handicap? About how often? Who participates in these discussions?

THIS MAY SEEM IRRELEVANT, BUT IT REALLY IS NOT. WE CAN EXPLAIN LATER IF YOU ARE INTERESTED:

B. How and when did you first learn about sex?

1. Do you remember wondering about sex very often? What did you used to wonder?

2. What did you do when you wondered?

3. Did you ask questions about sex? Whom did you ask?

4. Were they answered to your satisfaction?

5. How does your family feel about questions about sex? (Are they comfortable about these questions?)

6. How did and do you feel about questions about sex?

7. How do you feel about discussing sex with your parents?

C. Did you ever wonder about anything concerning your family? (If SibH asks what, for example, say: Is there anything about your family that you do not know and would like to know?)

1. If you wondered, what did you do about it?

2. What did your parents do about your asking?

D. Have you ever considered the possibility of having a handicapped child? (When did this first occur to you?)

1. How do you feel about it?

V Aggression*

A. How do your parents feel about fighting among the children in the family? (When SibH says fighting, find out whether he means just verbal or also physical conflict.)

---

* These data were not used in the analyses and discussion of the results. Although covering an important topic, the responses to our questions were too difficult to score and understand to allow the material to have statistical meaning. For example, it was impossible to distinguish between parental prohibition of aggression toward H and a young adult sibling's own sense of the wrongness of expressing aggression toward a handicapped child.

1. What did you do when you got mad at H? At your brothers and sisters?

2. What would your parents say or do if you fought with H?

3. What would they say or do if you fought with your other brothers and sisters?

4. What did your brothers and sisters do when they got mad at H? At you? At each other?

5. Did your parents ever say you shouldn't fight with your H because of his handicap? (Do not accept yes or no; get examples.)

6. Did your parents ever say you shouldn't fight with your sister(s) because she was a girl?

7. What did your parents do when they got mad at H? At you? At your brothers and sisters?

VI SibH's Adjustment

A. What is your grade point average? How do you feel you are doing at ——— (name of college)? (If SibH is a freshman, ask the latter.)

B. Have you found it easy to make friends at ——— (college name)? About how many close friends would you say you have— either here or if a freshman—last year?

C. Have you had many dates at ——— (college name)? (Or last year?) About how often do you date? Do you date as often as you like?

D. Have you participated in school activities here? What and how often?

E. Do you participate in sports other than physical education here? What and how often? (Ask about whether the season makes the difference, if it is not clear to you.)

DO YOU HAVE ANY QUESTIONS YOU WOULD LIKE TO ASK US ABOUT WHAT WE ARE UP TO WITH THE RESEARCH?

Appendix D

INFORMATION TEST*

NAME: ....

DATE: ....

Here are some questions about retardation. Briefly answer each question as well as you can. If you have no idea, simply put "I don't know."

1. What is mental retardation?
2. What IQ level defines retardation?
3. What are two causes of mental retardation?
4. What is Mongolism?
5. Under what circumstances can retarded people improve their level of intellectual functioning?
6. Under what circumstances might this improvement occur?
7. Name two kinds of retardation that are present at birth.
8. Do some retarded people have seizures?
9. Are retarded people capable of having babies?
10. Can people with IQ's below 70 ever learn to read and write?
11. Name two state laws about retarded people.
12. Name two sources of support for the institutions for the mentally retarded in your state.
13. Do most retarded people look different from normal people?
14. Are mentally retarded people different from those people who are emotionally disturbed?
15. What is cerebral palsy?

* Maximum score on all items is 2 points.

References

Aberle, D.F. and Naegele, K.D., "Middle-Class Fathers' Occupational Role and Attitudes Towards Children," *American Journal of Orthopsychiatry*, 22 (1952), 366–78.

Ackerman, N., "Prejudice and Scapegoating in the Family," in G.H. Zuk and I. Boszormenyi-Nagy, Eds., *Family Therapy and Disturbed Families* (Palo Alto: Science and Behavior Books, 1967).

Adams, F.K., "Comparisons of Attitudes of Adolescents Towards Normal and Retarded Brothers," *Dissertation Abstracts*, 27, 3–A (1966), 662–63.

Adams, M., "Siblings of Retarded: Their Problems and Treatment," Paper presented at meeting of the American Association for Mental Deficiency, Chicago (1966).

Altus, W.D., "Birth Order and Its Sequelae," *Science*, 151 (1965), 44–49.

Ausubel, D.P., *Ego Development and the Personality Disorders* (New York: Grune & Stratton, 1952).

Bateson, G., Jackson, D.D., Haley, J. and Weakland, J.H., "Toward a Theory of Schizophrenia," *Behavioral Science*, 1 (1956), 251–64.

Becker, D. and Margolin, F., "How Surviving Parents Handled Their Young Children's Adaptation to the Crisis of Loss," *American Journal of Orthopsychiatry*, 37, 4 (1967), 753–57.

Begab, M.J., "Impact of Education on Social Work Students' Knowledge and Attitudes About Mental Retardation," *American Journal of Mental Deficiency*, 74, 6 (1970), 801–808.

Benda, C.E., *The Child with Mongolism (Congenital Acromicria)* (New York: Grune & Stratton, 1960).

Berlyne, D.E., "A Theory of Human Curiosity," *British Journal of Psychology*, 45 (1954), 180–91.

Blalock, H.M. Jr., *Causal Inferences in Nonexperimental Research* (Chapel Hill: University of North Carolina Press, 1961).

Blatt, B. and Kaplan, F., *Christmas in Purgatory* (Boston: Allyn & Bacon, Inc., 1966).

Braginsky, D.D. and Braginsky, B.M., *Hansels and Gretels: Studies of Children in Institutions for the Mentally Retarded* (New York: Holt, Rinehart and Winston, 1971).

Brim, O.G. Jr., "Family Structure and Sex Role Learning by Children: A Further Analysis of Helen Koch's Data," *Sociometry*, 21, 1 (1958), 1–16.

Brodie, R.D. and Winterbottom, M.R., "Failure in Elementary School-boys as a Function of Traumata, Secrecy and Derogation," *Child Development*, 38, 3 (1967), 701–11.

Caldwell, B.M. and Guze, S.B., "A Study of the Adjustment of Parents and Siblings of Institutionalized and Noninstitutionalized Retarded Children," *American Journal of Mental Deficiency*, 64 (1960), 845–61.

Carver, J.N., "Reactions of Parents of Severely Retarded Children at a State Training School," Unpublished doctoral dissertation, Yale University (1956).

Dittes, J.E. and Capra, P.C., "Affiliation: Comparability or Compatibility?" *American Psychologist*, 17 (1962), 329.

Ehlers, W.H., *Mothers of Retarded Children: How They Feel, Where They Find Help* (Springfield, Illinois: Charles C Thomas, 1966).

Emch, M., "On 'The Need to Know' as Related to Identification and Acting Out," *International Journal of Psychoanalysis*, 25 (1944), 13–19.

Farber, B., "Family Organization and Crisis: Maintenance of Integration in Families With a Severely Mentally Retarded Child," *Monographs of the Society for Research in Child Development*, 25, 1 (1960).

———, "Interaction With Retarded Siblings and Life Goals of Children," *Marriage and Family Living*, 25 (1963), 96–98.

———, *Family: Organization and Interaction* (San Francisco: Chandler Publishing Co., 1964).

———, *Mental Retardation: Its Social Context and Social Consequences* (Boston: Houghton Mifflin Company, 1968).

Farber, B. and Jenné, W.C., "Family Organization and Parent-Child Communication: Parents and Siblings of a Retarded Child," *Monographs of the Society for Research in Child Development*, 28, 7 (1963), serial no. 91.

Farber, B., Jenné, W.C. and Toigo, R., "Family Crises and the Decision to Institutionalize the Retarded Child," *Council for Exceptional Children*, NEA, *Research Monograph Series* (1960), no. A–1.

Farber, B. and Ryckman, D.B., "Effects of Severely Mentally Retarded

Children on Family Relationships," *Mental Retardation Abstracts*, 2 (1965), 1–17.

Farrell, M.J., "The Adverse Effects of Early Institutionalization of Mentally Subnormal Children," *American Journal of Diseases of Children*, 91 (1956), 278–81.

Felzen, E.S., "Mothers' Adjustment to Their Mongoloid Children," Unpublished doctoral dissertation, Cornell University (1970).

Fowle, C.M., "The Effect of the Severely Mentally Retarded Child on His Family," *American Journal of Mental Deficiency*, 73, 3 (1968), 468–73.

Giannini, M.J. and Goodman, L., "Counseling Families During the Crisis Reaction to Mongolism," *American Journal of Mental Deficiency*, 67, 5 (1963), 740–47.

Graliker, B.V., Fishler, K. and Koch, R., "Teenage Reaction to a Mentally Retarded Sibling," *American Journal of Mental Deficiency*, 66, 6 (1962), 838–43.

Green, A.W., "The Middle-Class Male Child and Neurosis," *American Sociological Review*, 11 (1946), 31–41.

Hall E. and Barger, B., "Attitudinal Structures of Older and Younger Siblings," *Journal of Individual Psychology*, 20, 1 (1964), 59–68.

Hall, W.T., "Family Disorganization as Associated with Severity of Handicap (by Cerebral Palsy) of a Minor Child," Unpublished doctoral dissertation, University of Minnesota (1961).

Hanks, J.R. and Hanks, L.M., "The Physically Handicapped in Certain Non-Occidental Societies," *Journal of Social Issues*, 4, 4 (1948), 11–20.

Jaffe, J., "Attitudes of Adolescents Towards the Mentally Retarded," *American Journal of Mental Deficiency*, 70, 6 (1966), 907.

Jervis, C.A., "The Mental Deficiencies," in S. Arieti, Ed., *American Handbook of Psychiatry*, Vol. 11, Ch. 63 (New York: Basic Books, 1959).

Kaplan, F., "Some Effects of Anxiety and Defense in a Therapy-Like Situation," *Journal of Abnormal Psychology*, 71, 6 (1966), 449–58.

———, "Siblings of the Retarded," in S.B. Sarason and J. Doris, Eds., *Psychological Problems in Mental Deficiency*, 4th ed. (New York: Harper & Row, 1969).

———, "One Approach to Aiding the Multi-Problem Family," in F. Kaplan and S.B. Sarason, Eds., *The Psycho-Educational Clinic: Papers and Research Studies* (Boston: Massachusetts Department of Mental Health Monograph Series, 1970).

Kaplan, F. and Colombatto, J., "Head Start Program for Siblings of Retarded Children," *Mental Retardation*, 4, 6 (1966), 30–32.

Kaplan, F. and Fox, E.M., "Siblings of the Retarded: An Adolescent Group Experience," *Community Mental Health Journal*, 4, 6 (1968).

Kessler, J.W., *Psychopathology of Childhood* (Englewood Cliffs: Prentice-Hall, 1966).

Kirk, S.A. and Bateman, B.D., Compilers, *Ten Years of Research at the Institute for Research on Exceptional Children* (University of Illinois, 1964).

Koch, H.L., "The Relations of Certain Formal Attributes of Siblings to Attitudes Held Toward Each Other and Toward Their Parents," *Monographs of the Society for Research in Child Development*, 25, 4 (1960), serial no. 78.

Kramm, F.R., "Families of Mongoloid Children," *U.S. Children's Bureau Publication*, No. 401 (1963).

Kushlick, A., "Assessing the Size of the Problem of Subnormality," in J.E. Meade and A.S. Parkes, Eds., *Genetic and Environmental Factors in Human Ability* (New York: Plenum Press, 1960).

Lasko, J.K., "Parent Behavior Toward First and Second Children," *Genetic Psychology Monographs*, 49 (1954), 97–137.

McArthur, C., "Personalities of First and Second Children," *Psychiatry*, 19 (1956), 47–54.

McCandless, B.R., *Adolescents: Behavior and Development* (Hinsdale, Illinois: Dryden Press, 1970).

Maccoby, E.E., "Sex Differences in Intellectual Functioning," in E.E. Maccoby, Ed., *The Development of Sex Differences* (Stanford: Stanford University Press, 1966).

Macgregor, F.C., Abel, T.M., Bryt, A., Louer, E. and Weissmann, S., *Facial Deformities and Plastic Surgery: A Psychosocial Study* (Springfield, Illinois: Charles C Thomas, 1953).

Menolascino, F.J., "Parents of the Mentally Retarded: An Operational Approach to Diagnosis and Management," *Journal of the American Academy of Child Psychiatry*, 7, 4 (1968).

Meyerson, L., "Physical Disability as a Social Psychological Problem," *Journal of Social Issues*, 4, 4 (1948), 2–10.

Orne, M.T., "Demand Characteristics and Quasi-Controls," in R. Rosenthal and R.L. Rosnow, Eds., *Artifact in Behavioral Research* (New York: Academic Press, 1969).

The President's Panel on Mental Retardation, *Report to the President: A Proposed Program for National Action to Combat Mental Re-*

tardation (Washington, D.C.: Government Printing Office, October 1962).

Rapaport, L., "The State of Crisis: Some Theoretical Considerations," *Social Services Review*, 36 (1962), 211–17.

Rosenthal, R., "Self-Fulfilling Prophecy," *Psychology Today*, 2, 4 (1968), 44–51.

Rosenthal, R. and Rosnow, R.L. "The Volunteer Subject," in R. Rosenthal and R.L. Rosnow, Eds., *Artifact in Behavioral Research* (New York: Academic Press, 1969).

Ryckman, D.B. and Henderson, R.A., "The Meaning of a Retarded Child for His Parents: A Focus for Counselors," *Mental Retardation*, 3, 4 (1965), 4–7.

Saenger, G., *Factors Influencing the Institutionalization of Mentally Retarded Individuals in New York City* (Albany: New York Interdepartmental Health Resources Board, January 1960).

Sarason, S.B., "The Content of Human Problem Solving," *Nebraska Symposium on Motivation* (1961), 147–74.

Sarason, S.B. and Doris, J., *Psychological Problems in Mental Deficiency*, 4th ed. (New York: Harper & Row, 1969).

Sarason, S.B. and Gladwin, T., *Psychological Problems in Mental Deficiency*, 3rd ed. (New York: Harper & Row, 1959).

Sarason, S.B., Levine, M., Goldenberg, I.I., Cherlin, D.L. and Bennett, E.M., *Psychology in Community Settings: Clinical Educational Vocational, Social Aspects* (New York: John Wiley & Sons, 1966).

Sarason, S.B. and Mandler, G., "Some Correlates of Test Anxiety," *Journal of Abnormal and Social Psychology*, 47 (1952), 810–17.

Schonell, F.J. and Watts, B.H., "A First Survey of the Effects of a Subnormal Child on the Family Unit," *American Journal of Mental Deficiency*, 61 (1956), 210–19.

Schreiber, M. and Feeley, M., "Siblings of the Retardate: A Guided Group Experience," *Children*, 12, 6 (1965), 221–25.

Slobody, L.B. and Scanlan, J.B., "Consequences of Early Instutionalization in Mental Retardation," *American Journal of Mental Deficiency*, 63 (1959), 971–74.

Staver, N., "The Child's Learning Difficulty as Related to the Emotional Problem of the Mother," *American Journal of Orthopsychiatry*, 23 (1953), 131–42.

Stevens, H.A., "Overview," In H.A. Stevens and R. Heber, Eds., *Mental Retardation: A Review of Research* (Chicago: University of Chicago Press, 1964).

Stevens, H.A. and Heber, R., Eds., *Mental Retardation: A Review of Research* (Chicago: University of Chicago Press, 1964).

Stone, N.D., "Family Factors in Willingness to Place the Mongoloid Child," *American Journal of Mental Deficiency*, 72, 1 (1967), 16–20.

Stubblefield, H.W., "Religion, Parents, and Mental Retardation," *Mental Retardation*, 3, 4 (1965), 8–11.

Stuckert, R.P., "Occupational Mobility and Family Relationships," *Social Forces*, 41 (1962–63), 301–307.

Sutton-Smith, B. and Rosenberg, B.G., "Age Changes in the Effects of Ordinal Position on Sex-Role Identification," *Journal of Genetic Psychology*, 107 (1965), 61–73.

Tooley, K., "A Developmental Problem of Late Adolescence: Case Report," *Psychiatry*, 31, 1 (1968), 69–83.

Wechsler, D., *Wechsler Adult Intelligence Scale: Manual* (New York: Psychological Corporation, 1955).

Westley, W.A. and Epstein, N.B., "Family Structure and Emotional Health: A Case Study Approach," *Marriage and Family Living*, 22 (1960), 25–27.

Westley, W.A. and Epstein, N.B., *Silent Majority* (San Francisco: Jossey-Bass, 1969).

Wolfensberger, W. and Kurtz, R.A., Eds., *Management of the Family of the Mentally Retarded: A Book of Readings* (Follett Educational Corporation, 1969).

Wood, A.C., Friedman, C.J., and Steisel, I.M., "Psychosocial Factors in Phenylketonuria," *American Journal of Orthopsychiatry*, 37, 4 (1967), 671–79.

Wright, B.A., *Physical Disability—A Psychological Approach* (New York: Harper & Brothers, 1960).

Wunsch, W., "Some Characteristics of Mongoloids Evaluated in a Clinic for Children With Retarded Mental Development," *American Journal of Mental Deficiency*, 62 (1957), 122–30.

Yannet, H., "When to Institutionalize the Retarded Child," *Connecticut Health Bulletin* (June 1963).

Zuk, G.H., Miller, R.L., Bartrum, J.B. and Kling, G.F., "Maternal Acceptance of Retarded Children: A Questionnaire Study of Attitudes and Religious Background," *Child Development*, 32 (1961), 525–40.

Index

3